Racism and Borders

RACISM AND BORDERS: REPRESENTATION, REPRESSION, RESISTANCE

JEFF SHANTZ, EDITOR

Algora Publishing
New York

Library of Congress Cataloging-in-Publication Data —

Racism and borders : representation, repression, resistance / Jeff Shantz, editor.
    p. cm.
  Includes bibliographical references and index.
    ISBN 978-0-87586-807-3 (soft cover: alk. paper) — ISBN 978-0-87586-808-0
(hbk.: alk. paper) — ISBN 978-0-87586-809-7 (ebook) 1. Border security. 2. Racism. 3.
Emigration and immigration—Social aspects. I. Shantz, Jeff.
  JV6225.R36 2010
  363.28'5—dc22
                    2010027860

Front cover:
Above: Jeff Shantz. "Stop Deportations." 2010. Photograph.
Below: Peter Fine. "Barbed Flag." 2008. Photograph. From the collection of the artist.

ACKNOWLEDGMENTS

I must begin by acknowledging the work being done every day, in various locations, by people organizing to defend immigrants and refugees, and opposing border restrictions. I must also acknowledge those who struggle simply to live their lives free of harassment, surveillance, and punishment, who face injustice simply because they have moved in an effort to better their lives.

In terms of the current project, I would like to thank all of the contributors for their timely work, and for responding to editorial requests in a careful manner. They are all doing work, beyond the scope of this collection, that engages with pressing questions and challenges of these difficult times.

Finally, I must thank Saoirse and Molly Shantz for generously granting me the time to work on this volume. They too have felt the restriction of borders, even at their young ages. Both have given up much playtime to make this possible. An inestimable contribution.

TABLE OF CONTENTS

INTRODUCTION: CONTEMPORARY BORDER STRUGGLES

Growing up in a border city (Windsor, Ontario—right across the Detroit River from Detroit, Michigan), I have had my share of strange, even startling, experiences at the border. Over the years, I have seen a range of interactions between travelers, typically working class, and border security agents, immigration officers and various other State representatives of Canada and the United States. I have also observed and experienced first-hand the changes in border security, especially the tightening of border policies and the increasingly restrictive approach to border crossing, even where it involves the movement of working folks doing a little shopping or sightseeing. These policy shifts have been accompanied by a pervading sense of fear and panic, approaching paranoid levels, at and around borders.

One of the more memorable of personal border crossing experiences occurred a few years after the passage of the North American Free Trade Agreement (NAFTA). On one attempt to enter Detroit to take in a Tigers baseball game, I was pulled aside by the border officer and sent to the waiting room where people were being processed, suspended in the nowhere land between here and there, between passage and detention. At one end of the room, taking up most of the wall space was a large, framed NAFTA document proclaiming the supposed benefits of the trade agreement and lauding its contributions to the easier flow of goods and services across the border into the US. It would ease the movement of people between Canada, the US, and Mexico. The promise of the relaxed border, a boon to all. Ironically, however, this mounted wall document was hanging, almost mockingly, over rows of people for whom the border was in no way relaxed—for whom dreams of easier access had evaporated over the course of hours-long waits, frustration, and anxiety. So much for movements and flow across borders.

Notably, many of the people stuck in the room of the great tribute to NAFTA were US citizens. Men and women alike. Older folks and adolescents, and ages in between. Most were blue collar working class or middle income. Incredibly, and tellingly, all were African American or Latino/a.

Of course, over the last decade there have been even more dramatic, and harmful, examples of border security, surveillance and repression. On Friday, April 23, 2010, Arizona Governor Jan Brewer signed into law the toughest immigration bill in the United States. The controversial new law, SB 1070, is designed to strengthen the ability of the state's law enforcement agencies to identify, prosecute, and deport non-status migrants. The law would make it a crime for individuals to fail to carry immigration documents. In addition, citizens are now allowed to sue local agencies if they believe immigration law is not being fully enforced. Cities and towns are required to increase patrols. Even more it would give police broad powers to target and detain people believed, on questionable grounds, to be in the country without status. Law officers can arrest and detain people without warrant. Critics have identified the law as an invitation to racial and ethnic profiling, and a justification for harassment and discrimination against people, particularly, those believed to be Hispanic. The law has already contributed to a heightened climate of fear and distrust. With the law, Arizona becomes the first US state to require people to carry identity papers, a move many suggest harkens to authoritarian and racist governments, such as those in Nazi Germany and apartheid South Africa. SB 1070, far from being a stand alone piece of legislation, an anomaly, actually comes after a year, 2009, in which a record 222 immigration laws were enacted in 48 states. In addition there were a record 131 resolutions passed. Clearly the issue of racism, profiling and borders is a pressing one that requires greater critical scrutiny.

Key in understanding contemporary border tightening and restrictions on population flow and mobility is the context of neo-liberalism. The North American Free Trade Agreement, for example, more than a simple policy initiative, is one of the prominent manifestations of neo-liberal social transformation—the widespread shifting of resources upwards, from poor to wealthy, and the reorientation of society toward further dominance of the market in determining social matters. Society is placed in service of the market rather than the market being placed in the service of, as one aspect of, society. Neo-liberalism has provided the ideological justification for the expansion of markets, both domestically and globally, and the deployment of social resources (public funds and tax breaks as well as military force and punishment regimes) in support of markets.

The late-1970s witnessed the emergence of a series of significant social, political, and economic shifts in Western liberal democracies, including the US, Canada, and the UK, ushering in a neo-liberal period capitalist development that continues to the present day. Neo-liberalism, accompanied by what are sometimes called New Right social visions, advocated and initiated profound alterations in public and social policy, impelling a move from the social the social citizenship or social welfare state policies of the post-WWII period (marked by social programs and public spending that softened the blow of capitalist economies on working class and poor people) toward economic rationalist programs for dealing with social issues. Economic efficiency and market operations, rather than public welfare, became the reason of state above all else. Social citizenship rights gave way to an emphasis on taxpayer privileges which, rather than being inherent, could be removed or reduced as the state (or capital) deemed necessary or saw fit. People were discouraged or prevented from making claims on the state at the same time as states (and capital) could make growing claims (increased work, consumption taxes, laws and restrictions) on the people. This saw a reduction of universal provisions for the disadvantaged, such as accessible tuition, welfare or social housing, and an increase in tax breaks and grants for the wealthy and corporations.

In response to growing economic hardships and poverty, including crisis-level increases in homelessness and economic refugees leaving former industrial centers like Detroit, governments, at federal and local levels, replaced social programs with law and order policies and a growth of what has been come to be called the prison-industrial complex. Under neo-liberalism, poor and racialized communities have been subjected to a series of civil wars—the "War on Drugs" and the "War on Terror" among them.

Neo-liberal policy makers (in parties of the Left and Center as well as the Right) have presented a view of society as disordered, "out of control," and requiring discipline and punishment to restore order. Perceived criminals of various sorts (including later terrorists) have been constructed as a separate category of people who are beyond normal rules and responses in society. Politicians have sought and nurtured public consent for a more powerful and punitive state—the "national security state" marked by increased, widespread surveillance, tightened borders, heavier policing (of specific communities), tougher sentences, and more punitive measures. It includes the criminalization of minor forms of behavior not previously criminalized. The national security state focuses especially on control and surveillance of the poor, racialized minorities and the politically active (not only terrorists but activists, protesters, and community advocates, particularly of the Left or anti-capitalists). Indeed activists have been referred to as "domestic terrorists" and threatened with anti-terror legislation (see Shantz 2003).

Neo-liberalism has made political and economic capital from an emphasis on "chaos" or "anarchy" that supposedly needs policing to restore "law and order" or "national security." It plays upon fear mongering and moral panics over imagined increases in crime, especially among racialized youth. Neo-liberalism ignores, or denies, structural inequalities almost entirely, looking at inequality as a result of personal market failings to be resolved through training and work. It assumes a social consensus exists around security, risk, and fear, but never asks whose morals and values are actually being promoted or who motivates and benefits from this claimed consensus.

One of the great ironies of the neo-liberal period of globalization has been the fact that as politicians ideologically proclaim globalization and the opening of borders and flow across borders, the increased movement of goods and transactions has been accompanied by an increased immobility and restriction for large numbers of the general population—the working class and poor especially. The globalization of capital, investment and speculation, has been accompanied by, even facilitated by, the forced territoriality, the immobility or repressive mobility, of the working classes in much of the world, including those countries that have forcefully promoted so-called "free trade" and (corporate) globalization—Canada and the US. While capital is able to move around almost at will, pulling up and moving workplaces and disrupting local economies, working people find it more difficult to follow their former employers, to cross borders, to move in search of a better life, to share in the mobility that is such a central part of neo-liberal ideology. Even weekend shopping trips to Michigan or Ontario become fraught with worry or subject to harassment.

A key feature of neo-liberal "law and order" policies has been racialization and the construction of threat along racialized lines. Race and crime, and their meanings, are socially constructed. The term racialization denotes a social process in which differences in appearances are made to stand for biological, and in some forms social, properties, inherent in specific individuals or communities. Notions of race are, of course, discursively constructed, as effects of power, and such designations can be applied to multiple, differing meanings. At the same time racism is real and is felt as such.

Specific groups are constructed and linked to particular crimes and individuals within, or perceived to be within, those groups are constructed as being prone to commit specific crimes. Crimes by people of color are always labeled by race, while whiteness is almost never raised as part of crime reports or news stories.

19th century "scientific" attempts to catalog racial types linger in present-day notions of race. The use of classification is a system of power, what some call biopower—power exercised through constitution and control of physicality. It goes beyond simple classification, of course, as classification opens the door to other practices of power, including the policing of boundaries and enforcement of classification schemes. States seek to restore order if one part of the system seeks to cross or blur boundaries. Thus issues of representation, in contexts of racialization and the exercise of biopower, become key aspects of social context and struggle. Representations are always presentations of power and hegemony. At the same time they are confronted by opposition, counter-power and counter-hegemony.

Racial profiling, as in much contemporary security practice, is an aspect of racialization. It relies upon stereotypes rather than reasonable suspicion to single out people arbitrarily for scrutiny and/or punishment. Since September 11, 2001, racial profiling has become a regular, and as the legislation in Arizona shows increasingly widespread, impactful, and normalized, feature of border control, migration restriction, security, and surveillance practices as part of the "War on Terror" within liberal democracies that otherwise claim to have respect for individual rights and freedoms, and civil liberties.

Official liberal and neo-liberal versions of law, as in contemporary liberal democracies like the US, Canada, and the UK, present legal processes and legislation as neutral and impartial. Suggestions that individuals are disadvantaged because of group associations contradicts liberal versions of the law. To speak of communities as marginalized or subjected to racism, and to suggest that this must be addressed in discussions of legal practice poses a fundamental challenge to legal notions in Western liberal democracies (Henry and Tator 2000) From the perspective of critical race theories, the universal legal being is actually a male and white being who must be integrated into the market system.

Critics suggest that the legal system, its laws, and policies, are themselves racist. In any event, critics note that the legal system in countries like the US and Canada has certainly had a racist history and been used for racist ends. Far from being neutral, laws facilitated and maintained slavery, enabled and legitimized the theft of indigenous lands and cultures. Laws prohibited African-Americans from learning to read and write and forbid indigenous people from using their languages and practicing their beliefs. The laws have long been used to restrict the entry of racialized minorities into these countries and into public life within these countries upon arrival. Laws are not neutral. Rather they are political and have been deployed for political and economic ends. As Kobayashi (1990, 449) notes: "The law has been wielded as an instrument to create a common sense justification of racial differences, to reinforce common sense notions already deeply embedded within a cultural system of values." To address this, Kobayashi (1990, 449) suggests that legal theory and practice must be situated within social, political, and economic circumstances. Juridical procedures must be interpreted according to dominant ideologies. Legal systems, laws, and policies cannot be studied in separation from the material social relations they claim to regulate and order. As Henry and Tator (2000, 149) suggest: "The legal system produces and reproduces the essential character of law as a means of rationalizing, normalizing, and legitimizing social control on behalf of those who hold power and the interests they represent." The essays in the present collection seek to uncover and examine these processes of power and normalization, as expressed in dominant discourses and practices around borders, race, and security—as means of contesting and challenging them. The liberal argument that law is objective masks a fear that more situated approaches that identify race, sex, and class will shift emphasis from law to activism. The present volume seeks to pose these questions, including, even especially, the need for activism.

The first four chapters of *Racism and Borders: Representation, Repression, Resistance* examine in detail the repressive policies and practices of border controls in the contemporary context. They outline measures taken by governments and the impacts of these measures within specific contexts, particularly the US, the UK, and Canada.

Michael Kilburn notes that racial profiling is typically constructed and perceived as an issue of civil liberties within the context of specific nations. The focus is generally on the abrogation of constitutional rights such as equal protection and due process. Yet, as Kilburn argues, profiling is not merely, or primarily, an issue of inconvenience, undue scrutiny, or harassment. In his view, the state sanctioned classification by race, ethnicity, or religion may also be the early stages of genocide. Kilburn notes that racial profiling has received renewed attention and rationalization in the so-called "War on Terror," with screenings of travelers at airports and border crossings, and targeted assassinations in Baghdad and Waziristan and draws connections between these forms of profiling.. He highlights the common roots of racial profiling and other human rights abuses and atrocities and seeks to open a cross disciplinary dialogue to assess and address them in their complexity and commonality. He suggests that an interdisciplinary approach to the investigation and mitigation of racial profiling might enhance the protection of human as well as civil rights.

Elvira Doghem-Rashid examines the UK police use of the "extraordinary" section 44 stop and search powers bestowed on the police by the Terrorism Act (2000). In effect since February 2001, the Act gives police the ability to stop and search people without probable cause of a criminal activity. Doghem-Rashid's chapter provides a review of the key public debates on section 44, and discusses these debates in the context of a detailed analysis of police stop and search data. The data are unique in that they detail the full range of police ethnic codes—including Arab—which are not published in the police monthly monitoring reports. The analysis also draws on a wide range of published material, reports and interviews in order to present the public and government responses to the ongoing debates. Analyzing extensive data, Doghem-Rashid explores the question regarding whether police stops are disproportionately targeting Asians and Arabs, as a proxy for Muslims, as part of a racial profile in the UK?

An active organizer of immigrant and refugee defense movements in Canada, Harsha Walia examines ways in which Canadian state policies, economic relations in the global economy, strategic discourses of nationalism, and hierarchies of race, class, and gender have been mobilized in constructing the category of migrant workers. Walia further examines how shifting political and economic relations, relations of power, have created the legal, social, political, and economic conditions for the exploitation of migrant workers. For Walia, changes in Canada's immigration policy, have reflected and contributed to an increased reliance on migrant workers. Extending migration controls and the legal distinction between citizen and non-citizen, in various policies and legislation enacted recently, has allowed the Canadian state to pursue economic growth while protecting the ideology of "White Canada." Walia concludes her chapter by emphasizing resistance, examining current examples and further possibilities of strengthening alliances across diverse social movements in BC in order to advance the collective interests of diverse poor and working class communities.

Heidi Rimke provides a detailed analysis of techniques of governing under neo-liberalism, a discussion of which is often missing in debates over border security in the current period. Her chapter develops a critical theoretical framework by analyzing the image of the monster as a political technology of neo-liberalism. Rimke focuses on two contemporary social forces: 1) psychopolitics, or the entrenched psychocentrism characteristic of a culture dominated by "psy" discourses that simultaneously depoliticize the political while capitalizing on the emotional, especially fear, paranoia, and anger; and, 2) the post-911 explosion of the security industry/apparatus. Within that context, the chapter examines several related themes: the politics of emotions and the emotions of politics, the politics of security and insecurity, and the politics of dangerization, victimization, and dehumanization. In order to demonstrate how neo-liberalism feeds upon and governs through mass-mediated, hyper-consumption of monstrous spectacles, Rimke's analysis relies upon Baudrillard's (2010) characterization of society as organized around carnivalization and cannibalization. Rather than normalizing psychocentrism, the chapter provides a sociopolitical analysis of emotional practices of power productive of neo-liberal subjectivities inextricably intertwined with the governance of populations under capitalism. In this way, Rimke offers a genealogical approach to the psychopolitics of emotional governance of the insecure, cannibalistic society as a means to critically interrogate the social production and consumption of fear and terror intrinsic to dominant and dominating rationalities that govern through insecurities.

The middle chapters (Five and Six) critically examine issues of representation, racialization and national security. Issues of border controls, race and repression are, of course, constructed through various means. These chapters show the deployment of power, and resistance through artistic frameworks in literature and art. The contemporary context reflects ongoing anxieties and practices that have been played out in different, though familiar, ways in American history.

David Magill's chapter presents a wider view of the 1920s cultural panic over national borders, understanding it as an outgrowth of white masculinity's anxieties about its own constitution in relation to national identity's privileges and powers. Using Eve Sedgwick's notion of "border panic," Magill suggests that the structural and psychic anxieties arising from a fear of mobility gives rise to strict regulatory boundaries for determining identities and movement. Migrations into and across the United States exacerbate white male tensions because those fluid spatial movements reflect materially the social mobility claimed by disenfranchised groups and physically the ways migration undermines the distinct borders constructed as a property claim on national identities. Mobility becomes a key term of power as well as a marker of modernity. White masculinity manages and defers these tensions through legislative mandates, judicial rulings, and social policies that strategically re-define America's "imagined community" as exclusively white and male through assertions of spatial boundaries, assertions that simultaneously point up the constructedness of these boundaries. Magill reads John Dos Passos' *Manhattan Transfer*, George Owen Baxter's *Tigerman* (1929) and Harold Bell Wright's bestseller *The Mine With the Iron Door* (1923) as texts that register the ongoing "border panic" in US culture and contribute a voice to the cultural panic over immigration and national borders, contextualizing them within various legislative enactments of the day. These Jazz Age texts present an archive of Americanization and its discontents, commenting on the representativeness of art and law as spaces where white masculinity converges with national identity.

Visual artists Peter and Aaron Fine start from concerns with extraordinary rendition in order to offer a vantage point from which to compare and connect political disappearances with what they see as the parallel process of racial passing in America. Their chapter, entitled "White-Out," examines an environment where specific forms are made to become invisible. Border controls in America suggest to them the dangers of losing sight of one another. Blending in means becoming lost. To white-out suggests to erase an error, a fault, or a failing, or even more, to paint over anything "wrong," any "stray character," and make it "white." Legal and extra-legal measures—detention, deportation, profiling, internment, and so on—represent one side of a two-sided process of assimilation and control. Disappearance—of one form or another—is the stick. Access to American-ness is the carrot that encourages racial and ethnic minorities to pass over and into whiteness. Exploring the visual record they seek the blind spots of border enforcement.

It is not enough merely to document and understand representation and re-pression with regard to tightened borders, profiling and security. The point is to change the situation, to resist repression in its various guises. The final two chapters look at resistance in varying, even quite disparate forms.

Graciela Susana Boruszko takes a very personal, indeed autobiographical, ap-proach to overcoming separation, exclusion, and "othering" by borders. Beginning with the premise that people participate in a collective history while developing a personal history through a private story, she uses her own personal intercul-tural journey as a compass to explore the interrelation of the self with "the other." She outlines a particular journey in the shaping of a personal identity that reveals her own personal vocation. While some would use Christian ideology as a justi-fication for profiling and the closing of borders (especially to non-Christian "oth-ers"), Boruszko proposes a Christian notion of hospitality as a starting point for thinking about openness, or solidarity, across and beyond borders For Boruszko, the practice of hospitality, of making room for the other was deeply ingrained in her own "migratory" journeys. The disposition to serve offers a reverse side of the contemporary migratory currents that pursue globalization from the perspective of personal profit. Between exclusion and liberal indifference, Boruszko locates a middle ground of mutual respect. This is hospitality—making room for the other as part of becoming closer to one's self.

Recent state practices in a range of Western liberal democracies, most nota-bly the criminalization of migrants, the punishment of alternative globalization activists, and the extension of security forces since 9–11, have exposed the repres-sive nature of globalization. These practices, and responses to them, suggest that struggles against borders, rather than diminishing under globalization and free trade, are perhaps the key struggles of our times. The final chapter in *Racism and Borders* re-situates the state as an active and crucial part of developing globaliza-tion processes. Rather than a diminished state, as proponents of corporate globalization promise, this chapter highlights the many interventions by the state, especially around control of population movements, that play a crucial part in transforming and regulating social relations in the context of globalization. The chapter also examines emergent strategies and analyses deployed by new movements contesting transformed state practices. Such movements call at once for self-determination and global connectivity while confronting the new realities of statist border practices. They develop creative strategies to organize against the local agents of global capital, including national states, while seeking to create political spaces and communities that go beyond appeals for state protectionism. Consisting primarily of poor people, unemployed workers, and dispossessed people of various backgrounds No One Is Illegal movements have provided a pole of attraction for struggles against local regimes of neo-liberal global governance. Through direct actions, rank-and-file militance and community organizing based on appeals to a solidarity of the excluded, they have impelled a recomposition of class struggle forces across the borders that divide oppressed and exploited people. In doing so these movements provide important insights into the bridging of sectoral differences among movements of poor people, immigrants, and refugees.

Racism and Borders provides a multi-national perspective on an issue of great and growing concern in the context of neo-liberal governance and corporate globalization. Most existing studies of racial profiling have examined domestic policies within specific national contexts. The present volume, on the other hand, seeks to broaden the discussion, examining issues of profiling, border security, repression and resistance from transborder perspectives, with significant analyses of policy and practice. The chapters making up *Racism and Borders* raises important questions about the movement, restriction, and regulation of people within neo-liberal capitalist globalization. At the same time attention is given to global grassroots movements that organize across borders to oppose racial profiling and border tightening.

It is hoped that the book will serve as an important resource for human rights groups, advocacy movements and community organizations. It should prove particularly valuable for community groups supporting immigrants and refugees as well as those supporting members of racialized non-migrant communities.

REFERENCES

Baudrillard, Jean. 2010. *Carnival and Cannibal or The Play of Global Antagonism*. Translated by Chris Turner. Calcutta: Seagull Books.

Henry, Frances and Carol Tator. 2000. *The Colour of Democracy: Racism in Canadian Society*. Toronto: Harcourt Brace Canada.

Kobayashi, Audrey. 1990. "Racism and the Law in Canada: A Geographical Perspective." *Urban Geography* 11(5): 447–473.

Shantz, Jeff. 2003. "Chief Plans Police State in Ontario." *Green Left Weekly*. 535. http://www. greenleft.org.au/node/27757 (Accessed June 10, 2010).

CHAPTER 1. RACIAL PROFILING AT THE BORDERS: IMPLICATIONS FOR NATIONAL AND HUMAN SECURITY

Michael Kilburn

> Racially biased policing is at its core a human rights issue. While some may view it as merely a public relations problem, a political issue, or an administrative challenge, in the final analysis, racially biased policing is antithetical to democratic policing." (Police Executive Research Forum)

> The practice of profiling by race, ethnicity, religion, or national origin runs counter to what is arguably the core principle of American democracy: that humans are created equal and entitled to be treated equally by the government irrespective of immutable characteristics like skin color faith and ethnic or national origin. (ACLU 2004)

In 2003, Donato Garcia, a Latino man, was approached by Dallas police as he sat in his car waiting for his wife and his two young children. When he questioned the reason for being asked to present identification, he was maced, dragged from the vehicle, beaten and arrested. Living in a predominantly white neighborhood, he had been stopped by police dozens of times and even ticketed in his own driveway (Amnesty International n.d., n.p.).

In April 1994, Alphoncina Mutuze was stopped at a roadblock in Kigali. Even without her identity card, she was identified as a Tutsi by her "soft hair," height, and facial features. Thus profiled, she was beaten, raped, enslaved and threatened with death. Her mother and most of her family were murdered after being identified as Tutsi (Olejede 2004. See also UN n.d., n.p.).

These two examples illustrate the scope and range of human rights violations that could fall under the rubric of racial profiling. In each case, individuals were targeted by police or private militia for interdiction, harassment, and worse on the basis of an identity-based suspect classification. In each case, the interaction with state or proxy agents was non-crime specific, based solely on a discriminatory and generic profile of otherness which easily escalated to more serious and substantive violations. While not suggesting that the individual trauma and social injustice of racial profiling is the moral equivalent of genocide, the human rights perspective suggests that the difference may be one of degree rather than kind. All violations of human rights proceed from this fundamental betrayal of the first principle: "that all human beings are born free and equal in rights and dignity" (Universal Declaration of Human Rights). Procedurally disregarding this basic premise leads directly to the dehumanization that makes possible the full range of human rights violations.

Yet only the first of these scenarios would typically be construed as "racial profiling." The case of Ms. Mutuze, owing perhaps to its horror, geographical otherness, or invocation of scale, appears to transcend the civic context normally associated with the term, rising to the level of "atrocity," "crimes against humanity," or "grave breaches of international humanitarian law." By contrast, racial profiling is most often construed in the United States, and perhaps the West generally, as a violation of civil, rather than human, rights. The two categories obviously overlap but treating racial profiling narrowly as an abridgment of *constitutional* rights (specifically 4th amendment protocols on the reasonableness of search and seizure, or 14th amendment guarantees of equal protection and due process) rather than a substantive violation of integrity and fundamental human dignity has important consequences in terms of recognizing the systematic scope and social impact of the problem as well as the efficacy of the remediation.

A human rights perspective can offer a broader context than is normally applied to studies of racial profiling. While many minorities suffer the indignity, inconvenience, and perhaps abusive treatment at the hands of police and other law enforcement agents, millions of others worldwide are threatened with violence or even death at borders and checkpoints simply by virtue of their racial, ethnic, or religious identity. In situations of ethnic conflict or genocide, racial profiling is used to classify, segregate, and systematically exterminate entire classes of people. Government identity cards listing ethnicity, family names, physical features, and even personal relationships with the victim (Komar 2008, 176) are used to categorize potential targets. When Tutsi are slaughtered at roadblocks,

Bosnian Muslim houses selectively destroyed, Palestinians arbitrarily detained at checkpoints, and Sunni or Shia targeted for assassination or displacement in their own neighborhoods, it is clear that racial and ethnic profiling is a serious human rights abuse with potentially deadly consequences. Indeed, in these extreme circumstances, profiling may be seen as a functional component in the early stages of genocide: classification; symbolization; and dehumanization.

This chapter suggests that reframing racial profiling as a substantive human rights issue rather than a question of police procedure or public policy has several advantages. Greater attention to the common premise and conduct of racial profiling with other human rights violations may facilitate a cross disciplinary discourse to consider and investigate the phenomenon in its full scope, social effects, and implications. A global perspective on traditional legal and policing approaches to the issue may suggest linkages to underlying issues of social injustice, while a critical consideration of the applicability of criminological justice models of analysis of the phenomenon can only enrich, ground, and clarify the broader political, sociological, and cultural perspectives of the human rights approach. Finally, and hopefully, such collaborative, interdisciplinary research might lead to the development of effective protocols against racial profiling and other identity-based human rights violations.

HISTORY

There are historical as well as institutional reasons for framing racial profiling as a question of civil, rather than human rights. Racial profiling has been a consistent feature of policing and social policy in the United States since its founding, and successive groups of ethnic, racial, and religious minorities have suffered under its arbitrary gaze. Native Americans, Irish, Italian, Hispanics, Japanese, and particularly African-Americans have all suffered from suspect classification. The profiling and harassment of ethnic immigrants, particularly Jews, during the Palmer raids of the 1920s prompted the organization of the ACLU and its advocacy for civil rights protections and due process. Yet it has really only been in the past 30 years with the rise of civil rights consciousness that racial profiling was finally recognized by law enforcement as not only constitutionally insupportable but counterproductive to the broader mission of public safety. Just as consensus appeared to have been reached among the Department of Justice, state and local police agencies, and public opinion, that racial profiling was "unconstitutional, socially corrupting, and counterproductive" (ACLU 2009, 9) the terror attacks of 9/11 recast the debate. Since then, despite official disavowal and anti-discriminatory rulings and policies, the practice remains pervasive and the post

9/11 climate has complicated efforts to combat it both legally and in the court of public opinion. Yet the same logical and strategic flaws that make racial profiling ineffective and counterproductive as a policing tool also undermine its efficacy in counterterrorism.

A brief overview of the history of racial profiling should illuminate the institutional basis and bias of the practice and suggest how a human rights perspective might prompt its reconsideration. Racial profiling and suspect classification generally have been consistent, even integral, features of American society from its founding. The genocide and expropriation of the native population under the ideology of "manifest destiny" was a founding principal of the country, underwriting subtler forms of social disenfranchisement. Various laws, both state and federal, singled out entire classes of people for surveillance, preemptive interdiction, and unequal treatment. The institution of slavery, uneasily recognized in the US Constitution, is perhaps the most egregious example, but many other minorities—Chinese, Irish, Jews, Latinos—were legally accorded only second class citizenship and widespread racist and xenophobic attitudes maintained cultural discrimination even where the laws did not do so explicitly.

Even after the civil war and the abolition of slavery, discriminatory "black codes" and terroristic campaigns by the Ku Klux Klan (KKK) and other paramilitary groups, often with the complicity if not active support of local police, effectively kept minority populations "in their place." Federalism made any challenge to discriminatory laws and practices piecemeal, and the structure of the appeals process and composition of the Supreme Court made successful challenges to discriminatory laws arduous and remote, particularly following the infamous decision in *Plessy* v. *Ferguson* reaffirming the principle of "separate but equal." Still, the gradual incorporation of Constitutional rights to the states following the due process clause of the 14th Amendment made for some progress in the 20th century, particularly through the Civil Rights movement after World War 2. The Civil Rights Acts of 1964 and 1968 eliminated much de jure discrimination, though their full application to the states has proven a long and contested battle. While momentous progress has been made, and while racial attitudes have undoubtedly improved, vested systemic racism, manifest in broad social inequality and institutionalization, particularly in the criminal justice system, has proven more difficult to overcome.

Even as broad policies of biased policing diminished in the face of increased federal oversight and enhanced civil rights protections, a series of unrelated developments gradually reintroduced a stealth version of the practice that would reach epidemic proportions by the 1990s. The first development was the application of behavioral science to criminal profiling as a supplement to traditional investigative techniques in select, high profile, difficult to solve cases such as the "mad bomber" of New York City in the 1950s and the Boston strangler of the 1960s (Heumann and Cassak 2003, 12-13). The development of the Behavioral Sciences Unit at the FBI in the 1970s broadened its scope and applicability, but maintained a level of elitism and highly selective application (see also McCann 476).

The social disruptions of the 1960s, not least the assertion of political rights and voice by African-Americans and other minorities but also including youth counterculture, women's liberation and the antiwar movement, appeared to threaten traditional American values and produced a conservative reaction among what Richard Nixon's presidential campaign called the "silent majority." A spate of riots, bombings, and skyjackings in the late 1960s only added to the sense of impending anarchy and gave Nixon's promise of law and order a broad mandate. His "war on drugs" brilliantly distilled these fears and prejudices into a single policy initiative and provided a pretext for preemptive policing through the development of skyjacker and drug courier profiles.

The Supreme Court decision in *Terry* v. *Ohio* (1968)—itself perhaps influenced by social demands for law and order—created the legal basis for the expansion of profiling beyond case specific investigations by allowing for investigative stops without probable cause (Heuman and Cassak, 22). In the context of the veiled racism of Nixon's war on drugs—the justicial corollary to his "Southern strategy"—and the newly minted Drug Enforcement Agency's (DEA) broadened application of profiling and other proactive law enforcement tactics, the Terry decision opened the door to the proliferation of racial profiling. With the veneer of objectivity from its social science roots, imprimatur of legitimacy from the Supreme Court decision in Terry, and national security mandate from Nixon's war on drugs, the practice circumvented the otherwise broad gains in civil rights. As it expanded to street level crime and deputized law enforcement personnel untrained in its subtleties, the social scientific expertise and probabilities of criminal profiling were diluted to stereotypes and hunches and became susceptible to racial bias. Crucially, as Heumann and Cassak point out; profiling became a tool of preemption rather than investigation:

> Profiling was increasingly less the reactive application of information and methodologies by specialists, drawing from the behavioral sciences in the course of a crime investigation, and more the proactive approach by law enforcement personnel generally (and those working with them) to uncover planned or potential criminal activities. (2003, 33)

Under the guise of public safety, and with the complicity of the Supreme Court, which in a series of cases over the next 20 years (see Heumann and Cassak 2003, 64–65 for an overview) either upheld the use of profiles or refused to directly address their constitutionality, an entire class of citizens became suspect. As the war on drugs expanded under the Reagan administration—including a forebodingly preemptive foreign policy in Latin America—racial profiling, along with homelessness and other social injustices, became normalized in public consciousness, reflected in the phrase "driving while black" and T-shirts worn by young African-Americans with bulls-eyes and the phrase "Born Suspect."

SCOPE AND EFFECTS POST 9/11

As the practice expanded and evolved from the "reasonable suspicion" standard of Terry to pretextual traffic stops, police across the country became increasingly brazen in their inclusion of race in profiling and increasingly aggressive in their conduct of stopping and searching. The media began covering stories of egregious cases of racial profiling and a number of lawsuits were filed. The Civil Rights division of the US Department of Justice began investigations and lawsuits, issuing a number of consent decrees to the worst offenders. The shooting of four unarmed teenagers during a traffic stop by New Jersey state police in 1998 finally brought the issue to national attention and achieved a political consensus against the practice.

Both candidates in the 2000 presidential race came out strongly against racial profiling, with Democratic candidate Al Gore promising that banning it would be the first Civil Rights Act of the 21st century. The scope of the problem was addressed by President Bush early in his presidency. In an address to a joint session of Congress in February 2001 he stated flatly: "Too many of our citizens have cause to doubt our nation's justice, when the law points a finger of suspicion at groups, instead of individuals. All our citizens are created equal, and must be treated equally . . . [Racial profiling is] wrong and we will end it in America." Attorney General John Ashcroft condemned it as "an unconstitutional deprivation of equal protection under our Constitution" (cited in Alvarez 2009, n.p.) and directed his Department to work towards its eradication. Two years later, in June 2003, the US Department of Justice issued its *Guidelines Regarding the use of Race by Federal Law Enforcement* Agencies, which prohibited the use of "generalized stereotypes" and "race or ethnicity to any degree, except in suspect specific descriptions" (n.p.).

Despite its claim to ensure an end to racial profiling in law enforcement, however, these guidelines fell short on several counts, not least of which was their issuance as guidelines rather than an enforceable executive order or legislative Act. The guidelines did not apply to state or local law enforcement and contained no provisions for data collection, education, retraining, or enforcement. Moreover, the racial and ethnic mandate was too narrow and did not cover profiling based on religion appearance or national origin. There were also blanket exemptions made to the guidelines in matters of national security and border integrity. A draft report by the US Commission on Civil Rights summarized its shortcomings.

> The guidelines begin a national solution and are commendable for the precedent they set in presidential action against profiling. No past President has attempted to resolve the problem of racial profiling in such a comprehensive manner. But the problem is far from resolved. The guidance needs a mechanism to enforce or track noncompliance; it only applies to federal agencies, leaving state and local law enforcement unaffected; and it has broad exceptions for national security and immigration purposes. (2004, 87)

Of course there were other events in 2001 that would vastly expand the scope of profiling in the United States and render even these cursory and rhetorical guidelines moot. Following the terror attacks of 9/11, there was a vast expansion of profiling by federal state and local law enforcement. In the words of a 2004 report by the ACLU, racial profiling became "sanctioned bias." The response of the Bush administration to the terrorist attacks of September 11, 2001 was not simply an extrapolation of "driving while black" to "flying while Arab," but shifted the entire focus of federal law enforcement to an aggressively and inductively preemptive stance. An astonishing memo issued by Attorney General Ashcroft on November 8, 2001, announced the transformation of the core mission of the Department of Justice from upholding the Constitution and the rule of law to subordinating civil liberties in the prosecution of the war on terror.

> The Department of Justice is the guardian of liberty in our land and our mission is to preserve the constitutional rights and freedoms of all Americans and our sacred responsibility is to protect those who are weak, vulnerable, or oppressed... this department exists to protect American's constitutional rights from threats foreign and domestic that would rob us of our basic liberties... we exercise sweeping powers and vast resources... in the days following September 11... [T]he president charged us with a critical mission... [T]he fight against terrorism is now the first and *overriding* priority of the Department of Justice. (Ashcroft 2001, n.p. [emphasis added])

In one stroke the constitutional basis for protection against violations of civil liberties such as racial profiling—not to mention the very philosophical premise of democratic government—was subverted to the dictates of national security. In case the implications of this memo weren't clear enough, the Department of Justice's Office of Legal Counsel also issued a raft of memos asserting the authority of the president as Commander-in-Chief to override Constitutional rights in the name of national security. One, apparently revoking *posse comitatus*, envisioned the deployment of US military forces within the United States and stated flatly that "the fourth amendment has no application to domestic military applications" (cited in Conyers 2009, 29).[1]

The implications for individual civil liberties and rights in the face of this paradigm shift were immediate. It retroactively legitimized and perpetuated the arbitrary detention of thousands of Arab, Muslim, and South Asian men initiated immediately after 9/11, the first large-scale preventative detention of a population based on ancestry since the internment of Japanese-Americans during World War II. These random detentions without charge, some lasting more than a year (but averaging about 3 months), were followed by a program of coercive interviews and mandatory registration of target populations fitting a profile according to immigration status and national origin. In June 2002, the NSEERS program (National Security Entry/Exit registration System) was instituted, entailing mandatory registration for aliens from certain countries or who met a broad profile allegedly signifying elevated risk to national security. Nearly 100,000 were registered in the first year, of which almost 10 percent were subject to deportation. Not one terrorism related charge was brought.

In spite of protestations by some state and local law enforcement agencies, who expressed skepticism at the crude and discredited tactics, racial profiling became official government policy in the war on terror. Many police officials lamented that the public trust and cooperative relationships that had been painstakingly built within these communities should be compromised from above. In short, just as it was discredited as a policing tactic on the local level, profiling became the tool of first resort in a re-prioritized justice system. Even as the Department of Justice rhetorically condemned racial profiling as 2003 guidelines, the broad exclusions for border control, national security indicate a continued reliance on these measures in its domestic agenda. Not surprisingly, by November 2004, the US Commission on Civil Rights—an independent government agency—reported that the post-9/11 policies of the Department of Justice on Homeland Security had exacerbated racial and ethnic profiling despite the president's admonitions against it (USCCR n.d., n.p.).

A broadly construed Muslim/Arab/Middle Eastern suspect classification was not the only target of profiling in the post-9/11 period. The Office of Legal Counsel, under John Yoo's expansive interpretation of executive power, also provided the legal rationale for the domestic surveillance program, the scope of which is still coming to light. Millions of Americans are now routinely profiled through secret surveillance and fast drift-net data mining operations conducted by the FBI and NSA with the complicity of private telecom companies. This "total information awareness" program illustrates on a society-wide scale the betrayal of the social contract heretofore experienced only by minority populations. The philosophical implications of this Hobbesian turn bode even worse for democracy. A government proactively searching for enemies, rather than operating deductively from actionable intelligence, creates a climate of fear and paranoia and undermines civil society. Just as racially biased enforcement compromises community policing, a government that regards its own citizens is a pool of potential enemies rather than constituents, is fundamentally undemocratic.

If the domestic costs of suspect classification were not bad enough, the inductive logic of profiling redefined foreign policy as well. The logic of preemption is evident in the 2002 US National Security Strategy, which asserts that, "as a matter of common sense and self-defense, America will act against such emerging threats before they are fully formed" (NSS 2002–2009, 2). This was profiling writ large, to foreign policy ends. Alleged "rogue nations" were indicted by "underlying prejudices and presumptions of guilt," randomly associated with a vaguely defined "axis of evil." The posture of responding aggressively to perceived and hypothetical threats "before they could materialize" was the corollary to expand profiling in domestic law enforcement. The presumption of guilt and aggressively pretextual interdiction was facilitated by lowered standards in oversight and multi-agency initiatives made possible by the Patriot Act and other anti-terror legislation intended to preempt threats to public safety and order, both domestic and foreign.

The post-9/11 world has seen a Hobbesian sacrifice of rights and liberties for the promise of security and the shift to a more aggressive unilateral foreign policy. This was not simply imperial overreach by an ostensibly unitary executive, as asserted in Rep. John Conyers' January 2009 report, "Lessons and recommendations relating to the presidency of George W. Bush," but had broad support in Congress and the mainstream media, and among most Americans. As a 2004 US Commission on Civil Rights report succinctly put it: "The terrorist attacks of September 11, 2001, shattered the emerging public consensus that racial and ethnic profiling is wrong and should be eliminated" (USCCR 2004, n.p.). A survey in 2000 indicated that in the United States 80 percent thought racial profiling should be abolished; scarcely a year later, following the September 11 attacks, a majority supported it, at least for "Arabs," and thought those fitting a broad terrorist profile should be required to carry special identification. A surge in hate crimes against those of "middle-Eastern descent" (broadly construed) and tolerance for identity-based surveillance and interdiction was also widely evident.

Even as Arabs, South Asians, and Muslims were subjected to increased levels of racial and ethnic profiling, the practice also continued unabated against the usual suspects, African-Americans and Latinos. According to a 2004 report by Amnesty International's domestic human rights agency, more than 32 million US citizens (the population of Canada) reported being racially profiled, with 87 million more considered to be "at high risk" of arbitrary stops, searches, detention, and other harassment simply because they belong to ethnicities commonly targeted by police. While the numbers are clearly a function of the report's broad and agenda-driven methodology, by Amnesty's reckoning this would make racial profiling the most common rights violation in the United States. Yet even a human rights organization such as Amnesty International deferred to the civil rights framework both rhetorically and substantively when considering racial profiling. The key findings of the 2004 Amnesty International report, "Threat and Humiliation" called for the elimination of "this extremely prevalent human rights problem" (vii), but limited its recommendations to constitutionalism and domestic legal remedies, such as passing Senator Russ Feingold's "End Racial Profiling Act (S 2481; HR 4611), encouraging and enforcing state and local ordinances against the practice; maintaining databases and independent monitoring bodies; and training and public education. While these are certainly credible and necessary steps toward ending the practice, they fall somewhat shy of Amnesty's customary tactics and institutional reference points when addressing other types of human rights abuses. The American Civil Liberties Union's (ACLU) report on racial profiling, "Sanctioned Bias: Racial profiling since 9/11," issued in the same year as the Amnesty Report, uses similar language and reaches similar conclusions, stating: "Only through federal legislation can the problem of racial profiling be comprehensively identified and ended" (ACLU 2004, 2).

CIVIL VS. HUMAN RIGHTS

As outlined above, there are historical, cultural, and strategic reasons for the prevalence of the civil rights paradigm in dealing with racial profiling, even after 9/11. The Constitutional design of checks and balances, rule of Law, and incorporation of the Bill of Rights continues to hold out the promise of a "more perfect union." While incomplete and inconsistent, there has been undeniable progress in the field of civil rights for African-Americans and other minorities over the past few generations. Challenges to discriminatory practices have been argued most effectively, if painstakingly, on constitutional grounds through the legal system. The legitimacy of rights claims, both in court and in public opinion, were underwritten by a disciplined commitment to non-violence, a reverent nativism that resonated with mainstream American values, and a strict constructionist invocation of US Constitutionalism: "to rise up," as Dr. Martin Luther King Jr. put it, "and live out the full meaning of its creed." The gradual momentum towards greater constitutional rights for minorities in the 20th century, and the attendant normative shift in cultural attitudes, is one reason that opponents of racial profiling have continued to frame it in terms of civil rather than human rights. The discourse of human rights may have a clearer moral and universal basis than the shady, compromised history of constitutionality, but it is not justiciable. As Dr. Sam Holliday points out somewhat cynically in an article in *Politeia*,

> In practice, however, civil rights have continued to prevail and the march to universal human rights has been slow... Historically rights have been gained through custom and tradition, status, accomplishment, or force. Only in the last 300 years, through acceptance of social contracts, have rights for all citizens of a state even been considered. Under a social contract, between citizens and their government, rights and responsibilities are specified by a constitution, or through laws determined by some legislative body. Then these rights are adjudicated by some legal system. But these are civil rights, and they are by no means universal. (2004, n.p.)

According to Holliday, human rights are not exactly "nonsense on stilts," but no basis for substantive social progress.

Frustrated with the slow pace of change and uncomprehending of the docile tactics of the SCLC during the civil rights struggles of 1960s, Malcolm X made the internationalist case for framing equal rights for African-Americans in terms of human rights, arguing that the pre-political, ethical recognition of African-Americans was a prerequisite to the full realization of civil and political rights.

> The common goal of 22 million Afro-Americans is respect as human beings, the God-given right to be a human being. Our common goal is to obtain the human rights that America has been denying us. We can never get civil rights in America until our human rights are first restored. We will never be recognized as citizens there until we are first recognized as humans. (X, 1964, n.p.)

Malcolm X's radicalism, however, his refusal to renounce violence in self-defense, his Muslim religion, and his internationalist vision and sympathies, alienated mainstream audiences. In the Cold War context of the 1960s, "internationalism" was a suspect classification in itself and talk of human rights appeared to betray leftist sympathies and possible Communist affiliations. Strategically, then, the civil rights discourse was the only possibility for moderate progress within the law.

Despite the invocation of unalienable human, or "natural," rights in the Declaration of Independence and other foundational texts of US political philosophy, *human rights*, with its fey aura of universality and implicit endorsement of supranational governance, rings alien to American political discourse. Until quite recently, this has been especially so in the judicial branch, where the supremacy of the US Constitution is *sine qua non* and where questions of rights are decided. As Justice Alito's furious dissent from the bench in the juvenile death penalty case *Simmons* v. *Roper* (2004) illustrated, "Acknowledgement' of foreign approval has no place in the legal opinion of this Court." While extreme in its parochialism, Alito's position reveals a common political ideology of reflexive unilateralism in foreign and especially domestic policy in the United States; the reluctance to accede unambiguously to global norms or concede the legitimacy of global monitoring bodies. Perhaps this is evolving somewhat as Barack Obama attempts to mend the fences trampled by Bush administration's preemptive and unilateralist policies, but it is still a powerful current in American political discourse.

This tendency is reflected, for example, in the reservations and declarations listed in US accessions to several treaties including the ICCPR and the Convention on the Elimination of All Forms of Racial Discrimination (ICERD), which consistently reassert the supremacy of the United States Constitution over international obligations and refract rights and obligations through American definitions and precedent. There is also a generalized bias in American rights discourse toward first-generation (civil and political) rights over second-generation (social and economic rights), which tends to downplay systemic patterns of social discrimination.

For strategic, institutional and cultural reasons, then, civil rights, constitutionality and due process have been the preferred modes of discourse in attempts to remediate racial profiling. Since the attacks of 9/11, however, and particularly in response to the conduct of the nation in the so-called war on terror, the discourse of human rights has become increasingly salient in framing the practice of racial profiling, broadly construed. With the legal status and requisite Constitutional protections of so-called enemy combatants unclear, human rights advocates were thrust to the forefront of opposition to the Bush administration's policies of torture, rendition, surveillance and profiling. With the mandate of national security overriding its traditional mission to uphold Constitutional rights and protections—a position not yet overturned by the Obama administration—the Department of Justice was no longer a reliable ally in the struggle for civil rights. Stonewalled by claims of national security and executive privilege, or outmaneuvered by the cynically creative machinations of the Office of Legal Counsel, lawyers and advocates for the detained, rendered, and surveilled in the war on terror had to resort to innovative means, including appeals to transnational human rights institutions and networks, to move their clients' cases forward. When, for example, the Supreme Court upheld the Bush administration's assertion of state secrets privilege and dismissed a lawsuit against George Tenet for the rendition and torture of Khaled el-Masri, the ACLU petitioned the Inter-American Commission on Human Rights, a body of the Organization of American States (OAS), which demanded a substantive response from the US State Department (Satterthwaite 2008, 575–577). While the US routinely ignores decisions of the IACHR and OAS lacks any means to enforce its decisions against a sovereign state, the case does illustrate the broad potential for a human rights paradigm to broaden the scope of responses to domestic rights violations.

It is perhaps ironic that the ACLU, which pioneered civil rights advocacy and litigation, has been foremost in recognizing the potential of the human rights paradigm against racial profiling and other abuses of power. Shortly after the publication of its report on racial profiling in 2004, the ACLU initiated its Human Rights Program, which employs an international human rights framework and mechanisms to ensure US compliance with international human rights treaties and to advocate for its domestic rights agenda. Frustrated with the lack of progress on racial profiling—including the failure of Congress for 8 years to pass ERPA—as well as other ongoing rights violations by the Bush administration, the HRP submitted reports to the Human Rights Council and United Nations Committee on the Elimination of Racial Discrimination, the monitoring bodies of the ICCPR and ICERD, which the United States has ratified. This prompted a critical visit by the UN's special rapporteur on racism and resulted in a landmark declaration by that body against the practice of racial profiling in the United States. While the conclusions took the form of "decisive observations" and were not enforceable, employing the framework and prestige of the United Nations in racial profiling illustrates how a holistic human rights approach can help move the issue forward in ways that were not possible when approaching it strictly as a technical domestic civil rights issue. As the ACLU reported:

> By invoking international human rights sources, the ACLU has been able to make advances when previous concerns were dismissed by the courts. Having adopted an integrative approach to human rights advocacy that incorporates community organizing and coalition building, in addition to utilizing litigation and legislative strategies, HRP is strengthening its work to advance human rights in the United States (2007, n.p.).

Twenty years after the end of the Cold War, Malcolm X's insight that institutionalized racism is fundamentally a human rights issue may finally be politically acceptable. Given the failure of civil rights strategies to effectively mitigate the practice of racial profiling, and considering the ongoing social costs in terms of individual dignity, community disenfranchisement, the legitimacy of police and other public institutions, not to mention the extraordinary stakes for effective strategies in counter-terrorism, it may now be worth considering a broader shift in perspective and tactics. The conclusion of the paper will outline the potential benefits to considering racial profiling through a lens of human rights.

ADVANTAGES OF THE HUMAN RIGHTS PARADIGM

One advantage over the traditional criminological approaches to racial profiling is that the human rights paradigm is more holistic and sensitive to the broader costs and consequences of systemic affronts to dignity. With an emphasis on individual civil and political rights, traditional legal and criminal justice approaches to the problem simply cannot give a comprehensive accounting of the social costs of racial profiling. Victims of racial profiling may suffer not only the immediate effects of the event violation of human dignity shame, depression and a loss of faith in the system but also long-term effects of trauma and related of related stress. This is particularly true for children who witness the encounter (see Amnesty International 2004, 21). An appreciation of these aftereffects entails a shift of emphasis on substantive rather than just procedural rights and takes seriously the sometimes unquantifiable effects of such violations, both for the individual and the community.

In addition to individual humiliation, families and communities are also negatively affected by racial profiling. Discriminatory practices can lead to resentment, suspicion and anger. These are not just attitudes, but have empirical consequences as well, leading to distrust and a lack of cooperation with authorities, social segregation, and political disenfranchisement. (Walker 2003). Fear and alienation undermines the legitimacy and effectiveness of law enforcement, poor community relations breed further suspicion on both sides and the reluctance to cooperate with the police or report crime increases frustration and more aggressive interactions. The profile thus becomes an autocatalytic process that institutionalizes racial disparity throughout the criminal justice system. Glaser (2006), for example, has mathematically correlated racial profiling to the disproportionate incarceration of minorities, a kind of self-fulfilling prophecy. The prioritization of individual rights in legal and criminological approaches, however, and the emphasis on procedural rather than substantive rights, can render the cumulative social trauma and injustice invisible. But by tempering the traditional emphasis on civil and political rights with 2nd generation social rights, the human rights perspective is better positioned to capture the collective impact of this practice on minority communities and track its reverberating social costs.

Besides a subtler appreciation of the social consequences of rights violations, the human rights perspective also points toward potentially positive outcomes.

Civil and political rights are normally construed as *negative* rights, that is, rights which are realized by their non-abrogation: the right not to be tortured, for example, or not to have the transparency of justice sullied by government intervention and prejudice. An integral human rights perspective, however, also recognizes *positive* rights, not only in the traditional sense of rights that need affirmative action by government for their realization, such as the right to food, education, or social security, but in the sense that a positive recognition of rights and dignity yields a mutually beneficial and substantive result. The idea, somewhat counter-intuitive to the Hobbesian thesis of a zero sum game between rights and security, is that respecting human and civil rights actually increases security and the common good. This notion is manifest in the preamble to the Universal Declaration of Human Rights, which states clearly in its first line that, "recognition of the inherent dignity and of the equal and inalienable rights of all members of the human family is the foundation of freedom, justice and peace in the world" (UNGA 1948, n.p.).

In terms of racial profiling, this approach would suggest that it is not sufficient for effective policing to simply not engage in discriminatory practice; one should affirmatively engage the public in a respectful and collaborative manner. This would entail not merely observing standard protocols and statistical equity, but to the qualitative aspects of the interaction. Research data, including testimony collected by Amnesty International (2004) indicate that racial profiling, laden as it is with prejudice and the presumption of guilt, leads disproportionately to disrespect, excessive force, and other violations of dignity. Racial profiling not only does not work in terms of increasing hit rates, but is actually counterproductive in terms of wasted resources, alienation and resentment. A positive affirmation of the rights and dignity of the public might yield better intelligence and community relations.

The human rights implications are even clearer for profiling in the post 9/11 environment. The expansion and institutionalization of these discredited police tactics in the so-called war on terror created a legacy of distrust and paranoia in the target communities, undermining cooperation and diminishing the already meager intelligence resources. Lengthy arbitrary interrogations, detentions, and deportations have had a devastating effect on families, businesses and communities, not to mention the legitimacy of the government's moral and civilizational claims. Citing the 2003 report by the Office of the Inspector General, the ACLU (2004) concluded that not only were civil rights violations by the FBI, INS and other federal agencies in the aftermath of 9/11 "deliberate and wholesale," but also quite ineffective, with not one of the 762 detainees reviewed found to have any links to terrorism (cited in ACLU 2004).

Beyond the domestic misapplication of ethnic and national profiling for counterterrorism, the same tactics writ large for a purportedly preemptive foreign policy and deployed in the streets of Baghdad and Kandahar have proven not only ineffective and counterproductive, but deadly. Here, racial and ethnic stereotypes are compounded by cultural ignorance and a confounding patriotism on both sides, deepening the divide between security forces and the community. Conducting neighborhood sweeps, preventative detentions, and mass arrests according to a generic and culturally uninformed profile has led to widespread resentment and open resistance to the American occupation. These tactics have had severe blowback on American troops, international goodwill, and the legitimacy of the missions. Besides this collateral damage, the policies have not even been effective, something that should have been obvious from the literature on domestic racial profiling well before 9/11. The arrogance, ignorance, and disrespectful conduct of the allied forces have alienated the local population and undermined the common struggle against extremists.

An affirmative respect for human rights, cultural diversity and positive community policing practices would go a long way to build mutual trust and cooperation. A human rights perspective recognizes the positive correlation between respecting human rights and effective law enforcement. Dick Cheney's protestations aside, there is ample evidence that violating human rights through profiling, torture, rendition, and other abuses have not made us safer, whereas FBI interrogations, for example which abjure abusive tactics and rely on rapport, respect, and co-dependency have yielded the most actionable intelligence. All police and surveillance work involves profiling to a degree but racial, rather than behavioral profiling is a distraction. The point where it violates the subject's rights is not coincidentally also the point of diminishing returns. The security response to the attempted Christmas day airline bombing over Detroit is a case in point. Having missed the behavioral profile of a would-be attacker (paying in cash for a one way ticket, traveling with no coat or luggage and so on), the Obama administration responded by profiling travelers from 14 countries with suspected links to terrorism. Given al-Qaeda's stateless transnational affiliations, such a policy seems reactive and counterproductive, squandering security resources and international relations on racial, ethnic and national profiling rather than enhancing behavioral surveillance.

BENEFITS FOR RESEARCH

Besides the practical applications of more holistically accounting for the social costs of racial profiling and the constructive effects of affirmatively recognizing human rights in law enforcement and national security, there are also theoretical advantages to considering a human rights perspectives on the question of racial profiling. An adoption of the human rights paradigm might be beneficial to racial profiling research first of all by providing as meta-level of analysis to facilitate cross disciplinary research. Engel and Calnon (2004) have suggested that the lack of a coherent theoretical paradigm for racial profiling hampers research, particularly an understanding of the causal mechanisms and broader social trauma. Triangulating data sources as suggested by Warren, Tomaskovic-Devey, Smith and Mason (2006) is an important methodological innovation, but does not address the larger theoretical incoherence. A recent article by Robin Engel identified at least four discourses operating in racial profiling research: a) legalistic; b) criminological; c) normative; and d) economistic. Each discourse is limited in its own purview, with the procedural and technocratic language of legal and criminological research often unappreciative of the normative social implications. Human rights research tends toward the normative, but often at the expense of empirical and statistical integrity. The claim in the 2004 Amnesty International report "Threat and Humiliation," that 87 million Americans are potential victims of racial profiling, "because they belong to a racial, ethnic, or religious group whose members are commonly targeted by police for unlawful stops and searches" is as empirically vague as it is alarmist. Strategic overstatement is one thing, but analytical clarity and methodological soundness might be just as effective and more sustainable in making the case for intervention. Perhaps the broader scope and true interdisciplinarity of human rights scholarship could provide a framework for cross-disciplinary dialogue and collaborative research on racial profiling and associated civil and human rights violations.

With its integrationist approach—that all rights are equal and mutually implicated—and global perspective, the human rights perspective might even suggest that racial profiling is a systemic flaw, a function rather than a dysfunction, of a racially-biased justice system. As Jack Glaser (2006) points out, racial profiling is functionally linked to other racial disparities in the US criminal justice system, including rates of prosecution, sentencing, and incarceration. The legalistic and criminological approaches, with their emphasis on procedural rights and narrower methodologies, may miss the larger human rights concerns, particularly social, economic and cultural issues such as widespread economic inequality, social injustice and the "cradle to prison pipeline" (CDF 2007, n.p.) that feeds an increasingly privatized corrections system with disproportionate numbers of minorities.

The United States has the highest incarceration rate in the world both per capita and, incredibly, in terms of sheer numbers. That this country should have a million more of its citizens in prison than China has, with only one-quarter the population, and that the imprisoned population should be so racially disproportionate, indicates a more deeply flawed criminal justice system than procedural abuses could account for. Thousands of articles analyze, quantify, and theorize various aspects of racial profiling, but few works in the criminal justice literature capture the moral outrage. The cold calculus of quantitative analysis strikes one from outside the discipline as the moral equivalent of counting the silverware while the Titanic sinks.

Offering a broader cross-cultural and comparative perspective (and conversant in moral outrage) human rights scholars are well-positioned to supplement traditional approaches to racial profiling, as well as other issues of criminal justice and law enforcement. The predominantly domestic focus of Criminal Justice is challenged both theoretically and practically by the demands of the post 9/11 security environment. While racial profiling has been seen and treated (if only topically) as an essentially domestic and procedural affair, the broader context of racial profiling at the borders is clearly global in scope, raising issues of state sovereignty, international law, and transnational politics and culture beyond the purview and expertise of criminology and related disciplines. With a sober assessment of the limits of law—particularly international law—in remediating human rights violations, and experience dealing with rogue states, human rights scholars and practitioners may also bring a healthy dose of cynicism to the prospect of effective legal remedies. Bridging the disciplines of criminal justice, law, international relations, and with a fundamentally internationalist and normative approach, human rights can make a positive contribution to a more expansive consideration of these issues.

The anthropocentric focus of human rights can also perhaps compensate for the institutional, procedural and quantitative bias of criminal justice, which often prioritizes the state/offender dyad to the exclusion of the victim. Focused on the dignity of the person, a human rights perspective can refocus attention on the position of victims of racial profiling and other rights violations. The sub-discipline of victimology is perhaps a natural bridge between these disciplinary perspectives and might facilitate collaborative research and dialogue (Kilburn 2007).

In sum, human rights scholarship has much to offer traditional disciplinary approaches to the broader understanding of racial profiling. As an interdisciplinary subject, it can facilitate dialogue among the various registers and discourses of research. Its broad social perspective and holistic definition of rights can compensate for the individualistic, civil and political focus of law and criminal justice. Combined with a normative agenda, this critical macro view may reveal systemic inequities. And the combination of a global perspective and anthropocentric focus can orient and contextualize the domestic research agenda and rehabilitate the status of the victim at the heart of the issue. Finally, the proactive understanding of rights—that public safety/national security follows from human security, and not vice versa—provides a more promising policy orientation than the discredited Hobbesian *dictat* of recent history.

Of course, the traditional disciplinary paradigms of law, psychology and criminal justice have much to offer human rights scholarship as well; theoretically, methodologically, and tactically. Careful monitoring and sophisticated statistical analysis of incidents of profiling and discrimination can help ground the righteous alarmism that sometimes animates rights advocacy groups. With clear social scientific standards for research methodologies and analysis, established protocols for evaluating incidents of racial profiling, and experience navigating the prevarications of legal regimes, the insights of psychology, law, and criminal justice might be fruitfully applied to other types of racial and ethnic differentiation. A clearer social scientific basis for analyzing racial profiling as both a rights violation in itself and a harbinger of greater atrocities could prompt clearer, swifter, and more effective countermeasures. Sound data collection procedures, clear analytical models, and domestic expertise in litigation could help track and more effectively intervene in the early stages of genocide and other wide scale systematic human rights abuses. As may be seen from the current situation in Darfur, compelling narratives and normative moral appeals are not enough to compel action. Human rights violations do not speak for themselves. Even when a situation is identified as genocide, the slightest ambiguity in the data or smallest loophole in the legislation can forestall intervention. If the threshold were analytically clearer, then perhaps effective countermeasures might be more forthcoming. Hopefully, a cross-disciplinary consensus on upholding civil and human rights will ultimately yield more accurate monitoring, more sophisticated and socially grounded analysis, and a deeper understanding and appreciation of the human and social cost of this practice. As the normative discourse of human rights informs and is grounded by the legalistic and criminological, studies should also lead to more effective remediation, and ultimately an end to racial profiling in all its manifestations.

CONCLUSION

With the persistence of racial profiling in policing worldwide, and particularly with its application to border controls and other national security measures in the conduct of the so-called war on terror, there is an urgent need for dialogue among the various agencies, groups and disciplines engaged in the practice. The various perspectives and discursive modes operating on the issue of racial profiling: the legalistic approach of the constitutionalists with a focus on due process rights; the criminological approach of police and criminal justice scholars; the normative approach of the human rights scholars and advocates; and the economistic considerations of social policy experts, will hopefully discipline each other and lead to deeper understanding and more effective countermeasures. Recent initiatives by the ACLU may indicate the beginning of such a convergence wherein civil rights and human rights groups work more effectively together, sharing tactics and expertise and realizing their common purpose. Scholars should follow the lead of the activists to collegially, collaboratively, and critically develop a body of interdisciplinary scholarship that assesses racial profiling in its full complexity and informs social policy toward the protection and realization of both civil and human rights. The normative discourse of human rights could contribute a moral imperative to such a reconsideration, and the realization that respect for human rights and dignity is the foundation of a just and secure social order.

As Mccann (1994) once called for a robust interdisciplinary dialogue on criminal profiling, drawing on the "empirical and theoretical strengths of the behavioral sciences as well as the practical experience and needs of law enforcement" (1994, 480–481), a critical reevaluation of racial profiling with a priority on *human* rather than *national* security might help salvage some of the original promise of the methodology. An end to identity-based profiling and the development of protocols for more targeted and sophisticated criminal/behavioral profiling would lead to better security and a greater exercise of fundamental rights for all. Just as the historical experience of racial profiling has demonstrated that the sacrifice of civil liberties does not lead to greater public safety, the violation of human rights in the name of national security violates the very principles we seek to preserve and promote. As Benjamin Franklin famously put it, "Those who would give up essential liberty to purchase a little temporary safety, deserve neither liberty nor safety."

NOTE

1. The fact that this memo was written by John Yoo, author of the infamous torture memos, was uncovered by the ACLU through a FOI application.

REFERENCES

Alvarez, L. 2009. "Ashcroft Meets With Black Lawmakers Who Opposed His Nomination. *The New York Times*, A21.

American Civil Liberties Union. 2004. *Sanctioned Bias: Racial Profiling since 9/11*. New York: Author. http://www.aclufl.org/take_action/download_resources/racial%20profiling%20report.pdf.

American Civil Liberties Union. 2007. "About the ACLU's Human Rights Program." http://www.aclu.org/human-rights/about-aclus-human-rights-program.

American Civil Liberties Union. 2008. "International Human Rights Experts Denounce US Record on Racial and Ethnic Discrimination." http://www.aclu.org/human-rights/international-human-rights-experts-denounce-us-record-racial-and-ethnic-discrimination.

American Civil Liberties Union. 2009. "UN Human Rights Body Issues Decisive Observations on Racial Discrimination in US." http://www.aclu.org/human-rights_racial-justice/un-human-rights-body-issues-decisive-observations-racial-discrimination.

American Civil Liberties Union and the Rights Working Group. 2009. *The persistence of racial and ethnic profiling in the United States: A follow-up report to the Committee on the Elimination of Racial Discrimination.*

Amnesty International. n.d. Testimony from Amnesty International USA's Hearings on Racial Profiling. http://www.amnestyusa.org/us-human-rights/other/rp-while-driving/page.do?id=1106662.

Amnesty International, US Domestic Human Rights Program. 2004. *Threat and Humiliation: Racial Profiling, Domestic Security, and Human Rights in the United States*. New York: AIUSA.

Ashcroft, J. 2001. "Memorandum for Heads of Department Components: Comprehensive Review and Reorganization of the Department of Justice to Meet Counterterrorism Mission." http://fas.org/irp/news/2001/11/ag-reorg-110801.html

Bush, G. W. 2001. "State of the Union." http://www.let.rug.nl/usa/P/gwb43/speeches/state_union_2001.htm.

Children's Defense Fund. 2007. *America's Cradle to Prison Pipeline*. http://www.childrensdefense.org/child-research-data-publications/data/cradle-prison-pipeline-report-2007-full-highres.pdf

Conyers, J. 2009. "Reining in the Imperial Presidency: Lessons and Recommendations Relating to the Presidency of George W Bush. (House Committee on the Judiciary Majority Staff Report to Chairman). http://judiciary.house.gov/hearings/printers/110th/IPres090113.pdf

Engel, R.S., J.M Calnon, and T.J. Bernard 2002. "Theory and Racial Profiling: Shortcomings and Future Directions in Research." *Justice Quarterly* 19:249–273.

Engel, R.S. and J.M. Calnon. 2004. "Examining the Influence of Drivers' Characteristics During Traffic Stops With Police: Results From a National Survey." *Justice Quarterly* 21(1): 49–90.

Engel, R.S. 2008. "A Critique of the "Outcome Test" in Racial Profiling Research." *Justice Quarterly* 25(1): 1–36.

Glaser, J. 2006. "The Efficacy and Effect of Racial Profiling: A Mathematical Simulation Approach." *Journal of Policy Analysis and Management* 25(2): 395–416.

Gregory, N. 2005. "Offender Profiling: A Review of the Literature." *The British Journal of Forensic Practice* 7(3): 29–34.

Harris, R.L. 2009. "Bollywood Star Detained at Newark Airport." *The New York Times*. A2.

Heufmann, M. and L. Cassak. 2003. *Good Cop, Bad Cop: Racial Profiling and Competing Views of Justice.* New York: Peter Lang.

Holliday, S. 2007. "Civil rights vs. human rights." *Politeia.* http://newcitizenship.blogspot.com/2007/12/d-r-sam-c.html.

Kilburn, M.J. 2007. "Criminology, Victimology and Human Rights: Towards a Synthetic Paradigm." Presented at the Annual Meeting of the International Studies Association, 48th Annual Convention, Chicago.

Komar, D.A. 2008. "Variables Influencing Victim Selection in Genocide." *Journal of Forensic Science* 53:172–177.

Lichtblau, E. 2003. "Threats and Responses: Law Enforcement; Bush Issues Racial Profiling Ban But Exempts Security Inquiries." *The New York Times*, A1.

McCann, Joseph T. 1992. "Criminal Personality Profiling in the Investigation of Violent Crime: Recent Advances and Future Directions." Behavioral Sciences and the Law 10: 475–481.

National Security Strategy of the United States. 2002. http://georgewbush-whitehouse.archives.gov/nsc/nss/2002/

Olojede, D. 2004. "Genocide's Child." *Orlando Sentinel.* http://www.orlandosentinel.com/topic/ny-rwanda-day1,0,357350.story

Satterthwaite, M.L. 2008. *The Story of El-Masri v. Tenet: Human Rights and Humanitarian Law in the War on Terror* (New York University Public Law and Legal Theory Working Papers). New York University School of Law: NELLCO.

Scalia, A. 2004. "Dissent in *Roper v. Simmons.*" http://www.deathpenaltyinfo.org/u-s-supreme-court-roper-v-simmons-no-03-633.

UN General Assembly. 1948. *Universal Declaration of Human Rights*, 217 A (III). http://www.unhcr.org/refworld/docid/3ae6b3712c.html.

UN Human Rights Council. 2009. "Report of the Special Rapporteur on Contemporary Forms of Racism, Racial Discrimination, Xenophobia and Related Intolerance, Doudou Diène: Addendum, Mission to the United States of America, 101-102, U.N. Doc. A/HRC/11/36/Add.3" http://www2.ohchr.org/english/bodies/hrcouncil/docs/11session/A.HRC.11.36.Add.3.pdf.

UN. (n.d.). "Lessons from Rwanda: Survivor Testimony." http://www.un.org/preventgenocide/rwanda/testimonies.shtml.

US Commission on Civil Rights. (n.d.). "Civil Rights Implications of Post-September 11 Law Enforcement Practices in New York." http://www.usccr.gov/pubs/sac/ny0304/ch1.htm.

US Commission on Civil Rights. 2004. "Redefining Rights in America: The Civil Rights Record of the George W. Bush Administration." http://www.law.umaryland.edu/marshall/usccr/documents/cr12r24.pdf

US Department of Justice. 2003. "Fact Sheet: Racial Profiling." http://www.usccr.gov/pubs/sac/ny0304/app.pdf.

US Department of Justice, Civil Rights Division. 2003. "Guidance Regarding the Use of Race by Federal Law Enforcement Agencies. http://www.justice.gov/crt/split/documents/guidance_on_race.php.

Walker, B.A. 2003. "The Color of Crime: The Case Against Race-Based Suspect Descriptions." *Columbia Law Review* 103: 662–669.

Warren, P., D. Tomaskovic-Devey, W. Smith, M. Zingraff, and M. Mason. 2006. "Driving While Black: Bias Processes and Racial Disparity in Police Stops." *Criminology* 44(3): 706–738.

X, Malcolm. 1964. "Racism: The Cancer that is Destroying America." *Egyptian Gazette*. http://www.africawithin.com/malcolmx/quotes.htm.

CHAPTER 2. RACIAL PROFILING

Elvira Doghem-Rashid

> "Racial profiling—the use of race or ethnic appearance as a factor in deciding who merits police attention as a suspicious person—has undergone a sudden and almost complete rehabilitation [since September 11]." (Harris 2002b, 8)

> "Since September 11th, racial profiling is no longer the dirty phrase that it once was." (Sharma 2003, 299)

> "Ignoring [that the 9/11 he hijackers were Arab or Middle Eastern men] amounted to some kind of political correctness run amok in a time of great danger." (Harris 2002b, 9)

These quotes highlight the ease with which the once widely accepted proposition that ethnic profiling as ineffective, divisive and discriminatory has crept back into conventional practice with little public outcry after the events of 9/11 shocked the world. It appears that the events that unfolded, and the danger posed by this new terrorist threat, have cloaked ethnic profiling in a veil of respectability.

While ethnic profiling in everyday policing matters is recognized as a pernicious form of discrimination, somehow the threat from terrorism is considered an exception to the rule. The exceptional nature of terrorism is illustrated by the fact that the UK government introduced the Terrorism Act (2000) which gave the police what the Government calls "extraordinary powers," to be used in short-term limited operations to detect and stop terrorism. Section 44 (s44) powers are intended to disrupt, deter or detect terrorist action (Home Office 2004). Although time has shown that s44, as it has been used, has relatively low detection powers resulting in arrest rates of less than 0.5% in 2009 (calculations based on MPA Dec. 2009 data). In response the official line is that the main objective of s44 is to "create a hostile environment for terrorists," a phrase regularly cited by senior police officers and Ministers.

In the same year as the Terrorism Act, the Government also introduced The Race Relations (Amendment) Act (2000), which brought all public services—including the police service—within the scope of UK anti-discrimination legislation. This was the first time that the police force were legally obliged to ensure racial equality of service delivery, so while previously ethnic profiling may have been the undesirable face of "institutional racism," the Act made it illegal: "Under the Act, it is unlawful for a police officer to discriminate in carrying out any of his or her functions including conducting stop and searches...If a person believes they have been stopped and searched on the grounds of their race or ethnicity... they can complain of racial discrimination. (Bowling and Phillips 2007, 941)

Only a year prior to the enactment of these two pieces of legislation the Macpherson report, resulting from the inquiry into the death of Black teenager Stephen Lawrence, declared that the police were institutionally racist.[1] The term institutional racism arguably encompasses informal ethnic profiling, with the report citing the disproportionate use of Police and Criminal Evidence Act 1984 (PACE) stop and search powers by the police as an example of institutional racism in practice. Bearing this landmark report in mind and the history of reported disproportionality in police exercise of regular stop and search powers, the introduction of a stop and search power requiring less justification in terms of reasonable suspicion of wrongdoing could easily see the historic disproportionality trends continue unconstrained. Thus the parallel inclusion of the police within the realm of anti-discrimination legislation may have had the power to prevent. The discourse since early 2001, when the Terrorism Act came into effect, to the present suggests that this has not been the case.

Over time the Home Office has been challenged on the use of s44 and been forced to issue guidance to police on its use. For example, in 2003 civil liberties and human rights organization Liberty challenged the Metropolitan Police and the Home Office to a judicial review of the authorizations of s44 which resulted in the Home Office issuing guidance to Chief Police Officers in 2004 (circular 038/2004). This did not abate the debate, as illustrated by minutes from the Stop and Search Action Team Community Panel in 2005, which in response to the issue noted "specific guidance to police says that the power should not be based on racial profiling" (Meyrick 2005c, 4). As a result of the ongoing criticism of the operation of s44, updated guidance notes were issued to the police in 2006 (circular 022/2006) and most recently in 2008 (circular 027/2008).

This research examines the documented discussions surrounding the operation of s44 and the statistical data of stops using this extraordinary power in order to assess the criticisms in the light of empirical data.

CRITICISMS OF S44 POLICING POWERS USED AS "ROUTINE"

Given that s44 powers were introduced as "extraordinary powers," there has been much criticism of the police, in some areas of the country, for the considerable number of people that they have stopped using s44 powers. Over time this has led to claims that the police are abusing these powers and using them as part of their toolkit in everyday policing, affording them greater freedom to stop people without the usual grounds of "reasonable suspicion" required under other stop/search powers such as PACE.

Both of the major opposition parties have been critical of the use of s44 powers enacted under the Labour government. Conservative Shadow Home Secretary Chris Grayling commented: "People will be highly suspicious about the scale of stop/search under terror laws. This will only serve to reinforce the view that many anti-terror powers are being used for unrelated purposes." (SkyNews 2009, n.p.). Meanwhile Liberal Democrat Shadow Secretary of State for the Home Department Chris Huhne noted that "figures demonstrate the blanket use of these powers, and the lack of intelligence used to direct them" (2010, n.p.).

Lord Carlile, the independent reviewer of terrorism legislation for the government since 2001, has also commented in his annual reports that the powers are used by some forces "without full consideration" and that "I am sure beyond any doubt that s44could be used less and expect it to be used less....Whilst arrests for other crime have followed searches under the section, none...has ever related to a terrorism offence" (2008, 29–30). His 2008 singled out the MET police for criticism, for having s44 authorizations in force throughout the entire London area, and called on them to limit tier use of s44. There have been reports in the press that undercover police officers have used s44 powers, as well as community police officers searching people under s44.

The fact that in five (known) instances the police used s44 powers when there was no authorization in place further indicates that some police forces are taking it for granted that the powers are available to them as standard, and using it as part of their everyday policing toolkit. The fact that the five incidents were not in five separate areas, but in fact that in two instances the violation was repeated in the same area at different points in times reinforces the implication denigration of the exceptional aspect of s44 and its use in everyday policing. The steady stream of media reports about the use of s44 powers against clearly non-terrorist targets, such as an octogenarian heckler at a party political conference, protesters, photographers (with reported cases of officers deleting images—which is illegal) and children, often cited as use of the powers in everyday policing.

TARGETING MUSLIM, BLACK AND ASIAN ETHNIC GROUPS

The Terrorism Act has been charged with specifically constructing the Muslim community as a "suspect" community (Kundnani 2009; Spalek, El Awa, and MacDonald 2008), with police use of "hard" policing tactics such as s44 stop and search claimed to be targeting Muslims and using Asian ethnicity as a proxy for identifying Muslims. The associated suspicion bestowed upon the Muslim community as a result of the Terrorism Act and its implementation has "grave consequences" for individuals and their families (Spalek, El Awa, and MacDonald 2008, 9). Not least of these consequences is the common media portrayal of the Muslim community in a negative light and the ongoing problem of anti-Muslim hostility that is creeping into accepted norms of attitudes as a result (Khan 2007, 11).

This has not been lost on the authorities, with the MPA noting that "[s]ince the events of July 7 2005, members of the Asian community perceive that they are being unfairly targeted for searches under the Terrorism Act" (2008a, 3) and that "[w]ithin the young generation of some Arab communities there is a general feeling that they have been targeted because of their ethnicity, while older generation support S44as long as it doesn't target Arab of Moslems [*sic*]" (2008a, 5).

As alluded to in the introduction, in the post-9/11 era ethnic profiling appears to have not only crept back into conventional practice (some may argue it never left) but been given a new sense of "common sense" respectability. The widespread media demonization of Muslims and the recorded rise in Islamaphobia will no doubt have a strong influence on the shaping of public perception of ethnic profiling, be it formal or informal. This is supported by Doghem-Rashid (2004), who found that in the fight against terrorism, the public seemingly endorsed the ethnic profiling of young Asian men. The research interviewed a nationally representative sample of 491 people (aged 15+), asking about a range of topics related to (then) current issues related to multiculturalism and ethnicity. Respondents were presented with statements, with which they were asked to agree or disagree, one of which was the statement: "The increased police 'stop and search' of young Asian men is reasonable in the fight against terrorism." Some 44% agreed (either strongly agreed/agree) with the statement and only 30% disagreed to any extent. Interestingly, analysis of newspaper readership of both daily and Sunday broadsheets revealed statistically significant relationships in response to the statement, with readership of a daily or Sunday broadsheet more significantly related to greater agreement with the statement.

RACIAL PROFILING: HISTORY, DEFINITION, PROOF

The term "racial profiling" and its ensuing debate first arose in the United States in the 1990s, triggered by a US offensive against drugs that led to the development of profiles of drug couriers to aid police officers in deciding whom to consider suspects (Engel, Calnon, and Bernard 2002), that resulted in police targeting certain ethnic groups for stop/search operations. The colloquial expression "driving while Black" was a popularized description of the police practice of stopping African-American (or other ethnic minority) drivers in disproportionate numbers (Harris 1999) and has since been used more generally to refer to the influence of race in law enforcement decisions.

The use of race to form a suspect profile is justified, by proponents, on the grounds of a purported correlation between certain racial groups and certain criminal activity (Holbert and Rose 2006; Steel 2001). This is contested by many others, such as De Schutter and Ringelheim, who argue "ethnic profiling is a form of discrimination...whether or not a statistically significant relationship could be established between membership in a particular racial or ethnic group and certain forms of criminal behaviour" (2008, 360).

It is important here to clarify that the use of race as a descriptive indicator of a person that has committed a crime is clearly relevant to police officers who are looking for that person. Similarly, the use of race in "criminal profiling" [a practice developed in the US and mainly used since the 1970s in investigations of serial killers] may be plausible; as the profiles are used to aid police apprehend the perpetrator of a known crime. It is the move of profiling from a technique to detect known criminals, to seeking out unknown criminals, which raises issues of discrimination in use of race in profiles. This shift from know to unknown criminals was again spearheaded in the US, in the 1980s, in the "war" against drugs and an attempted crackdown on the transportation of drugs led to the development of profiles of drugs carriers (Harris 2002a). More recently, the technique of predictive profiling has started to be applied in the area of counter-terrorism, as evidenced by the EU recommendation of the development of terrorist profiles, data mining in German seeking potential terrorists, and almost certainly in the application of police stop/search powers in the UK (albeit informally in the latter).

APPARENT SANCTIONING OF FORMAL ETHNIC PROFILING

Despite racial profiling an being illegal for of discrimination under European human rights law (De Schutter and Ringelheim 2008, 360), the European Union has recommended to members states to construct "terrorist profiles" using characteristics including nationality and birthplace (Council of the European Union 2002), with a view to identifying terrorists before the execution of terrorist acts, in cooperation with the immigration services and the police. This policy also made the explicit link between terrorism profiles and immigration (CFR-CDF 2003, 29). Despite the fact that ethnicity, nationality, or country of birth are not the sole criteria in the profile, the risk of discrimination is still existent (CFR-CDF 2003) and nonetheless constitutes ethnic profiling (Harris 2002a).

While this example relates to a formalized policy of ethnic profiling, ethnic profile can also take the form of a de facto, informal, practice, by individual law enforcement officers. Their actions need not be purposefully or even consciously discriminatory, based on subjective experiences or internalized stereotypes, but represent no less a danger of discrimination (Harris 2002a). Police use of stop/search powers has a well documented relationship with informal ethnic profiling. The introduction of s44 stop/search powers in the UK can only serve to advance this relationship by eliminating the requirement of "reasonable suspicion," thereby removing behavioral cues and placing complete emphasis on individual officers' "instincts" and personal judgments about what constitutes suspicious and who may be a potential terrorist.

In the UK there has been mixed messages about the use of ethnic profiling and police use of stop/search powers. In 2001, talking about the overall drop in police use of PACE stop/search powers post the 1999 Macpherson report and its *indictment of the police as institutionally racist,* Tory home affairs spokesman Ann Widdecombe is quoted as saying:

> Not only has use of stop/search fallen off but arrests have as well. The police are simply not as confident in doing their jobs as they were before the Macpherson Report. If you are serious about law and order, there must not be any no-go areas. Police have to stop/search people who may be fine upstanding citizens. That in itself should not be a source of complaint. (Quoted in Hickley 2001)

The implication being that the disproportionate use of stop/search powers against Black communities (that led to the criticism in the Macpherson report of "institutional racism") was justified; that attributing criminality to a whole community which results in police stopping "fine upstanding citizens...should not be a source of complaint" (quoted in Hickley 2001).

More specific to s44 and racial profiling, Hazel Blears, the then UK minister responsible for counter-terrorism, addressed the Commons Home Affairs Committee Inquiry into the impact of anti-terrorist measures on community relations saying: "If a threat is from a particular place then our action is going to be targeted at that area.... It means that some of our counter-terrorism powers will be disproportionately experienced by the Muslim community" (2005, n.p.). Following criticism of the comments the Minister retracted the statements, clarifying that police stops would be intelligence-led (cited in Goldston 2006, 3).

A correlation between ethnicity and criminality was also put forward as a justification of police disproportionately stopping Black people pre-Macpherson, citing that the decrease in police use of stop/search powers post-Macpherson was accompanied by a corresponding increase in crime. While these two phenomena were widely linked in the British press, supported by anecdotal reports that police officers felt that this link was valid too—"some officers have also linked the rise [in crime] to a drop in police use of stop/search in the aftermath of the critical Macpherson report on the Stephen Lawrence case" (Steele 2001, n.p.)—a statistically significant correlation was not tested/established in the media. The claimed link was later disproven.

Although, even if a statistical correlation can be established between ethnicity and criminality, attaching the "myth of criminal propensity" to certain groups in order to justify using race as a proxy for criminality (Wang 2001, 225) in predictive profiles is: proven to be inaccurate (Sharma 2003); places whole communities under suspicion (Hassan 2009; Goldston 2006; Harris 2002a and 2002b); and is not justifiable grounds for targeting specific ethnic groups (OSI 2007; De Schutter and Ringelheim 2008). Furthermore, using racial profiling places whole communities under suspicion and thus significantly increases the number of people that the police need to expend resources stopping and searching. Increasing the scope of suspicion to whole communities will thus invariably divert important law-enforcement resources from potentially more effective intelligence-led terrorism detection work, or even divert policing resources away from everyday policing.

The other effect of ethnic profiling in anti-terrorism stops is that history has proven time and again that such profile are under-inclusive and that several attacks (successful and foiled) have been perpetrated by people that do not fit the ethnic profile. For example, in the 1970s the IRA recruited and used female bombers in order to circumvent the police profile of an IRA bomber as male. More recently in the UK, White Muslim convert Nicky Riley attempted to detonate an explosive device in Exeter in May 2008 and was convicted and sentenced in January 2009 (Fresco 2010).

PROVING ETHNIC PROFILING

US law enforcement officers Holbert and Rose (2006), in relation to police stopping of cars, claim that in order to prove racial profiling two conditions must be satisfied: that minority groups must be proven "no more likely than Whites to violate traffic laws," and that police routinely stop drivers who are of a certain minority group at a higher rate than Whites. By this definition racial profiling cannot exist if the targeting of certain racial groups can be linked to criminality, a position which also appears to be supported by the statements made by some Ministers in the UK (see previous comments by Widdecombe and Blears).

This definition of ethnic profiling is contested by De Schutter and Ringelheim: "It should not matter...that a statistically significant relationship can be shown to exist between certain criminal behaviours and membership in such targeted groups" (2008, 384). The generally accepted indicator of evidence of racial profiling is disproportion in the use of stop/search powers against certain ethnic groups. Although they caution that where disproportion is observed, further investigation should be carried out in order to establish whether the disproportion can be justified by legitimate factors. If, after investigation, "objective and legitimate factors" cannot be found to account for the disproportion then it can be taken as a sign that the police are unfairly targeting certain ethnic groups (2008, 380). Bowling and Phillips also support the proposition that disproportionality is indicative of informal profiling of ethnic minorities, based on their assessment of research evidence showing that "racial prejudice and stereotyping are widespread within the British police and that this has an effect on policing practice" (2007, 960).

The Metropolitan Police Service itself recognizes that disproportionality is an indication of possible ethnic profiling:

> The policy and standard operating procedures are not discriminatory, however research across the MPS shows that more Asian men are disproportionately stopped and searched under Section 44. To a lesser extent black males are also disproportionately stopped. Disproportionality is viewed by some parts of the community as discriminatory. Disproportionality is not the same as discrimination but it may be an indicator. (MPS 2008, 3)

The issue of measuring disproportionality itself has also been the subject of debate. It has been argued that when examining data on police stops the location and time of day of specific police operations may mean that the "street population" available for stops include greater numbers of those from minority background, and so in this context stops are in proportion, as opposed to the disproportionality observed when comparing stops data to resident population figures

(FitzGerald and Sibbitt 1997; MPA 2004; Miller 2005). Despite this suggestion, the Government continue to produce statistics that report on the number of police stops in relation to resident population figures, believing that this is still a valid and useful measure.

ANALYSIS AND METHODOLOGY

The analysis presented is based on section 44 stop/search data from the Metropolitan Police Force (MET). The MET polices the London area. The reason that the MET is presented for detailed is analysis is due to the fact that in 2007/08 some 87% of all s44 stops nationally were carried out by the MET, making them the largest user of s44 powers.

Based on analysis of the public discourse of s44 powers and media reports between 2001 and 2009, the data were examined with a view to statistically assess the following research questions:

- Are the Asian and Arab communities (as both majority Muslim communities and those ethnic groups representing the ethnicities of the known perpetrators of 9/11 and 7/7) disproportionately subject to s44 stops?

- Are the police increasingly stopping people of white ethnicity, while also increasing (to a lesser extent) or maintaining (but not decreasing) stops of other ethnic groups, thus reducing disproportionality in the figures?

The data under analysis was obtained using a Freedom of Information Act request, and details ethnicity by the full range of codes used by officers in recording officer perceived ethnic identity, unlike government published data which generally details only White/Black/Asian ethnic groups. Thus, this analysis represents the first time that data on s44 stops of the Middle Eastern ethnic group has been published. Data for the Chinese ethnic groups is also presented throughout the analysis, also the first time that this data has appeared in print, in order to provide context to the data for other ethnic groups. Some of the data presented in relation to the Chinese and Middle Eastern ethnic groups are from small bases, and subsequent advanced statistical analysis of these groups should be treated with caution.

NATIONAL TRENDS 2001–2008

As a precursor to detailed analysis of annual data by the MET, Table 1 is presented in order to contextualize the overall trends in s44 stops.

TABLE 1. ENGLAND & WALES NATIONAL POLICE AND MET POLICE SEC-
TION 44 STOP & SEARCH DATA, 2001/2-2007/8

	2001/2	2002/3	2003/4	2004/5	2005/6	2006/7	2007/8
Met. Police (London area police)	2,963	13,243	15,535	12,686	22,701	25,255	101,751
Total England & Wales	8,550	21,577	29,383	32,062	44,543	37,197	117,278
% Searches Carried Out by MET	35%	61%	53%	40%	51%	68%	87%

Source: Home Office/Ministry of Justice Statistics on Race and the Criminal Justice System Annual Reports 2002–2008, author's analysis.

It is evident that the number of s44 stops has increased dramatically since 2001, with the MET accounting for a growing proportion of stops in recent years. Even while the national England and Wales figure fell in 2006/7, the number of stops carried out by the MET continued to rise. The data shows a marked increase in s44 stops carried out by MET between 2006/7 and 2007/8. The BTP data shows a similar step up in the number of s44 stops between 2006/7 and 2007/8, with an earlier marked increase between 2004/5 and 2005/6. These two periods are notable for the fact that on 7th July 2005 a terrorist attack in London, involving four suicide bombers detonating devises on the London underground (3) and a London bus, resulted in 52 deaths and a reported 700 injuries. The attack was carried out by four Muslim men, three of Pakistani and one of Jamaican origin. The second period is notable for the discovery of two car bombs in London on 29th June 2007, that were both disabled before they could be detonated, and a foiled attack on Glasgow airport on 30th June 2007. The 29th and 30th attacks were linked, and were perpetrated by two Muslim men of Iraqi and Indian ethnic origin.

It is worth noting that the Terrorism Act (2000) was enacted onto the UK statue books and the powers enshrined within it available to the police before the terrorist attacks on the US in September 2001 (9/11). The data in Table 2 shows that between 2001/2 and 2002/3 there was a more than doubling of the use of s44 across England and Wales, with a steeper increase in the MET area, indicating that possibly the 9/11 attack had the effect of increasing use of s44. Although, it is not possible to definitively examine this, as the monthly breakdown of data for this period is not published by either the Home Office or Metropolitan Police Authority (MPA), and while this data was requested as part of the Freedom of Information (FoI) request that supported the rest of the MET data analysis in this report, the data were only made available from April 2003. Meanwhile, the BTP data shows no substantive increase in the use of s44 between 2001/2 and 2002/3, supported by the detailed monthly data which also showed no variation in the number of searches carried pre-/post-9/11.

Thus, the national data shows an increasing use of s44 over time, with terrorist attacks or attempts serving as a catalyst to increased application. Table 2 details the national and MET data by the White, Black and Asian ethnic groups. Given the longstanding debate on the use of disproportionality and the type of population data used to benchmark the stops data, Table 2 presents the total national compared to the total national population, but also presents the total national figures once the data and population for the MET/London have been removed from the data and population figures respectively. This is hoped to give a more representative picture of the proportions of ethnic groups stopped outside of the capital.

TABLE 2. ENGLAND & WALES AND MET POLICE SECTION 44 STOP & SEARCH DATA, BY ETHNIC PROPORTIONS STOPPED, 2001/2-2007/8

	2001/2	2002/3	2003/4	2004/5	2005/6	2006/7	2007/8	Relevant Population
Total England & Wales (E&W)								
White	78%	67%	70%	73%	69%	70%	63%	91%
Black	6%	8%	9%	8%	9%	10%	13%	2%
Asian	9%	14%	12%	11%	15%	15%	18%	4%
MET/London								
White	69%	63%	66%	66%	60%	61%	60%	71%
Black	9%	9%	11%	11%	12%	13%	14%	11%
Asian	15%	17%	15%	15%	20%	19%	19%	12%
Total E & W EXCL MET/London								
White	82%	73%	74%	77%	79%	88%	82%	95%
Black	5%	7%	7%	6%	6%	4%	5%	1%
Asian	5%	9%	9%	8%	10%	6%	9%	3%

Source: Home Office/Ministry of Justice 'Statistics on Race and the Criminal Justice System' annual reports 2002-2008, author's analysis

The data show that in London, there appears to a consistent under-representation of the White ethnic groups in s44 stops, with the balance being a consistent over-representation of the Asian Ethnic group in these types of stops. Even before any terrorist attacks were carried out on UK soil, there was a consistent disproportion in the number of s44 stops of carried out among Asians, of generally only 3 percentage points above the proportion of the London Asian population. In2001/02 the proportions of stops to the populations were not far from proportional. The increased stops of Asians seems to have become substantially more disproportionate in 2005/6, which saw Asian represent 20% of s44 stops compared to making up 12% of the London population. This heightened level of disproportion remained at similar levels in subsequent years. A slight and increasing disproportion can also been seen in the number of s44 stops involving the Black ethnic group 2005/6 onwards. The increase in disproportion against the Black and Asian groups in s44 stops 2005/6, indicates a prima facie case for ethnic profiling of these ethnic groups, likely precipitated by the 7/7 terrorist attack in London.

Nationwide, with the exclusion of s44 stops carried out by the MET and removal of the London population from comparative population data, there appears to a longstanding and consistent disproportionate use of s44 among the Black and Asian groups.

MET–LONDON

This section examines the MET use of s44 in more detail, with annual stop for 2004–2009 presented in Table 3. In line with previously discussed Home Office data, the MET has increased its utilization of s44 powers significantly in recent years. The likelihood that terrorists events on UK soil have acted as a catalyst to greater use of s44 are supported data, with step changes in the level of use witnessed in 2005 and 2007. Although, terrorist incidents do not fully explain the trend of increasing s44 stop, as the number of stops increased further after 2007, peaking in 2008 at 173,997, an increase of 140% on 2007.

Possibly as a result of increasing public pressure, the MET reported the first annual fall in the use of s44 in 2009, a contraction of 34% on the 2008 high. While this fall reportedly marks a shift in MET police operation of s44, substantively the level of s44 stops in 2009 is still significantly higher than in other years, such as 2005, when the UK was directly affected by terrorist events. There were nearly five times more s44 searches carried out in 2009 than in 2005.

TABLE 3. METROPOLITAN POLICE SECTION 44 STOP & SEARCH DATA, BY ETHNICITY, 2004–2009

	2004	2005	2006	2007	2008	2009
Number of Stops	11,917	23,232	23,196	71,804	173,997	115,435
Year on Year % Change	-	+95%	-	+210%	+142%	-34%
Proportions Stopped						
White	66%	60%	62%	59%	63%	64%
Black	11%	12%	12%	14%	14%	12%
Asian	15%	20%	19%	20%	17%	17%
Middle Eastern	4%	4%	3%	3%	2%	-
Chinese	2%	2%	3%	3%	3%	-
Other*	1%	2%	2%	1%	1%	7%
Total	100%	100%	100%	100%	100%	100%
Annual % Change	2004-05	2005-06	2006-07	2007-08	2008-09	
White	-	+78%	+2%	+196%	+158%	-33%
Black	-	+121%	-4%	+272%	+135%	-41%
Asian	-	+148%	-3%	+225%	+106%	-32%
Middle Eastern	-	+59%	-19%	+179%	+96%	-
Chinese	-	+89%	+25%	+206%	+166%	-
Other^	-	+262%	-24%	+141%	+82%	-31%
Total	-	+95%	-	+210%	+142%	-34%
Ratio to White Stops	2005	2006	2007	2008	2009	
Black	-	1.34	1.25	1.56	1.42	1.24
Asian	-	1.91	1.81	1.99	1.58	1.59
Middle Eastern	-	2.84	2.25	2.11	1.60	-
Chinese	-	2.52	3.07	3.17	3.27	-
ANY Ethnic Minority	-	1.63	1.53	1.71	1.45	1.39

*Other category includes Middle Eastern and Chinese for 2009; data for these groups not available separately at the time of publication
^including Middle Eastern and Chinese for 2008–9

Source: MET FoI request 2009090005680/MET FoI Review Reference 2009110002145, author's analysis

The proportions stopped show a persistent overrepresentation of Asians in MET s44 stops, ranging from a high of 20% in 2005 to a less disproportionate 17% in 2007. While this is improved, it is nonetheless a disproportionate given that the Asian ethnic group represent 12% of the London population. The Middle Eastern/Arab ethnic group is also consistently overrepresented in MET s44 stops. While accounting for an estimated 1% of the London population, Arabs represented 4% of those stopped in London in 2004 and 2005, and again while this proportion contracted in recent years, to 2% in 2008, this is still disproportionate to their numbers.

In 2004, Arabs were 3.19 times more likely than Whites to be subject to an s44 stop—the highest level of ethnic disproportion that year. The likelihood of an Arab being stopped has contracted every year since then, to settle at 1.60 times more likely than a White person being stopped in 2008. This level is similar to the likelihood of an Asian person being stopped (1.58 in 2008), whose chances of being stopped have hovered near the same level throughout the period presented but have fallen slightly since a peak of 1.99 in 2007. Similarly, 2007 was a high for stops of Black people, who were 1.56 times more likely than a White person to be stopped, having increased slightly year-on-year since 2004. Again, similar to the Asian ethnic group, the likelihood of Black stops fell back a little to 1.24 in 2009. These contractions are the result of the increased proportion of stops for White people in 2008 and 2009, 63% and 64% respectively, compared to the 2007 low of 59%.

Notably, the Chinese ethnic group has consistently experienced relatively high levels of likelihood of being stopped relative to the White ethnic group, and this has increased year-on-year throughout the period of analysis. While the data for this groups should be treated with caution, as the numbers are small, it reinforces the rest of the data in that it is in line with the trend that all ethnic minority groups are substantively more likely to be subject to a s44 stop than the majority White ethnic group. This also lends weight to the argument that s44 is possibly being used by the police as part of their everyday policing toolkit and using it to target ethnic minorities.

While the use of s44 appears to be affecting all ethnic minorities disproportionately (with the exception of Black in 2004), closer examination of the monthly data surrounding terrorist events illustrates that the proportion of searches of the Chinese population, for example, remains at roughly the same level throughout the year and is not affected by monthly fluctuations around events such as

7/7. Meanwhile searches of Asian, Black and Arab ethnic groups increased post-July 2005. Illustrating that at certain points, such as immediately post-terrorist events, disproportionality towards these ethnic groups increases. This could be an indicator of racial profiling, given the immediate proximity to a recent terrorist event involving people from these ethnic groups, which will be at the fore of officers' minds in deciding who to stop.

It cannot be ruled out that the increased disproportionality observed immediately following an event is not the result of specific intelligence, although this is far less likely than in the operation of other police stop powers such as under PACE. This is based on the knowledge that s44 searches are commonly applied to 'create a hostile environment' for terrorist to operate, rather than to specifically seek an individual in an area, led by specific intelligence, such as PACE may be applied.

Ethnic profiling of the Asian group is further supported by the fact that while the disproportionality of searches among the Black ethnic group increased directly after the event, proportions returned to previous levels within two months post-event—unlike the levels of searches of Asians, which remained higher than previous levels and increased the overall annual disproportions experienced by this group. This suggests that major events involving Asians/Muslims is providing impetus and/or justification for either formal or informal profiling.

TABLE 4. METROPOLITAN POLICE SECTION 44 STOP & SEARCH DATA BY 24-MONTH PERIODS PRE/POST 2005 AND 2007 INCIDENTS, JULY 2003-JUNE 2009

	Absolute Numbers			% Change	
	July 2003-June 2005	July 2005-June 2007	July 2007-June 2009	pre/post 2005	post 2005 / post 2007
White	17,890	31,238	191,935	+75%	+514%
Black	3,073	6,731	41,252	+119%	+513%
Asian	4,205	10,475	53,832	+149%	+414%
Arab/M.E.	1,115	1,635	6,732	+47%	+312%
	600	1495	9839		
			1,495		
Other	433	823	3,149	+90%	+283%
Total	27,316	52,397	306,739	+92%	+485%

Percentages				
	July 2003-June 2005	July 2005-June 2007	July 2007-June 2009	London Population¬
White	65%	60%	63%	71%
Black	11%	13%	13%	11%
Asian	15%	20%	18%	12%
Arab/M.E.	4%	3%	2%	1%*
Chinese	2%	3%	3%	1%
other	2%	2%	1%	3%
Total	100%	100%	100%	100%

Average Monthly Stops			Paired T Test - Comparing Means	
	July 2003-June 2005	July 2005-June 2007	July 2007-June 2009	pre/post 2005	post 2005 / post 2007
White	745	1,302	7,997	sig	sig
Black	128	280	1,719	sig	sig
Asian	175	436	2,243	sig	sig
Arab/M.E.	46	68	281	NOT sig	sig
Chinese	25	65	410	sig	sig
other	18	34	131	sig	sig
Total	1,138	2,183	12,781		

Chinese
¬ *At 2001 census*
* *based on Arab League country of birth data on 2001 census*
Source: MET FoI Request 2009090005680 / MET FoI Review Reference 2009110002145, author's analysis

The monthly average stops for the two year period before and after the London bombings in 2005 show a nearly doubling of the number of stops, while post-2007 incidents there was nearly a six-fold increase in the overall average number of monthly stops on the previous period. Examination of the monthly data for 2007 shows that the increase between June and July was marked, increasing from 2,843 stops to 11,834 stops respectively. The two year post-2007 event data analysis indicates that an increased level was sustained for more than the short term post-event.

After June 2007, while all ethnic groups saw an increase in s44 stops, those directed at Asians and Arabs were increased at a greater rate. This steeper increase in the stop of Asians and Arabs could have been intelligence led, but may also represent some level of ethnic profiling, given the perpetrators were Iraqi and Indian and both men were detained during the course of the attempted attack, not post-event though intelligence-led efforts or through other policing methods such as s44 stops. The greater increase in stop of Asians is reflected in the increased disproportion in July 2007 figures, with Asians comprising 24% of all stops, up from 21% the month earlier.

TABLE 5. MET SECTION 44 STOP & SEARCH DATA, BY ETHNICITY AND MONTH, JUNE–SEPTEMBER 2007

	Jun-07	July 2007	% change June/July	Aug-07	% change July/Aug	Sep-07	% change Aug/Sept	% change June-Sept
	2,843	11,834		9,907		7,148		
White	58%	55%	+291%	59%	-10%	60%	-27%	+157%
Black	14%	14%	+313%	14%	-18%	14%	-26%	+149%
Asian	21%	24%	+374%	20%	-29%	20%	-30%	+136%
Chinese	3%	3%	+303%	3%	+3%	3%	-22%	+224%
Arab	2%	3%	+477%	3%	-35%	2%	-41%	+123%
Total	100%	100%	+316%	100%	-16%	100%	-28%	+151%

Source: MET FoI Request 2009090005680 / MET FoI Review Reference 2009110002145, author's analysis

While the data in Table 4 illustrate the MET significantly increased its stops of all ethnic groups post June 2007, more detailed data for the months immediately following, as set out in Table 5, show that while the Asian and Arab ethnic groups saw the greatest increases directly following the event, s44 stops of these groups were also scaled back at a greater rate in August and September 2007 than for other ethnic groups. This meant that for the three months post-June, the Asian and Arab groups actually saw the least overall increases in the number of s44 stops. The disproportion of stops of Asians remained in spite of this, but this served to re-balance the proportions such that the figures returned to similar proportions as in pre-event.

In summary, the data supports the proposition that the MET are ethnically profiling the Asian, Arab and increasingly Black ethnic groups, and that this is amplified in month directly following a terrorist event in the UK. More recently, since the 2007, the MET has not specifically increased its stops of the White ethnic group in order to "balance the stats," but the data (Table 5) does illustrate that the MET have not scaled back s44 stops of the White ethnic group at the same rate as for other ethnic groups, resulting in the proportions masking potentially even greater disproportions in the Asian group which, as noted previously, experienced far greater s44 stops in July 2007.

The fact that the pattern of increases and decreases in s44 stops of the Chinese ethnic group, between June and September 2007, closely mirror that of the White ethnic group lends weight to the proposition that the greater increase in s44 of suspect communities in the immediate aftermath of an event was later masked by a slower scaling back of s44 among non-suspect groups in later months. The 24-month analysis post-June 2007 reinforces this, illustrating that specifically the Asian and Arab groups showed the lowest overall increases in s44 stops over the period (Table 4) at increases of +414% and +312% respectively, compared to the Chinese (+558%), White (+514%) and Black (+513%). Yet despite the lower overall rate of increases, the Asian groups persisted in being disproportionately represented in stops during this 24-month period, at 18% (compared to representing 12% of the London population).

ALIENATING AND STIGMATIZING COMMUNITIES

Given the observed disproportion in the use of s44 across the ethnic groups in the UK, there is strong evidence that police officers are discriminating against ethnic minorities by means of informal profiling. In addition to establishing that some ethnic groups are more affected than others by the powers, it is important to unequivocally establish what impact this disproportion has on individuals and communities.

Profiling is over-inclusive, it puts far more people under police suspicion of terrorist activity—i.e. whole communities—than can be warranted (Goldston 2006, 1; Harris 2002b, 12). Terrorists represent a very small minority of any ethnic group and their beliefs are "not a reflection of beliefs or values within communities" (Hassan 2009); the overwhelming remaining majority of people in a targeted the community being law-abiding, tax-paying individuals that are entitled to the equal protection of the police. While a detailed evaluation of the impact is outside of the scope of this research, key issues are highlighted.

The damaging effects of over-inclusion are to alienate and stigmatize people, a prevalent concern amongst many in the UK in relation to s44, which Iqbal Sacranie, Secretary General of the MCB, accurately captures: "Just as an entire generation of young black people were alienated through Stop/search practice, we are deeply worried that the same could now be occurring again, this time to young Muslim men" (2004, n.p.).

In addition to alienating communities in a broad sense, such as anger towards authorities (Harris 2002b, 12), stop/search practices that are perceived to target ethnic groups can have consequences on an individual and group level that are personally distressing. Research among young Muslims reveals that as a direct result of experiences of S44stops by police, their sense of personal security is violated and they feel threatened by the police (Ahmed 2009, 75).

It does not appear that the individual level effects of S44stops on targeted ethnic minorities are recognized or being given sufficient consideration by the authorities. For example the MPS Equality Impact Assessment (EIA) (2008) concluded that the s44 policy will not discourage participation in public life, something which anecdotal evidence collected during the course of this research has indicated may not be the case for those that are subject to repeated stops. Research by Wang (2001, cited in Sharma 2003) supports the proposition that racial profiling in policing can have a direct impact on the way people from ethnic minorities live their lives, such a "avoiding driving flashy cars or walking though a predominantly White neighborhood, for example." Furthermore, experience of being stopped by the police can "lead an individual to depression and isolation."

Aside from the potential personal and emotional issues arising from ethnic profiling in police stops, are the implications for ethnic minorities that the encounter put them at risk of further discrimination by other authorities in the future. The 2008 EIA concluded that the policy does not negatively affect equality of opportunity for those impacted; another contested assertion. Common practice in operating s44 powers means that personal identifying information is collected from people stopped (despite there being no legal obligation for those stopped to provide this information) which means that the vast majority of those stopped using the powers will be on record as having been stopped under terrorism law. This record of the stop itself has the potential to negatively affect an individuals' equality of opportunity and places people from ethnic minorities at higher risk of stigmatization and possible discrimination:

> The basic issue is about the rights of a person. The danger is that those who are subject to S&S are tainted by the stigma of having been stopped and searched under the suspicion of terrorism. The data may be passed to other intelligence agencies and this could even affect a person when travelling abroad or if they are applying for a job in security-sensitive areas. Without any redress, it is a further sign that civil liberties are being continuously eroded. (*The Muslim News* 2007, n.p.)

DISCUSSION: CHANGE THE LAW

It is clear that the current legislation is far too broad and open to misuse, in both its over-use and in its ability to allow racial profiling. Legal academics have called for the law to be amended or repealed (Bowling and Phillips 2007; De Schutter and Ringelheim 2008). The introduction of a "reasonable suspicion" in the operation of police stop/search has also been long recommended by several European Union bodies. For example, the Committee of Ministers of the Council of Europe in 2001 suggested adopting the European Code of Police Ethics which states that "[p]olice investigations shall, as a minimum, be based upon reasonable suspicion of an actual or possible offence or crime" (para 47). The EU Network of Independent Experts on Fundamental Rights (Opinion No 4 'Ethnic Profiling', December 2006), stated that EU Member States should "define with the greatest clarity possible the conditions under which law enforcement authorities may exercise their powers in areas such as identity checks or stop-and-search procedures." The European Commission Against Racism and Intolerance also recommends (*General Policy Recommendation n111* in paragraph 3) the introduction of a "reasonable suspicion" standard, according to which "powers relating to control, surveillance or investigation activities can only be exercised on the basis of a suspicion that is founded on objective criteria."

Following the challenge to the law, in the form of *Gillan and Quinton* v. *UK*, a change to the law may be on the horizon. The European Court of Human Rights (ECHR) ruling, in January 2010, unanimously decided that the lack of safeguards against racial profiling and discrimination in police powers of stop/search under s44 of the Terrorism Act (2000) was a violation of article 8 of the European Convention on Human Rights. The Home Office has declared it will challenge the ruling, which will in itself take some time to be heard, but if the challenge is unsuccessful it will mean a revision of the Act in some form.

While some would like to see the law amended with the introduction of reasonable suspicion to stop criteria, UK civil liberty and human rights organization Liberty that acted on behalf of the applicants Gillan and Quinton, argue that in some circumstances a law that allows searches without suspicion could be necessary:

> Liberty has always accepted that an exceptional power to stop/ search without suspicion may be justified in certain limited circumstances—for example where, due to a particular event or the nature of a particular area, it is reasonably believed that an act of terrorism may be planned; or where specific information linked to a place or event has been received which indicates the same.

As such the organization is campaigning for the current powers to be amended, not to include grounds of reasonable suspicion but such that the powers could be invoked only for short time periods, limited purposes and small geographical areas, with the key caveat that designated areas are also published so that the public is aware the powers are in use.

> We believe authorisations should also be published so everyone is aware that these powers are being used. This would enable the police to search everyone entering the area—more like the type of searches we all submit to on entering certain public buildings such as the Houses of Parliament. It would avoid the current racially discriminatory approach. (Corinna Ferguson, barrister and legal officer, Liberty, 24/02/2010)

However the law is potentially amended, it is clear that the Home Office is seeking to retain s44 powers in their current form for as long as possible and therefore safeguards against racial profiling need to be addressed in other areas of operation.

CLARITY AND TRANSPARENCY

Given the disproportions that the data of s44 reveals, it is no surprise that without people being given a clear reason for stops, some people will feel targeted on their ethnicity. Whether a duty of reasonable suspicion is introduced or not, what is clear is that at present there is a need for greater understanding of s44 powers among the public: "The [Muslim] community's distrust of the use of stops and searches is further fueled by the lack of clarity as to why they are being stopped" (MCB 2004, 19).

There is a clear need for greater awareness among the public, particularly the communities most greatly affected, of how s44 powers can be exercised and their rights. The fact that there is a lack of clarity at the level of the general public about the operation of s44 powers cannot be in doubt. For example, research among young Muslims found that their understanding of the Terrorism Act (2000) was "that the police have the power to stop any individual whom they feel is behaving in a suspicious manner...[yet] they are being targeted by police officers without good reason, and guidelines to stop/search are being breached by individual officers" (Ahmed 2009, 75). There is no requirement of suspicious behavior, yet the perception that there is such a requirement—combined with the knowledge that they were not engaging in such behavior—is fueling distrust and anger towards the police.

The public confusion is not entirely surprising when one considers the fact that even organizations such as the Policy Research Centre of the Islamic Foundation, who carried out the research, illustrated some confusion between the grounds for stops under PACE and s44 in their 2009 report[2]. When discussing respondents' feelings that they were being stopped without cause under the Terrorism Act (2000), the report cited guidelines that "police have powers to stop/ search individuals only when they have 'reasonable suspicion' that one of the following is being carried on the person: drugs, weapons or stolen property and items which could be used to commit a crime" (74). These guidelines relate to PACE powers of stop and search, not s44.

A systematic program of public awareness of the conditions of s44 stops and also their rights under the law may serve to foster trust in the police and a feeling of transparency in their use of S44powers. For example, under the law there is no obligation for a person stopped under s44 to provide their name—just to allow the search. Yet personal information is routinely collected during s44 stops, with officers requesting the information as standard; thus placing the onus on the person stopped to refuse to provide it. Senior Officers interviewed as part of this research explained that the information is asked as standard since it is a requirement for other types of search (the forms used in s44 stops are also the same as those used in other types of stop, there for have the personal data fields). The officers accepted that by virtue of an officer asking for this information there is an implicit indication that this is required information. Providing personal information in a stop related to terrorism, when a person thinks they have done nothing to justify being stopped, is likely to make the experience more personal and potentially more emotive. By officers informing people of their rights and making them aware that they do not have to provide their names if they don't want to, may in itself increase co-operation and trust in the police.

This issue of officers routinely asking people stopped under s44 for personal details and not informing them of their right to decline disclosing this information was raised by The Muslim News "on several occasions" with the British Transport Police (BTP) Chief Constable, Ian Johnston, "during past consultations after receiving several complaints from the Muslim community." Despite this, the BTP released a DVD in 2007 on stop and search under s44 which *The Muslim News* subsequently branded as misleading:

> The film informs us of what the public should expect when they are stopped at underground stations. But what the DVD fails to mention is that a stopped person does not need to provide his/her name or address. On the contrary, the public is being misled by the police by them insisting in the DVD on taking down the name and address of the person stopped. At no time is the victim informed of their right not to disclose this information. (2007, n.p.)

Examples such as this do nothing to instill trust in the police and ensure the transparent operation of these exceptional powers.

A senior Black officer interviewed, when asked about the issue of informing people stopped of their rights did not seem to appreciate why people may not wish to disclose their names during a stop, saying "in for a penny, in for a pound, why not give it?" The fact is that the person being stopped has not opted into the situation, they were selected by the officer, and in most cases they do not know why they were selected. This attitude highlights how officers see stopping people as a routine part of their job and may not fully appreciate that for people being stopped it may be an intimidating situation and that they may fear declining could lead to an escalation of the stop; or people's possible concerns about their name being recorded on a police database in association with terrorism and the potential future impact of this association.

The Muslim News reported evidence that in some cases people stopped by BTP and refusing to provide their personal details have been warned that failure to provide the information would resulting them being detained and not allowed to continue with their journey. Bowling and Phillips also note that refusal to answer questions during a stop may be interpreted as an indicator of guilt by officers and therefore it is may escalate the situation (2007, 952).

Officer training in respect of carrying out s44 stops and differentiating them from other types of stops may help officers be more sensitive to public concerns and so foster greater co-operation.

In order to make use of s44 powers transparent and clear to the public, the police should also consider narrowing the area designations to strategic locations and make the areas known to the public, as suggested by Liberty and other civil liberty campaigners. To date the government has resisted calls to publish the details of designated areas, claiming that this would give reduce the effectiveness of s44 powers and give terrorists an advantage (ICO 2010, 9).

In November 2007, civil rights campaign website SpyBlog UK asked the Home Office for details of the time, place and duration s44 stop/search authorizations since the Act came into force, using the Freedom of Information (FOI) Act. This information is highlighted as important to the public interest, in order to monitor use of s44 powers:

> Given that jobsworth private security guards have been reported as falsely claiming that the area or building which they are working at is supposedly covered by such Authorisations (which only give powers of stop/search to Police Constables in Uniform), we feel that the Home Office, or local Police forces, should publish ... areas which are currently subjected to such Authorisations, and to the extraordinary and exceptional powers which they grant. (Spy Blog UK, 2007)

FOI Legislation states that all requests should receive a response within 20 working days. The Home Office refused to release the information, a decision which the organization successfully appealed; despite this the Home Office still refused to release the information. In June 2009 the Information Commissioner's Office (ICO) formally sent a Section 51 Information Notice to the Home Office, giving them 28 days in which to release the information—action the ICO rarely takes. The consequences of the Notification are that, technically failing to release the information within the 28 days could result in the Home Office being taken to the High Court for Contempt of Court proceedings. That said, the Home Office did not release the information within the 28 days and was neither taken to the High Court. More than two years after the original request was made, the ICO issued a Decision Notice in February 2010, (partly) upholding the complaint against the Home Office for refused to release any information and identifying procedural breaches by the Home Office in responding the request for information. The ICO found that the in this case the Home Office was not co-operative and its approach was not within the spirit of the Act.

Julian Todd of the website WhatDoTheyKnow.com submitted a similar request for time, date and areas covered by the s44 powers. The request was submitted in June 2008, rejected, appealed and as of February 2010 still being investigated by the ICO. These two cases highlight the Home Offices' resistance to being open and transparent in the operation of s44 powers, which can only serve to reinforce the public perception that the powers, which were claimed as "extraordinary" on creation, are in fact being used by police forces as quite ordinary powers.

Lord Carlile states that in at least five instances the police have used s44powers where there was no authorization in effect[3] with the consequence of stopping hundreds of people illegally (Carlile 2008; McNulty 2007). Without the knowledge of when and where authorizations are in effect, such occurrences cannot be monitored openly.

ETHNIC MONITORING

In response to allegations of racial profiling by police in the US, many states set up systems to collect and analyze statistical data on motorists who are stopped by the police, including information on their racial/ethnic background, with a view to monitoring the officers' behavior (McMahon, Garner, Davis, and Kraus 2002; Weatherspoon 2004). In Europe, the UK is the only country to have a similar system of monitoring in place (Goldston 2006). Monitoring of PACE searches was introduced in 1993, although ethnicity data were reported in broad

White/ethnic minority categories and it did not differentiate between those within the "ethnic minority" category. Mandatory detailed ethnic monitoring was later introduced in April 1996 (FitzGerald and Sibbitt 1997), which recorded the ethnicity of people *searched* using PACE powers.

The monitoring of all those stopped (and not just those subsequently searched) was suggested in the Macpherson report, under Recommendation 61, in order to improve monitoring as a direct result of the disproportionate number of Black people in the data on people searched. On 17 September 2002 the Home Secretary announced that Recommendation 61 would be phased into practice. Recommendation 61 also suggested that monitoring should include the self-defined ethnic identity of people stopped, which was again phased into police monitoring, for example Greater Manchester Police introduced this in 2002, while the Metropolitan Police force introduced this in April 2003 (MPA Commissioner 2002).

In the UK, monitoring police practices are ahead of other European countries, but there are still areas which are not considered to be sufficiently covered by current monitoring procedures, such as disability, sexuality, religion and in some cases ethnicity. In the case of ethnicity, concerns have been raised by the Gypsy Traveller community over the use of stop/search powers directed at them (MPA 2008a; 2008b), for example, which if substantiated could be an indication of police use of s44 powers for non-terrorism searches (i.e. everyday policing). While the police 6+1 ethnic codes do not differentiate the Gypsy Traveller community, neither does the self-defined ethnicity 16+1 system, thus these community concerns cannot currently be assessed statistically.

> Several Borough scrutiny groups are of the opinion that the Home Office self-defined ethnicity categories are not suitable. This is because many of their communities would not readily be able to identify themselves in these categories. The scrutiny groups further believe that the lack of flexibility with the system may be a major obstacle to obtaining co-operation from the public on ethnic monitor. (MPA 2008a, 4)

Similar concerns of police targeting and use of s44 have been expressed by the Lesbian, Gay, Bisexual and Transgender community in certain areas of London (MPA 2008a). Again, since sexuality is not recorded, it is difficult to monitor police behavior in this respect. And it is hard to conceive why this community would be specifically targeted under s44, which again gives rise to the possibility of officers using these powers for non-terrorism policing.

Then there is, of course, the issue of the suspected ethnic profiling of Muslims post-9/11 and July 7, which is often put forward as the reason for the disproportionate stops of Asians — ethnicity being used as proxy for religion. The inadequacies of using racial groups as a proxy for religion have been highlighted (MCB 2004) and since information on religion is not collected by police, no analysis can be done in this respect to definitively test for disproportionality of stops in respect of Muslims. Despite calls for collecting data on religion by the Mayor of London and a range of organizations (Ali 2005), to specifically enable the examination of the proportions of Muslims stopped, it does not look likely that religion will be making its way on to police monitoring systems in the future: "National research has been conducted by the Home Office that shows that communities would be unwilling to disclose their faith at point of contact" (MPA 2008a, 5).

The national research referred to was commissioned by the Stop/search Action Team Community Panel, to assess the possibility of recording faith in stop/search encounters. The research comprised a series of workshops, in eight venues across the UK, involving over 200 young people. The vast majority were opposed to being asked to declare their faith during a stop/search encounter, with the strongest reaction from the Jewish and Muslim communities. The research found that young Muslims were particularly fearful that declaring their faith during a stop would result in more punitive treatment. Another phase of the research discussed the idea among adult representatives from various faiths hosted by the Met and again the reaction was negative (Ainsworth 2009). So while Muslim organizations are calling for a means to assess disproportionality of stops among their community, it appears that people within faith communities are reluctant to provide the necessary information as part of the stop encounter. Thus the means of proving possible discrimination against the Muslim community is likely to prove impossible collate in the foreseeable future, due to the fear of discrimination itself.

THE MEDIA AND OFFICER PERCEPTIONS

Aside from the recommended changes to official police procedure in operating s44 powers, it must be noted that given the indirect/unofficial nature of the discrimination observed, outside factors that contribute to officer perceptions of minorities, and thus their actions towards them, cannot be overlooked. As such, the media plays a pivotal role in "perpetuating negative perceptions" of minority groups, not only in the extremist press but in the mainstream media (Rostas 2005, 29). This has the effect of cloaking racism/faithism in respectability.

Shah and Thornton suggest that media reporting of racial interactions can influence the formulation of public policy and "can help justify official policies of social control of racial and other minorities" (1994, 156), as well as influencing individual readers' perceptions and subsequent behavior towards ethnic minorities. The critical role the media plays in shaping and reinforcing public perceptions of race relations, through reporting style and selection of sources, is well documented in academia. In the UK, some activists and organizations also appear keenly aware of these factors at play. For example, Hassan (2009) cites that media reporting in the UK after four Somali men were arrested in Australia, for an alleged terrorist plot, wrongly held whole communities accountable for the actions of a few. He claims that such reporting undermined the positive work of community groups in relation to community cohesion, and facilitates alienation. The MCB highlights how the media use of sources can be manipulated to affect public perceptions, citing the example of a police source leaking information to the press in April 2004 as having intentionally damaging consequences whose "only possible purpose could have been to feed anti Muslim hysteria" (2004, 22).

Given that s44 powers are implemented by individual officers, without the relatively objective grounds of 'reasonable suspicion' as an external check on personal prejudices, the impact of negative media reports relating to Muslims and ethnic minorities on officer behavior is potentially significant. After all, police officers are only human and subject to the same influences as everyone else. Like everyone else, police officers are likely to incorporate racial stereotypes into their perceptions of the world (Cole 1999) and act upon those stereotypes, even if unintentionally, "unconscious biases...can lead us to treat people differently based on race, but without intending to or even being aware that we are doing so" (Wang 2004, 1017). This is a view echoed by the MCB:

> It is difficult to pass a day without an aggressive tabloid and broadsheet newspaper piece that seeks to persuade its enthralled readership that Islam and Muslims present a threat to the UK. It is inevitable that decision-makers and enforcement agents will internalise prejudice and manifest this in their practice. (2004, 19)

Therefore, in order to achieve significant and sustained long-term change in practices of ethnic profiling, monitoring needs to "extend well beyond the criminal justice system" and should include sources of bias in wider society (Stone 2005, 4). With this in mind, the recommendation that the Metropolitan Police incorporate 'exception testing' into their monitoring systems is a positive step:

> The MPS...monitoring incorporate "exception testing," i.e. officers whose racial disproportion in stops and searches is significantly above the average for officers in their borough, and that regular quarterly reports be presented to the Equal Opportunities & Diversity Board (EODB) on the outcome of this monitoring Recommendation 27. (MPA 2004, 98)

Although, notably, no recommendations were made in respect of how to deal with any cases found and reported. Also of note is that the EODB was disbanded in September 2008 and examination of records does not show any reports relating to exception testing, confirming the fact that exception testing was not put into practice.

National adoption of exception testing, and public reporting, is suggested as a standard addition to the current monitoring mechanisms. It would be the first time that the behavior of individuals is the focus of monitoring, whereas past efforts have been focused on the institutional level. It has been suggested that getting officers to collect data on ethnicity for monitoring purposes may raise awareness of the risk of discrimination and internalized biases (De Schutter and Ringelheim 2008, 378–379), so it is plausible that regular exception testing could raise awareness among officers that those who consistently show disproportion relative to their peers will be highlighted. While exception testing will only highlight "exceptions," knowledge that individual officer behavior is under scrutiny may also potentially evolve the behavior of individuals and drive down levels of widespread profiling practice.

There is some potential that the exception testing will become part of the national police monitoring toolkit in respect of all stop and search powers, pending the outcome of the piloting of the Next Steps initiative by the National Policing Improvement Agency (NPIA) in 2010. The initiative is modeled on US practices and involves exception testing as one of the assessments of police.

CONCLUSION

There can be little doubt that the UK police forces examined are using their exceptional powers of stop/search under s44 of the Terrorism Act (2000) in a discriminatory manner against ethnic minorities, the likely result of informal ethnic profiling. The Asian ethnic group has consistently experienced higher rates of disproportion in the stops data under this power. Combined with the marked observed increase in disproportionate representation of Asians in stops in the immediately following the July 2005 bombings in London and the failed attempted bombings in Glasgow and London in June 2007, are indicative of the suspicion these events bestowed on this ethnic group, which translated into discrimination on the ground.

The business case against informal racial profiling in policing does not seem to be filtering through to officers on the beat, despite the fact that many must be aware that the police are viewed with suspicion in some communities and that hard policing tactics such as stop/search are not welcomed by many. If ethnic profiling is to be successfully eradicated there needs to be a holistic approach to the issue. The current inadequacies of the law to ensure public protection from discrimination must be addressed; the operation of s44 powers should be more transparent and clear to the public, to foster faith in the police; there needs to be greater understanding among officers of the impact of hard tactics on individuals/communities in the context of counter-terrorism and an empathy with the view from the other side; and monitoring of use of s44 needs to be more comprehensive and more widely publicized, in order to hold police accountable to the public they are mandated to protect and serve.

NOTES

1. Institutional Racism: In the Stephen Lawrence Inquiry, 'institutional racism' was defined as 'the collective failure of an organisation to provide an appropriate and professional service to people because of their colour, culture, or ethnic origin. It can be seen or detected in processes, attitudes and behaviour which amount to discrimination through unwitting prejudice, ignorance, thoughtlessness and racist stereotyping which disadvantage minority ethnic people. It persists because of the failure of the organisation openly and adequately to recognise and address its existence and causes by policy, example and leadership' (Report of an Inquiry by Sir William Mcpherson of Cluny, February 1999, cm 4262-I, para 6.34).

2. The researcher and author of the Policy Research Centre of the Islamic Foundation (PRCIF) report has a masters degree, is a Research Fellow, Trustee of the Interfaith Network UK, an Executive member of the Association of Muslim Chaplains and Co-Founder of the Young Muslims Forum; a highly educated professional person and an active community activist—yet the powers of the police under s44 were not clear to her; how can the government expect the average layperson to be clear about these powers and their rights under the law? Both the author and the Head of the PRCIF were contacted regarding this apparent confusion; neither responded.

3. Lord Carlile reported, in his annual review, that 12 people were illegally stopped in one incident, meanwhile McNulty—whose office informed Lord Carlile of the incident—reported 259 people were stopped in this same incident in his written statement to the House. This discrepancy was raised by the author in personal communication with Lord Carlile, who reiterated the figure of 12 people; the current Minister of State, has not responded to written requests for clarification of this discrepancy.

REFERENCES

Ahmed, S. 2009. *Seen and Not Heard: Voices of Young British Muslims*. London: Policy Research Centre.

Ainsworth, M. 2009. "Stop and Search Advisor, National Policing Improvement Agency." Personal email communications with author.

Ali, H. 2005. *Stop and Search Scrutiny Implementation Panel*. Metropolitan Police Authority. http://www.mpa.gov.uk/committees/x-eodb/2005/050310/10/ (Accessed October 29, 2009).

Ayres, M., D. Perry, and P. Hayward. 2002 *Arrests for Notifiable Offences and the Operation of Certain Police Powers under PACE 12/02, England and Wales, 2001/02*. Research, Development and Statistics (RDS) Directorate of the Home Office.

Bowling, B. and C. Phillips. 2007. "Disproportionate and Discriminatory: Reviewing the Evidence on Police Stop and Search." *The Modern Law Review* 70(6): 936–961.

Carlile, Lord. 2009. *Report on the Operation in 2008 of the Terrorism Act 2000 and of Part I of the Terrorism Act 2006*. Home Office. June. http://www.official-documents.gov.uk/document/other/9780108508349/9780108508349.pdf (Accessed October 30, 2009).

———. June 2008. *Report on the Operation in 2007 of the Terrorism Act 2000 and of Part I of the Terrorism Act 2006*. Home Office. June. http://security.homeoffice.gov.uk/news-publications/publication-search/terrorism-act-2000/lord-carlile-report-07/lord-carliles-report-2008?view=Binary (Accessed October 29, 2009).

———. 2007. *Report on the Operation in 2006 of the Terrorism Act 2000*. Home Office. June. http://security.homeoffice.gov.uk/news-publications/publication-search/terrorism-act-2000/TA2000-review061.pdf?view=Binary (Accessed October 29, 2009).

———. 2006. *Report on the Operation in 2005 of the Terrorism Act 2000*. Home Office. May. http://security.homeoffice.gov.uk/news-publications/publication-search/terrorism-act-2000/tact-2005-review?view=Binary (Accessed October 29, 2009).

———. 2005. *Report on the Operation in 2004 of the Terrorism Act 2000*. Home Office. http://www.statewatch.org/news/2005/may/terrorism-act-2004-rep.pdf (Accessed October 30, 2009).

———. 2004. *Report on the Operation in 2002 and 2003 of the Terrorism Act 2000*. Home Office. http://security.homeoffice.gov.uk/news-publications/publication-search/terrorism-act-2000/terrorismact-rpt.pdf?view=Binary (Accessed October 30, 2009).

(CFR-CDF) EU Network of Independent Experts in Fundamental Rights. 2003. *The Balance Between Freedom and Security in the Response by the European Union and Its Member States to the Terrorist Threats*. European Commission DG Justice and Home Affairs. http://ec.europa.eu/justice_home/cfr_cdf/doc/obs_thematique_en.pdf (Accessed October 30, 2009).

Cole, D. 1999. *No Equal Justice: Race and Class in the American Justice System*. New York: The New Press.

Council of the European Union, The. 2002. *Draft Council Recommendation on the Development of Terrorist Profiles*. Document 11858/02. http://register.consilium.europa.eu/pdf/en/02/st11/st11858.en02.pdf (Accessed November 2, 2009).

De Schutter, O. and J. Ringelheim. 2008. "Ethnic Profiling: A Rising Challenge for European Human Rights Law." *The Modern Law Review* 71(3): 358–384.

Doghem-Rashid, E. 2004. *Multiculturalism in the UK*. Unpublished Masters Dissertation.

Engel, R, J. Calnon, and T. Bernard. 2002. "Theory and Racial Profiling: Shortcomings and Future Directions in Research." *Justice Quarterly* 19(2): 249–273.

European Network Against Racism. 2009. *Ethnic Profiling*. ENAR Fact Sheet 40. June. http://cms.horus.be/files/99935/MediaArchive/pdf/FS40%20-%20ethnic%20profiling.pdf (Accessed November 4, 2009).

EHRC Registrar. 2010. "Press release issued by the Registrar—Chamber judgment - Gillan and Quinton v. the United Kingdom (application no. 4158/05)." http://cmiskp.echr.coe.int/tkp197/viewhbkm.asp?sessionId=42624724&skin=hudoc-pr-en&act

ion=html&table=F69A27FD8FB86142BF01C1166DEA398649&key=79298&high-light=4158/05#02000001 (Accessed February 24, 2010).

Ferguson, C. 2010. "Gillan & Quinton v UK: Racial Profiling and the Consequences of the ECtHR Judgment." Presented at Runnymede Trust eConference "Ethnic Profiling in the UK." http://www.runnymedetrust.org/events-conferences/econferences/ethnic-profiling-in-uk-law-enforcement/corrina-ferguson.html (Accessed February 24, 2010).

FitzGerald, M. and R. Sibbitt. 1997. *Home Office Research Study 173—Ethnic Monitoring in Police Forces: A Beginning*. Research and Statistics Directorate Report. London: Home Office. http://www.homeoffice.gov.uk/rds/pdfs/hors173.pdf (Accessed October 30, 2009).

Fresco, A. 2009. "Nicky Reilly, Muslim Convert, Jailed for 18 years for Exeter Bomb Attack." *The Times Online*. http://www.timesonline.co.uk/tol/news/uk/crime/article5619151.ece (Accessed February 25, 2010).

Goldston, J. 2006. "Ethnic Profiling and Counter-Terrorism Trends, Dangers and Alternatives." Presented to the Anti-Racism and Diversity Intergroup, European Parliament in Brussels, June 6, 2006. Open Society Institute (OSI). http://www.soros.org/initiatives/justice/focus/equality_citizenship/articles_publications/articles/counterterrorism_20060606/goldston_20060606.pdf (Accessed October 30, 2009).

———. 2005. "Toward a Europe Without Ethnic Profiling." *Justice Initiatives* 6–13. Open Society Institute (OSI). http://www.soros.org/initiatives/justice/focus/equality_citizenship/articles_publications/publications/juticeinit_20050610/justiceinit_200506.pdf (Accessed October 30, 2009).

Greater Manchester Police. 2005. *Ethnic Monitoring of Police Activity*. http://www.gmp.police.uk/mainsite/0/1BD5BFAD2FF27AFA802571040041606C/$file/Ethnic%20data%20monitoring%20of%20police%20activity.pdf (Accessed February 24, 2010).

Harris, D. 2009. "Leveraging the Politics of Racial Profiling to Effectuate Reform." *Criminology and Public Policy* 8(2): 381–386.

———. 2007. "The Importance of Research on Race and Policing: Making Race Salient to Individuals and Institutions Within Criminal Justice." *Criminology and Public Policy* 6(1): 5–24.

———. 2002a. *Profiles in Injustice—Why Racial Profiling Cannot Work*. New York: The New Press.

———. 2002b. "Flying While Arab: Lessons from the Racial Profiling Controversy," *Civil Rights Journal* Winter: 9–13. http://www.usccr.gov/pubs/crj/wint2002/wint02.pdf (Accessed October 30, 2009).

———. 2001. "When Success Breeds Attack: The Coming Backlash Against Racial Profiling Studies." *Michigan Journal of Race and Law* 6(2): 237.

———. 1999. "The Stories, the Statistics and the Law: Why 'Driving While Black' Matters." *University of Minnesota Law Review* 84(2): 265–326.

Hassan, M. 2009. "Criminalising Muslim Somalis is Counter-Productive." *The Muslim News*. September. http://www.muslimnews.co.uk/paper/index.php?article=4294 (Accessed October 28, 2009).

Hickley, M. 2001. "Police Stop and Search Arrests Fall." *Daily Mail*. March, 10.

Holbert, S. and L. Rose. 2006. "Making Sense of the Data: The Shortcomings of Racial Profiling Data Collection and Analysis." *Law Enforcement Technology* 33(7): 42–44.

Home Office. 2009. *Home Office Statistical Bulletin 04/09: Statistics on Terrorism Arrests and Outcomes Great Britain 11 September 2001 to 31 March 2008.* Research, Development and Statistics (RDS) Directorate of the Home Office, May.

———. 2008. "Authorisations of Stop and Search Powers under Section 44 of the Terrorism Act." Home Office Circular 027/2008. http://www.civilrenewal.communities. gov.uk/about-us/publications/home-office-circulars/circulars-2008/027-2008/ (Accessed May 23, 2010).

———. 2006. "Authorisations of Stop and Search Powers under Section 44 of the Terrorism Act." Home Office Circular 022/2006. http://www.civilrenewal.communities. gov.uk/about-us/publications/home-office-circulars/circulars-2006/022-2006/ (Accessed May 23, 2010).

———. 2004. "Authorisations of Stop and Search Powers under Section 44 of the Terrorism Act." Home Office Circular 038/2004. http://www.civilrenewal.communities. gov.uk/about-us/publications/home-office-circulars/circulars-2004/038-2004/ (Accessed May 23, 2010).

———. 2003. *Statistics on Race and the Criminal Justice System—2003.* A Home Office publication under section 95 of the Criminal Justice Act 1991.

———. 2002. *Statistics on Race and the Criminal Justice System.* A Home Office publication under section 95 of the Criminal Justice Act 1991.

Huhne, C. 2010. *Excessive Use of Stop and Search.* Presented at Runnymede Trust eConference "Ethnic Profiling in the UK." http://www.runnymedetrust.org/events-conferences/ econferences/ethnic-profiling-in-uk-law-enforcement/chris-huhne.html (Accessed February 24, 2010).

Humphreys, S. 2005. "The Case for Monitoring Ethnic Profiling in Europe." *Justice Initiatives* 44–52. Open Society Institute (OSI). http://www.soros.org/initiatives/justice/ focus/equality_citizenship/articles_publications/publications/juticeinit_20050610/ justiceinit_200506.pdf (Accessed October 30, 2009).

Information Commissioner's Office. 2010. *Freedom of Information Act 2000 (Section 50) Decision Notice,* Date: 8 February 2010. http://www.ico.gov.uk/upload/documents/decisionnotices/2010/fs_50198733%20.pdf (Accessed February 24, 2010).

Jones, A. and L. Singer. 2008. *Statistics on Race and the Criminal Justice System 2006/7: A Ministry of Justice Publication under Section 95 of the Criminal Justice Act 1991.* Ministry of Justice. uly. Available online: http://www.justice.gov.uk/publications/docs/stats-race-criminal-justice.pdf (Accessed October 28, 2009).

———. 2007. *Statistics on Race and the Criminal Justice System—2006: A Ministry of Justice Publication under Section 95 of the Criminal Justice Act 1991.* Ministry of Justice. http://www. justice.gov.uk/publications/docs/race-and-cjs-stats-2006.pdf (Accessed October 28, 2009).

Keenan, R. 2005. "Stop and Search: the Leicestershire Experience." *Justice Initiatives* 82–87. Open Society Institute (OSI). http://www.soros.org/initiatives/justice/focus/equality_citizenship/articles_publications/publications/juticeinit_20050610/justiceinit_200506.pdf (Accessed October 30, 2009).

Khan, F. 2007. *Islamophobia—The Impact on London.* Report by the Muslim Safety Forum. http://muslimsafetyforum.org/docs/Islamophobia&ImpactonLondon.pdf (Accessed November 13, 2009).

Kundnani, A. 2009. *Spooked! How Not to Prevent Violent Extremism*. Institute of Race Relations (IRR). http://www.irr.org.uk/pdf2/spooked.pdf (Accessed November 4, 2009).

Lamberth, J. 2005. "Benchmarking and Analysis for Ethnic Profiling Studies." *Justice Initiatives* 59–65. Open Society Institute (OSI). http://www.soros.org/initiatives/justice/focus/equality_citizenship/articles_publications/publications/juticeinit_20050610/justiceinit_200506.pdf (Accessed October 30, 2009).

Macpherson Inquiry. 1999. *The Stephen Lawrence Inquiry, Report of an Inquiry by Sir William Macpherson of Cluny*. London: Stationery Office. Parliamentary papers, Cm 4262

McNulty, T. 2007. *Written Ministerial Statement to Hansard (House of Commons Daily Debates)*. December. http://www.publications.parliament.uk/pa/cm200708/cmhansrd/cm071212/wmstext/71212m0002.htm#column_40 (Accessed October 29, 2009).

Metropolitan Police Authority. 2009a. *Stops and Searches Monitoring Mechanism*. July.

Metropolitan Police Authority. 2009b. *Stops and Searches Monitoring Mechanism*. August.

Metropolitan Police Authority. 2009c. *Stops and Searches Monitoring Mechanism*. December.

Metropolitan Police Authority. 2008a *Stops and Searches Monitoring Mechanism*. June.

Metropolitan Police Authority. 2008b. *Equality Impact Assessment on the Use of Section 44 Terrorism Act 2000 Stop and Search Powers*. Freedom of Information Act Publication Scheme, MPA. July.

Metropolitan Police Authority. 2007a. Stops and Searches Monitoring Mechanism. February.

Metropolitan Police Authority. 2007. *Counter Terrorism: The London Debate*. MPA. July. http://www.mpa.gov.uk/downloads/publications/counterterrorism/ctld-22feb07.pdf (Accessed October 28, 2009).

Metropolitan Police Authority. 2006. *Stops and Searches Monitoring Mechanism*. July.

Metropolitan Police Authority. 2004. *Report of the MPA Scrutiny on MPS Stop and Search Practice*. MPA.

Metropolitan Police Authority Commissioner. 2002. *Update on MPS progress in relation to Recommendation 61 of the Stephen Lawrence Inquiry*.

Metropolitan Police Authority Commissioner. 2003a. *Implementation of Recommendation 61*.

Metropolitan Police Authority Commissioner 2003b. *Implementation of Recommendation 61 of The Stephen Lawrence Inquiry*.

Meyrick, T. 2005a. "Minutes: 2nd Meeting of the Stop and Search Action Team Community Panel—8th February, 2005." Home Office.

Meyrick, T. 2005b. "Minutes: 3rd Meeting of the Stop and Search Action Team Community Panel—14th March, 2005." Home Office.

Meyrick, T. 2005c. "Minutes: 7th Meeting of the Stop and Search Action Team Community Panel—29th September, 2005." Home Office.

McMahon, J., J. Garner, R. Davis, and A. Kraus. 2002. *How to Correctly Collect and Analyze Racial Profiling Data: Your Reputation Depends On It!*. Final Project Report for Racial Profiling Data Collection and Analysis. Washington DC: Government Printing Office. http://www.cops.usdoj.gov/files/RIC/Publications/e06064106.pdf (Accessed October 30, 2009).

Miller, J. 2005. "Measuring and Understanding Minority Experiences of Stop and Search in the UK." *Justice Initiatives* 53–58. Open Society Institute (OSI). http://www.soros.

org/initiatives/justice/focus/equality_citizenship/articles_publications/publications/juticeinit_20050610/justiceinit_200506.pdf (Accessed October 30, 2009).

Moeckli, D. 2005. "Discrimination Profiles: Law Enforcement After 9/11 and 7/7." *European Human Rights Law Review* 5: 517–532.

Muslim Council of Britain. 2000. "Have Your Say on Police 'Stop and Search' Powers." October 6. http://www.mcb.org.uk/features/features.php?ann_id=500 (Accessed October 28, 2009).

Muslim Council of Britain. 2004. *Government Discussion Paper—Counter-Terrorism Powers: Reconciling Security and Liberty in an Open Society; A Response from the Muslim Council of Britain*, MCB. August. http://www.mcb.org.uk/library/ATCSA.pdf (Accessed October 29, 2009).

Muslim News, The. 2007. "Misleading Police DVD on Stop and Search." September 28. http://www.muslimnews.co.uk/paper/index.php?article=3144 (Accessed October 28, 2009).

Nagel, C. 2001. "Hidden Minorities and the Politics of 'Race': The Case of British Arab Activists in London." *Journal of Ethnic and Migration Studies.* 27(3): 381–400.

Open Society Justice Initiative. 2009. *Ethnic Profiling in the European Union: Pervasive, Ineffective, and Discriminatory.* Open Society Institute (OSI). May. http://www.soros.org/initiatives/justice/focus/equality_citizenship/articles_publications/publications/profiling_20090526/profiling_20090526.pdf (Accessed October 30, 2009).

Open Society Justice Initiative. 2007. *Ethnic Profiling in Europe: Counter-Terrorism Activities and the Creation of Suspect Communities.* Submission of the Open Society Justice Initiative to the Eminent Jurists Panel on Terrorism, Counter-Terrorism and Human Rights of the International Commission of Jurists. June. http://www.ecre.org/files/Ethnic%20profiling%20in%20Europe%20English.pdf (Accessed October 30, 2009).

Open Society Justice Initiative. 2004. *Racial Discrimination in the Administration of Justice: Submission of the Open Society Justice Initiative to the UN Committee on the Elimination of Racial Discrimination on the Occasion of its 65th Session.* Open Society Institute (OSI). August. http://www.soros.org/initiatives/justice/focus/equality_citizenship/articles_publications/articles/racialjustice_20040802/racial_justice.pdf (Accessed October 30, 2009).

O'Rawe, M. 2005. "Ethnic Profiling, Policing, and Suspect Communities: Lessons from Northern Ireland." *Justice Initiatives* 88–99. Open Society Institute (OSI). http://www.soros.org/initiatives/justice/focus/equality_citizenship/articles_publications/publications/juticeinit_20050610/justiceinit_200506.pdf (Accessed October 30, 2009).

Pantazis, C. and S. Pemberton. 2009. "From the 'Old ' to the 'New' Suspect Community: Examining the Impacts of Recent UK Counter-Terrorist Legislation." *British Journal of Criminology* 49: 646–666. http://bjc.oxfordjournals.org/cgi/reprint/49/5/646.pdf (Accessed November 4, 2009).

Reidy, C. 2008. *Metropolitan Police Service (MPS) Stop and Search Equality Impact Assessment.* Freedom of Information Act Publication Scheme, MPA. http://www.met.police.uk/foi/pdfs/policies/stop_and_search_eia_non_s44.pdf (Accessed November 4, 2009).

Riley, J., D. Cassidy, and J. Becker. 2009. *Statistics on Race and the Criminal Justice System 2007/8: A Ministry of Justice Publication under Section 95 of the Criminal Justice Act 1991.* Ministry of Justice. http://www.justice.gov.uk/publications/docs/stats-race-criminal-justice-system-07-08-revised.pdf (Accessed October 28, 2009).

Rostas, J. 2005. "ID Checks and Police Raids: Ethnic Profiling in Central Europe." *Justice Initiatives* 26–31. Open Society Institute (OSI). http://www.soros.org/initiatives/justice/focus/equality_citizenship/articles_publications/publications/juticeinit_20050610/justiceinit_200506.pdf (Accessed October 30, 2009).

Shah, H. and M. Thornton. 1994. "Racial Ideology in US Mainstream News Magazine Coverage of Black-Latino Interaction 1980–1992." *Critical Studies in Media Communication* 11(2):141–161.

Sharma, S. 2003. "Beyond 'Driving While Black' and 'Flying While Brown': Using Intersectionality to Uncover the Gendered Aspects of Racial Profiling." *Columbia Journal of Gender and Law* 275–318. http://www.sjsu.edu/justicestudies/docs/Beyond_Driving_While_Black_and_Flying_While_Brown.pdf (Accessed October 29, 2009).

SkyNews. 2009. "Police Use Of Stop And Search Powers Soar." http://news.sky.com/skynews/Home/UK-News/Anti-Terror-Legislation-Sees-Police-Use-Of-Stop-And-Search-Laws-Treble-In-England-And-Wales/Article/200904415272529 (Accessed February 25, 2010).

Spalek, B., S. El Awa, S, and L. McDonald. 2008. *Police-Muslim Engagement and Partnerships for the Purposes of Counter-Terrorism: An Examination (Summary Report)*. University of Birmingham. http://muslimsafetyforum.org/docs/summary%20report%20ct%20police%20community%20partnership%20bham.pdf (Accessed November 13, 2009).

Spy Blog UK. 2009. *ICO Serves an Information Notice on the Home Office Re Our Complaint about the Terrorism Act 2000 s44 Stop and Search Authorisations.* http://p10.hostingprod.com/@spyblog.org.uk/blog/foia/ho-terrorism-act-2000-s44-authorisations/ (Accessed October 29, 2009).

Spy Blog UK. 2007. *Home Office–Terrorism Act 2000 Section 44 Authorisations—A Full Response within the Next Month?.* http://p10.hostingprod.com/@spyblog.org.uk/blog/foia/2007/12/home_office_terrorism_act_2000_section_44_authorisations_a_full_response_within.html (Accessed November 2, 2009).

Steele, J. 2001. "Street Crime Still Rising in London." *Daily Telegraph*, April 20, 16.

Stone, C. 2005. "Foreword: Preparing a Fresh Assault on Ethnic Profiling." *Justice Initiatives* 1–5. Open Society Institute (OSI). http://www.soros.org/initiatives/justice/focus/equality_citizenship/articles_publications/publications/juticeinit_20050610/justiceinit_200506.pdf (Accessed October 30, 2009).

Terrorism Act, The. 2000. http://www.opsi.gov.uk/acts/acts2000/ukpga_20000011_en_1

Todd, J. 2009. *Section 44 Terrorism Act Areas: A Freedom of Information Request to Home Office by Julian Todd.* http://www.whatdotheyknow.com/request/section_44_terrorism_act_areas (Accessed October 29, 2009).

Wang, L. 2004. "Race as Proxy: Situational Racism and Self-Fulfilling Stereotypes." *DePaul Law Review* 53: 1013. http://ssrn.com/abstract=1367888 (Accessed October 30, 2009).

Wang, L. 2001. "'Suitable Targets'? Parallels and Connections between 'Hate Crimes' and 'Driving While Black.'" *Michigan Journal of Race and Law.* 6(2): 209–236. http://ssrn.com/abstract=1374368 (Accessed October 30, 2009).

Warren, P. and Tomaskovic-Devey, D. 2009. "Racial Profiling and Searches: Did the Politics of Racial Profiling Change Police Behavior?" *Criminology and Public Policy.* 8(2): 343–369.

Weatherspoon, F. 2004. "Ending Racial Profiling of African-Americans in the Selective Enforcement of Laws: In Search of Viable Remedies." *University of Pittsburgh Law Review* 65: 721–743. http://heinonline.org/HOL/PDF?handle=hein.journals/upitt65&id=731&print=section&section=30&ext=.pdf&collection=journals (Accessed October 30, 2009).

Wu, F. 2002. "Where Are You REALLY From? Asian Americans and the Perpetual Foreigner Syndrome." *Civil Rights Journal* Winter:14–22. http://www.usccr.gov/pubs/crj/wint2002/wint02.pdf (Accessed October 30, 2009).

CHAPTER 3. RACE AND IMPERIALISM: MIGRATION AND BORDER CONTROL IN THE CANADIAN STATE

Harsha Walia

The myth of Canadian benevolence, the ideology of Canadian peace-keeping, and the veneer of Canadian multiculturalism have served to cast Canada as a liberal counterpoint to aggressive US immigration enforcement tactics. In fact, the US has pointed to Canada's skilled worker program and temporary guest worker programs as models to implement for US migration policy.

The number of migrant workers in the Canadian province of British Columbia (BC) has doubled over the past five years, spurred on by the province's construction boom, the upcoming 2010 Olympics, and trans-provincial transport of the Alberta Tar Sands, as well as growth in BC's resource extractive and mining industries. The exceptional freedom of capital stands in contrast with the restrictions against those migrant workers whose precarious labor secures corporate profits. The vulnerability of these workers is often framed as a problem of bad employers, yet labor coercion is a basic characteristic of capitalism, especially for indentured workers, slaves, prison labor, and migrant workers. For migrant workers, labor exploitation is an inherent part of the process of making a national identity that naturalizes the status of their unfree labor (Arat-Koc 1993, 229-242).

Ironically, border controls are deployed against those whose recourse to migration results from the free license afforded to capital to ravage entire economies and communities in the global South. McKenzie Wark reminds us about the injustice of the entire global economic order that creates migration flows: "Migration is globalization from below. If the 'overdeveloped' world refuses to trade with the underdeveloped world on fair terms, to forgive debt, to extend loans, to lift trade barriers against food and basic manufactured goods, then there can only be an increase in the flow of people" (Wark 2002, n.p.).

This essay examines how Canadian state policies, capital relations in the global economy, strategic narratives of nationalism, and hierarchies of race, class, and gender have constructed the category of migrant workers and hence created the legal, social, political, and economic conditions for their exploitation. Shifts in Canada's immigration policy, most recently through the Security and Prosperity Partnership (SPP), have created an increased reliance on migrant workers. By legalizing migration controls and the distinction between citizen and non-citizen, for example through its Seasonal Agricultural Workers Program (SAWP) and Live-in Caregiver Program (LCP), Canada has been able to pursue economic growth while protecting the ideology of "White Canada." The chapter concludes by examining examples and further possibilities of strengthening alliances across diverse social movements in BC in order to advance our collective interests.

MIGRANT WORKER PROGRAMS: A MODEL OF TRANSIENT SERVITUDE

Capitalism's drive to maximize profit intrinsically involves a constant search for cheap labor and the need to perfect the mechanisms for controlling workers. Despite popular belief that the existence of the nation-state is in question because of the nature of the current globalized economy (Dobbin 2003) the reality is that although the character of the nation-state may change, its importance to capitalist expansions remains pivotal. The state creates the legal framework that guarantees the ownership of private property and provides support for disciplining the workforce, while maintaining an economic infrastructure for capital flows. Therefore, the nation-state is the political pillar that allows for the expansion of capitalism.

While borders were essential to unify national markets in nascent capitalism, today they are used to create differential zones of labor and surplus capital. The borders of the modern nation-state increase competition as governments try to offer cheap workforces to attract investments. The ability of the marketplace to transcend national boundaries results in the need for temporary exploitations of labor. As Harold Troper has noted, the denial of legal citizenship to migrant workers allows states to accumulate domestic capital by "in-gathering of off-shore labour" in order to compete in the global market (2004, 136). Therefore, despite its rhetoric, capital does not aim to eliminate the need for national borders.

Indeed, the very regime of Canadian border imperialism legalizes "foreign and temporary" worker programs for the benefit of capital interests.

The relationship between *exploitable* and *disposable* labor has developed over the past century in Canada. Up until the 18th and 19th century, indentured servants working off debt bondages from England accompanied white settlers. The enslavement of Indigenous and black people soon replaced indentured servitude as a preferred form of permanent bonded labor. With the growing abolition sentiment, transient servitude as a profitable form of labor began to develop. Transient servitude, especially in the form of (im)migrant labor, had many of the advantages of slave-labor as employers maintained both control of the labor *as well as* the laborer (2008, n.p.). Today, the denial of legal citizenship through temporary migrant worker programs ensures legal control over the disposability of the laborers, which in turn embeds exploitability of labor as an inherent feature of such programs. According to Gary Teeple, labor as a commodity is crossing borders more easily through the very restriction of those very bodies that represent labor power (2000, 9–23). Migrant worker programs allow for capital interests to access cheap labor that exists under precarious conditions, the most severe of which is the condition of being deportable. This assures a pool of highly exploitable labor, excluded from the minimal protections of the welfare state, and readily disposed of without consequences. As Nandita Sharma argues, "the social organization of those categorized as non-immigrants works to legitimize the differentiation of rights and entitlements across citizen lines by legalizing the indentureship of people classified as migrant workers...Their vulnerability lies at the heart of the flexible accumulation process" (Sharma 2001, 415–439).

The most well-known historical example of this form of indentureship in Canada is the experience of Chinese railway workers in BC during the late 1800s. After risking death and starvation on boats from China, the estimated 17,000 Chinese workers who came to build the Trans-Canada Railways were forced to work in dangerous and deplorable working conditions. Chinese coal miners earned $1 a day compared to the $2.50 earned by white workers and an estimated 1000–3500 died during the railway's construction (Annian 2006, 90–111). These workers were also not allowed to bring families because the Canadian government and contractor expected the workers to return upon the end of the contract.

While the push for Canada's current Temporary Foreign Worker Program, like the migrant Chinese railway workers, largely comes from employers, the exploitation of migrant workers is only made possible through state regulations. Canada formally institutionalized its foreign contract labor programs through the Non-immigrant Employment Authorization Program (NIEP) in 1973. As Nandita Sharma discovered, shortly after the NIEAP was introduced, most workers began to enter Canada as "unfree" wage workers (Sharma 2006, 5–14). In Canada today, more people are admitted annually under Temporary Employment Authorizations (238,093 in 2004) compared to permanent residents (235,708 in 2004). In 2006, Citizenship and Immigration Canada (CIC) reported admitting 112,658 new migrant workers, representing a 13 per cent increase from 2005 (Sharma 2006, 108–137).

Migrant workers represent the perfect workforce in an era evolving global capital–labor relations: commodified and exploitable; flexible and expendable. Fundamental features of migrant worker programs in Canada include being tied to the importing employer; low—and often less than minimum—wages and long hours with no overtime pay; dangerous working conditions; crowded and unhealthy accommodations; denial of access to public healthcare and employment insurance despite paying into the programs; and being virtually held captive by employers or contractors who seize their identification documents (North-South Policy Institute 2006, n.p.). Their temporary legal status is what makes migrant workers extremely vulnerable to abuse as any assertion of their rights leads not only to contract termination but also deportation. As Himani Bannerji notes: "Expressions such as...'foreigner'...and so on, denoting certain types of lesser or negative identities, are in actuality congealed violence or relations of domination" (1995, 24).

Access to citizenship is a tool that fuels multimillion dollar industries. Migrant worker programs are the flip side of the transnational phenomenon of capitalist outsourcing. Adriana Paz argues that such programs depend on huge surpluses of labor from the South that capitalism itself has displaced (2008, n.p.). It has been extensively documented how the North American Free Trade Agreement (NAFTA) has displaced over 1 million Mexican farmers and forced over 15 million Mexicans into poverty; many of whom now work as undocumented workers in the low-paying sectors of the US and Canadian economies. According to William Robinson,

> The transnational circulation of capital and the disruption and deprivation it causes, in turn, generates the transnational circulation of labor. In other words, global capitalism creates immigrant workers... In a sense, this must be seen as a coerced or forced migration, since global capitalism exerts a structural violence over whole populations and makes it impossible for them to survive in their homeland. (2007, n.p.)

As described by David McNally, Canadian corporations are amongst the most aggressive foreign investors in Asia, Latin America, and the Caribbean. From Guatemala to India, Canadian corporations, especially mining firms, have been responsible for environmental destruction, human and labor rights violations, and forced displacement of surrounding communities (McNally 2006b, n.p.). Consequently, the violence enacted on those bodies rendered *displaced* by Canadian trade and foreign policy is further enabled through the deliberate making of migrant workers as perpetually *displace-able* by Canadian immigration and labor policy.

SEASONAL AGRICULTURAL WORKERS PROGRAM: HARVESTING INJUSTICE

Canada's SAWP is seen as the model for migrant worker programs across North America. Historically, Canada's agricultural sector has relied on marginalized groups to supply labor. Farm work is one of the top five most dangerous sectors of work in Canada with an overall annual rate of 11.6 deaths per 100,000 farm population (Pickett, Hartling, Brison, and Guernsey 1999, 1843-1848). Around 1900, as family farms expanded to larger commercial operations, the federal government began accepting British orphaned boys to provide farm labor. From 1942–1946, many German prisoners of war, conscientious objectors from the Doukhobour and Mennonite faiths, and interned Japanese Canadians were forced to work on farms. In the 1960s and 1970s, the Canadian and BC agricultural labor force included Indigenous peoples, Quebecois migrants, and Portuguese and Caribbean immigrants (Preibisch and Santamaria 2006, 108–130).

In 1966, the federal government implemented the SAWP, though BC did not join until 2004. This was largely due to the significant increase in BC's workforce in the 1970s and 1980s by recently-arrived South Asian immigrants from working-class/farming backgrounds in Punjab, most of whom had little knowledge of English and were primarily elders and women. Often enduring 14-hour work days making $1 per hour and living in converted chicken coops, South Asian farm workers carried forward a momentous struggle including the historic founding of the Canadian Farm Workers Union. A grueling fifteen-month strike at the Jensen Mushroom Farms resulted in the first labor contract for farm workers in BC. The Money's Mushroom strike initiated by five Punjabi women effectively shut down the sale and distribution of mushrooms across BC. Despite limited English skills and support networks, the workers were able to exert significant pressure on the agricultural industry through community action (Bush 1995). Currently, the Progressive Inter-cultural Community Services (PICS) continues to provide workshops, trainings, advocacy, language classes, and general resources to farm workers.

As with earlier shifts in the labor force, the devolution from immigrant farm labor to the SAWP was due to the need for even more vulnerable labor. Although a perceived labor shortage was cited by BC farm owners, a report by the BC Federation of Labour found that "the number of employees bonded by the Farm Labour Contractors is virtually the same in 2003 (5915) as it was in 1999 (6000)" (BC Federation of Labour 2004, n.p.). Across Canada, the number of SAWP workers has increased from 264 in 1966 to over 19,000 in 2004, with exponential growth in the past few years. In BC, the number of workers has grown from 50 workers from Mexico in the first year of implementation in 2004 to over 3000 workers—primarily Mexicans—in 2008 (Canadian Centre for Policy Alternatives 2008, 17).

Through the SAWP, the federal government issues temporary employment visas which allow workers to stay in Canada for up to eight months but limits their work permits to the designated employer. A 2006 study by the North–South Institute concluded that, while Canadian law theoretically protects migrant workers, in practice it is difficult for investigations of labor abuse to occur given the workers' temporary status (2006, n.p.). Documented abuses in the SAWP include wages lower than Canadian counterparts and up to sixteen-hour workdays during peak season without receiving overtime or vacation pay. Many migrant farm workers are required to work with pesticides without proper training or safety equipment. Accommodations may be attached to greenhouses with seepage of chemicals and pesticides. Some employers retain passports, health cards, social insurance cards, and work permits. The laborers' plight is exacerbated by the fact that all farm workers have been excluded from various provisions of the provincial Employment Standards Act since 2004. Furthermore, workers can be sent home for filing complaints and a negative report from an employer at the end of a season can result in the suspension from the program for future seasons. Finally, for SAWP workers, there is no option of permanent residency regardless of the number of years—and sometimes decades—they continue to toil in the fields of Canada.

While the organizing by South Asian immigrant farm workers had significant consequences including firings, intimidation, and death threats, the overall consequences were not as severe as those faced by SAWP workers. This is of course intentional. As Stasiulis and Bakan observe:

> [T]he First World state's ability to deny Third World migrants access to naturalization becomes a legal and internationally sanctioned means of discrimination and withholding many basic human rights, and increasing oppression based on race and gender. Denial of citizenship guarantees also intensifies class exploitation, creating pools of labor cheapened and made vulnerable to abuse by threats of deporta-

tion, and by pitting recent immigrants against poor and working class citizens. (2005, 14)

Unlike in other provinces, migrant farm workers are allowed to unionize in BC, but attempts to collective organize and/or unionize have led to deportations. In 2005, a group of thirty-two migrant Mexican workers at Golden Eagle Farms in BC wrote a letter released to media which expressed concerns about their working and living conditions including lack of access to sheltered eating spaces or toilet facilities in the fields; violation of safety codes in the transportation vehicle including removal of seats to cram workers in; and violation of their employment contract for not being provided with appropriate work gear and for being forced to work outdoors in a blueberry field instead of an indoor greenhouse. A few months later, one of the workers faced contract termination and forced repatriation. He believed—and was supported by allies including Justicia for Migrant Workers, No One Is Illegal, and BC Federation of Labour—that his removal was a reprisal for the letter.

Despite such setbacks, the United Food and Commercial Workers (UFCW) runs migrant support centres across the country, has won rights for SAWP workers to access Employment Insurance parental benefits that they were required to pay into but could not collect, and in August 2008 celebrated the first union certification of SAWP workers in BC at Greenway Farms (Sandborn 2008, n.p.). In September 2008, a group of 14 Mexican farm workers at the Floralia Plant Growers in Abbotsford, BC were sent back to Mexico after filing papers to unionize through the UFCW. Nonetheless, despite much fear, the remaining workers went ahead with the vote and overwhelmingly voted to unionize. In response to these two historic certifications, the British Columbia Agriculture Council has launched a legal challenge stating that the provincial labor board cannot legally grant SAWP workers the right to unionize since the workers come under a federally negotiated program.

Simultaneously, increased outreach efforts with migrant workers by community groups aims to empower workers to lead their own struggles with the recognition that any long term change must be directed by those who are most directly affected. In a move that greatly embarrassed Canada's international image, the United Nations Special Rapporteur on the Human Rights of Migrants Jorge Bustamante stated in a newspaper interview that he received letters of complaint directly from Mexican SAWP workers (Collins 2008). Labor unions, community groups, and migrant workers in BC continue to tirelessly advocate for full labor and permanent residency rights for SAWP workers.

THE LIVE-IN CAREGIVER PROGRAM: THE FEMINIZATION OF MIGRATION

Migrant women of color on temporary work visas most directly experience the hypocrisy of liberal democracies that promise opportunity while creating categories of exploited workers. Unlike earlier nanny recruitment programs involving primarily white British women who were able to gain permanent residency in Canada, under the LCP, migrant women—predominantly Filipinas since the 1980s—enter Canada as temporary workers. Although the program calls for a maximum 49-hour workweek, the mandatory live-in aspect allows employers to call on the caregivers at any time. Reports by the Philippines Women's Centre of BC demonstrate that women endure unpaid or excessive work hours, additional job responsibilities, expectations of being on-call at all times, forced confiscation of travel documents, gross violations of privacy, and sexual harassment and sexual assault (Diocson 2003, n.p.). CIC explicitly states that it does not bear any responsibility for enforcement of contracts between the worker and employer (Pratt 2004, 100–102).

Women are required to work for 24 months within a window of 36 months in order to qualify for permanent residency. During this period, the woman must work only in the home of the employer whose name appears on the work permit. If she wants to change employers, she must find a new employer and obtain a new work permit, the time frame for which is used against the 24-month requirement. Even though LCP workers pay into Employment Insurance, they cannot take advantage of it and therefore must always be employed or face removal. As one domestic worker remarked: "We know that, under the LCP, we are like modern slaves who have to wait for at least two years to get our freedom" (Diocson 2003, n.p.). CIC maintains that there is no abuse inherent to the program as there are avenues for formal complaints against employers. Of course, such a statement ignores the precarious immigration status of these women which makes many of them reluctant to report employer or agency abuse. It becomes, as intended, a seeming "choice" that the women make to suffer daily indignities.

Since LCP workers are not able to bring their families until they become permanent residents, a significant impact of the LCP is intergenerational family separation—ranging from 4 to 10 years. According to a statement by the Filipino Canadian Youth Alliance of BC:

> Most newly-arrived Filipino youth face the trauma of migration, family separation and reunification. A recent study at the University of British Columbia found that Filipino youth experience an average of five-year separation from their parents who come to Canada under the LCP...When youth finally are able to enter Canada to be reunited

with their parents, they are reunited as strangers—the result of many years of separation. (Filipino–Canadian Youth Alliance n.d., n.p.)

Conversely, LCP workers who spend years building a life in Canada but cannot complete their work requirements are faced with deportation, sometimes with their Canadian-born children. In a recent, highly publicized, case, Vancouver-based Lilibeth Agoncillo and her one-year-old Canadian born baby are facing deportation because, despite living and working in Vancouver for three years, Lilibeth did not meet the 24-months live-in requirement due to her pregnancy and bureaucratic delays of her work permit as a result of changes in her employers (Mata Press Service 2008, n.p.).

In addition to the supply of cheap labor provided by migrant women under the LCP, the program serves other functions in the capitalist economy. One of the main justifications for the LCP is that there is a labor shortage of Canadians who want to perform domestic work. However, one could readily argue that the reason that there are so few willing Canadians is the devaluation of domestic work in a gendered economy. The LCP also masks the critical need for a universal childcare program in Canada. For rich and middle-class women there are tax exemptions and the luxury of replacement domestic labor in the private sphere of the household, while poor and working-class women are forced to earn a living while juggling their household and childcare responsibilities. Similarly, the LCP facilitates the entry of foreign-trained nurses who cannot be accredited to work in Canada in the field of private home care and home support for the elderly and people with disabilities. In fact, the program prefers workers who have undergone formal training in the health care field as part of the requirement since 1992 that women have at least two years of college education. This creates a quasi-privatized health care system provided for by women in the LCP to those who can afford it, while abrogating the state's responsibility to enhance public and universal healthcare services.

With nearly 100,000 Filipinas having entered Canada under the LCP, groups like the Philippines Women's Centre of BC and SIKLAB–Overseas Filipino Migrant Worker Support Group have been advocating and mobilizing towards the abolition of the "racist and anti-woman" LCP. On International Migrants Day in 2008, these groups—along with others in the Filipino Migrante BC Coalition—wrote the following:

> As part of a growing and marginalized Filipino community, Migrante BC affirms today our commitment to uphold and advance the rights and welfare of migrant workers...We unite with migrants of other nationalities locally and internationally as part of our effort to mount the

broadest front against the brutal dictates of neo-liberal globalization. (Migrante BC 2008, n.p.)

SECURING BORDERS AND LABOR FLEXIBILITY

As it quietly turns into official policy, the Security and Prosperity Partnership (SPP) has further entrenched Canada's reliance on migrant worker programs. The SPP was founded in March 2005 at a summit of the Heads of State of Canada, the US, and Mexico with the backing of powerful lobby groups including the US Council on Foreign Relations, Canadian Council of Chief Executives, and Mexican Council on Foreign Relations. The SPP calls for maximization of North American economic competitiveness in the face of growing exports from India and China; expedited means of resource extraction particularly oil, natural gas, water, and forest products from the Canadian provinces of BC and Alberta; secure borders against "international terrorism, and illegal migration"; standardized regulatory regimes for health, food safety, and the environment; integrated energy supply through a comprehensive resource security pact to ensure that the US receives guaranteed flows of the oil from the Alberta Tar Sands in light of Middle East insecurity and hostile Latin American regimes; and coordination amongst defense forces (Walia and Oka 2008). In short, the SPP is a NAFTA-plus-Homeland-Security model. However, unlike NAFTA and other continental free trade agreements, the SPP is not an official treaty. Made operational through 19 working groups that are outside the legislative process, over 300 policies and agreements are being implemented to realize the stated priorities. The North American Competitiveness Council (NACC) is the only formal advisory board to the SPP and is made up exclusively of corporate CEOs (Walia and Oka 2008).

A central goal of the SPP is to ensure increased mobility of capital. Capital mobility is constituted in the SPP through practices such as biometric pre-clearance programs, the liberalization of rules-of-origins under NAFTA, and the development of trilateral policy frameworks to enhance freer movement of goods, capital, and electronic commerce (Walia and Oka 2008). To facilitate transport of goods, the NAFTA Superhighway is being built, a several hundred meters wide corridor including rail lines and pipelines from Mexico to the Western Canadian border. Preferred citizens who represent capital are ensured border mobility through initiatives such as the Business Resumption and Partners in Protection Program and the Fast and Secure Trade Pass.

Simultaneously, in a post 9/11 climate with the never-ending "War on Terror" and its accompanying construction of a constant imminent threat to North America, the SPP fortifies the border security apparatus. Canada and US have signed the joint Smart Border Declaration, a 30-point plan which includes adoption of coordinated border surveillance technologies; increasing arming of border guards; implementation of biometric programs; and increased tracking of foreign nationals. The legislation of the 2004 Safe Third Country Agreement is, according to CIC's own statistics, disallowing up to 40 per cent of potential asylum seekers to Canada (Canadian Council of Refugees 2005, n.p.). This "virtual" border wall denies, with some exceptions, entry to refugee claimants arriving at Canada through the US border.

In this way, the SPP intensifies the practices of both state selection and state expulsion. As the number of permanent residents and asylum seekers both drastically decrease, removals have also increased: CIC has reported an increase in deportations from approximately 9,000 in 2001 to 12,517 in 2006 (CIC 2006, 14). From 2006–2007, over 12,000 people were detained, with renewed calls by the Minister for Public Safety for tighter exit controls and increased detention to ensure deportation. According to Anna Pratt, "[d]etention and deportation are the two most extreme and bodily sanctions of this immigration penalty, which constitutes and enforces borders, polices non-citizens, identifies those deemed dangerous, diseased, deceitful, or destitute, and refuses them entry or casts them out" (2006, 1). The extolled multiculturalism of the handpicked diaspora exists parallel to what Peter Nyers has termed the "deport-spora" (2003, 1069–1093)'. The introduction of recent policies such as Bill C50 and the Canadian Experience Class create an increasingly hostile climate to family class immigrants, refugees, and working-class permanent residents. Instead, such programs favor those who can pay a high price for citizenship: either through the investment of foreign capital or as bonded labor in migrant worker programs.

The SPP's reliance on migrant worker programs resolves the seeming contradiction between the state's interests in tightening border controls and immigration crackdowns on the one hand, and the corporate lobby demanding freer border crossings to facilitate the secure movement of goods and capital, on the other. The NACC has stressed that "Every measure that adds to the cost or time to cross borders within North America is in effect a tax on enterprise" (North American Competitiveness Council 2007, n.p.). Thus the implementation of border security measures must not interfere with North American economic hegemony.

Migrant workers become central to resolving this paradox and constitute a distinct category of workers in relation to capital and the nation-state in a globalized economy. They allow for capital interests to subsidize economic production through precarious labor. The condition of being deportable assures the ability to super-exploit as well as to readily dispose of especially during moments of labor unrest or economic recession. The state is also able to exercise repressive social control through denial of basic rights and access to services afforded to citizens.

More importantly, migrant workers maintain the sanctity of racialized cultural identities and the purity of national identity by legalizing the "foreign-ness" of migrant workers. This is critical in the racist cycle required to dehumanize them and other migrants as "illegal" or "undesirable" (or in the post 911 climate as "potential terrorist threats") in order to justify their deplorable working conditions and state securitization processes that disproportionately target them. This naming of migrant workers as "temporary" creates a hierarchical order based on race that is legitimized through citizenship, which the state relies on to expand this pool of exploitable labor without the "threat of coloring" Canada (Sharma 2006, 18).

Although different eras have been dominated by different perceptions of what has constituted threats to the nation-state, each era has formulated threats as being external to the nation-state, thus justifying exclusionary immigration policies. (Importantly, this is regardless of the actual location of the so-called threat; for example within days of the attack on Pearl Harbor, Japanese *in* North America were seen as "enemy aliens"). This reinforces the normalization of Whiteness as Canadian-ness and justifies the deployment of state repression against those within the nation-state marked as "Other." Phrases like "immigrants" do not actually reflect one's legal citizenship status; it is a euphemism for racialized migrants from the Third World. The ability to designate and attack the hyphenated citizen—from Japanese Canadian to Arab Canadian—depends on the configuration of the Canadian nation as White supremacist, despite the shallow rhetoric of multiculturalism.

Here we see another critical connection between immigration controls and the expansion of migrant worker programs. It is not in the interests of Canadian state to deport all non-status migrants or to close down the border to all racialized immigrants. Rather, as David McNally observes: "It simply wants this labour on its own terms: frightened, oppressed, vulnerable" (2006a, 137). The political purpose of tightened security and immigration measures is to demobilize racialized populations within Canada in order to ensure collective social discipline and an internalized sense of non-belonging. As noted by Bhattacharyya, Gabriel and Small: "Capitalist expansion has depended so heavily on mythologies of race and their attendant violences that the double project of racial economic subjugation is a constitutive aspect of this expansion" (2002, 34).

Therefore through the SPP, the state is able to guarantee the free flow of capital across the border; legally sanction the denial of permanent residency to a growing number of migrants to ensure an exploitable and expendable pool of labor; and entrench a racialized national consciousness by arbitrating who legitimately constitutes the nation. According to Stasiulis and Bakan: "Multilateral state discussions now take as their priority the curbing of unwanted migration—as illegals, asylum seekers, designated 'criminals' or 'terrorists,' and so on—while selectively promoting the circulation of desired human capital" (2005, 28).

THE APARTHEID OF CITIZENSHIP

We live in a time where borders are concurrently transgressed and fortified and in which, as Hardt and Negri (2000) argue, territorial borders are highly integrated spaces of national identity. The nation-state and its resulting machinery of sovereignty are viable only as long as an "imagined community" within its borders is distinguishable from those beyond its borders. Canadian nationalism has consistently emphasized the nation as a contained entity threatened by outside forces. Anna Pratt (2006, 149–178) traces how immigrants to Canada have been portrayed as floods of disease-ridden people, criminals, frauds, or security threats, thus constructing their "undesirability" and fostering waves of moral panic about the "border." The physical, social, and metaphorical dimensions of nationhood have an undeniable effect on the production and reproduction of social exclusion and apartheid. As prime minister Mackenzie King declared in 1947: "I wish to make it quite clear that Canada is perfectly within her rights in selecting persons whom we regards as desirable future citizens...The people of Canada do not wish, as a result of mass immigration, to make any fundamental alteration in the character of our population" (2644–2646).

Discursive borders reinforce the physical border as notions of "Canadianness" maintain the power of the state to define the ideological ground of who belongs and who, in King's words, makes up Canada's population. The category of temporary foreign workers suggest that these people are not Canadian, are not working alongside Canadians, and are in some way working in opposition to Canadian workers. Similarly, the term illegal does not conjure up images of Americans who illegally overstay their tourist visas or Australian students illegally working without work permits. Rather, the phrase is a constructed one that facilitates the maintenance of social hierarchies based on race and class. As soon as someone is branded as illegal, their presence is erased from within (Dauvergne 2008, 130–146). Regardless of their contributions or length of residence, their membership within the nation is seen as infringement of Canadian sovereignty. In this sense, the constant imagining of Canadian identity is ultimately linked to the deliberate actions of nation-building.

It is important to note that the very foundation of Canada is based on legislating apartheid against Indigenous peoples through a colonial system of reservations, residential schools, the Indian Act and the fundamental denial of the nationhood of Indigenous peoples through forced assimilation. This makes it even more evident that the regulation of citizenship is far more than a legal exercise; the denial of Indigenous self-determination is closely linked with the exclusion of racialized immigrants, migrant workers, and refugees. The granting or withholding of citizenship rights—both immigrant status and registered Indian status—becomes the way for the state to determine and regulate who is part of the national community (Hussain 2004, n.p.), or, as Nandita Sharma observes, "their categorization positions them within Canadian space in particular, always hierarchically-organized, ways" (2006, 140).

Many movements in Canada have focused on the concept of full equality of citizenship rights as a strategy for social justice. However, the discourse of citizenship is deeply problematic. As Stasiulis and Bakan write: "Citizenship plays a role in accessing a wide range of rights, but as importantly in creating and reproducing inequality among individuals and groups in the context of contemporary globalization" (2003, 12). Despite their citizenship status, the lives of immigrant women of color and Indigenous women are characterized by extreme poverty as they labor in dangerous and precarious industries including garment factories, domestic work, the sex trade, and the service sector. Alongside them are those without citizenship, the numbers of whom are growing exponentially. Migrant and undocumented workers fall between the cracks of legal protection due to their very status as non-citizens. For example, common law doctrines hold that an employment contract will not be binding since the worker is considered illegal to begin with (Dauvergne 2008, 21–23). This makes it even more critical to challenge social movements organized on nationalistic lines and instead forces us to exercise our sovereignties differently, to think of human interconnectedness rather than social exclusion, and to configure our alliances and solidarities based on shared experiences and visions.

BUILDING ALLIANCES OF SOLIDARITY NOT CHARITY

Canada's perpetuation of genocidal policies, reliance on migration controls, distinctions between citizens and illegals, and stratification of women of color into low-wage work in order to maintain colonial relations and pursue economic growth are being resisted through strengthening alliances.

GOOD ENOUGH TO WORK, GOOD ENOUGH TO STAY

In the past three years BC's organized labor sector has undertaken courageous unionization drives, legal challenges, and advocated for permanent status for migrant workers. In addition to the work of UFCW with SAWP workers highlighted above, the British Columbia and Yukon Territory Building and Construction Trades Council has been supporting migrant workers employed in the construction industry. The Council won a BC Human Rights Tribunal complaint against an employer accused of intimidating workers; a discrimination suit against companies paying Canadian workers $10 an hour more than the Latin American migrant workers; and was involved in labor arbitration regarding poor working conditions such as wages of $5 per hour and 54–66 hour work weeks without overtime pay. Such organizing is in sharp contrast with the role that the Knights of Labour played in the Asiatic Exclusion League in the 1880's in calling for immediate restrictions on Asian immigration and participating in the 1907 race riots that destroyed Chinatown and Japantown in Vancouver, BC.

However, the current labor leadership including BC Federation of Labour does employ the rhetoric of protecting Canadian jobs while ignoring the ways in which global capital and racist neocolonial policies have created and maintained a global pool of migrant workers. It reveals the ways in which foreign workers are viewed as a threat to Canadian labor, destroying potential solidarities that cross the boundaries of exclusionary nationalism. In addition, concerns are being raised about the character of union organizing with its hierarchical structure and a predominately white middle-class leadership that perpetuates patterns of paternalism rather than facilitating the independent formation of migrant worker unions (Paz 2008). Finally, although the slogan "Good Enough to Work, Good Enough to Stay," adopted by the BC Federation of Labour, encourages permanent residency rights for migrant workers, it begs questions about the right of *human beings* to migrate and not simply be viewed as economic units that serve capital interests within a capitalist, racist, and sexist market.

STOLEN LABOR ON STOLEN LAND

Canada's state and corporate wealth is largely based on the subsidies provided by cheap migrant labor and the theft of Indigenous resources. The project of colonial conquest in Canada was designed to ensure forced displacement of Indigenous peoples from their traditional territories; the destruction of autonomy and self-determination in Indigenous self-governance; and the annihilation of Indigenous peoples' cultures and traditions. In recent years, the assertion of legislative authority over Indigenous peoples' resources has resulted in Canada's most profound act of colonization. From a legal standpoint, BC is unique to Canada since this province is unceded territory: virtually no treaties were made in the occupation and settlement of the province. This was, and continues to be, in violation of the 1763 Royal Proclamation which legally bound the British to make treaties to claim the "surrender" of Indigenous territory (Hill n.d., n.p.). This proclamation continues to form the basis of Canadian (colonial) law and most of the province remains unsurrendered Native land which neither the Canadian nor the BC governments have the moral or legal authority to govern.

These are the same imperialist forces that have perpetuated the dispossession and displacement of migrants to North America. In addition, migrants of color and Indigenous communities face similar conditions of unequal citizenship within Canada: They are underpaid, face high rates of incarceration and surveillance, are denied equal access to social services, suffer gross health inequities, and are subject to the daily reality of systemic poverty and racism. However there are many challenges that prevent this shared terrain of struggle from developing into genuine solidarity, especially the tangible role of (im)migrant workers in facilitating the removal and theft of Indigenous land and resources. As Indigenous activists called for the cancellation of the 2010 Olympic Games in BC under the banner, "No Olympics on Stolen Native Land," an increasing number of (im)migrant workers are being employed in those same industries that are expediting the rate of sport tourism and mining on Native lands. While there is no argument that capitalist profiteering—not migrant workers—is ultimately responsible for the devastation of Indigenous lands, as the Native Youth Movement has queried, how can one be a miner or a logger and still support Indigenous peoples' defense of the Earth (Native Youth Movement 2007)?

Anti-colonial and anti-capitalist migrant justice groups like No One is Illegal have prioritized solidarity with Indigenous struggles and acknowledged that demands of migrant communities will be short-lived if it is gained at the expense of Indigenous self-determination. While alert to trivializing the differences within and between these two communities, strong alliances have been built amongst grassroots Indigenous and migrant justice groups (Walia 2003). In BC, immigrants and refugees have participated in several delegations to Indigenous blockades, while Indigenous communities have extended their solidarity through rally slogans such as "No One Is Illegal, Canada Is Illegal" and the offering of protection and refuge for migrants facing deportation. This on-the-ground organizing has gone a long way to develop trust and to break down the divisions between Indigenous and racialized migrant communities that are mediated by white settler colonialism. As Indigenous warrior Gord Hill states:

The purpose of the colonial strategy is to either destroy or assimi-
late the Indigenous peoples and other oppressed social sectors. This
is inherent in colonization, which seeks to impose one world onto
another. The strength of our alliance, unlike the shifting alliances
made between ruling elites, is ultimately based on trust and solidarity.
(Quoted in Walia 2003, n.p.)

ONE FOR ALL, ALL FOR ONE

Immigration and labor policies in general are inextricably connected, as evident in worker vulnerabilities and income inequities in sectors dominated by immigrant workers, and particularly immigrant women. Under provincial employment standards, it is possible for workers who are new to the labor force to be
paid a $6 per hour training wage, instead of the regular minimum wage, for the
first 500 hours of work. Another endemic problem is that immigrants who are
trained within non-western educational traditions experience face great difficulties in gaining recognition for their training. In light of this onslaught of labor
flexibilization and deskilling, thousands of non-unionized and unionized immigrant workers in BC have been demanding better working conditions as part of
the Living Wage Campaign (Walia 2006).

While the oppression of various generations and categories of (im)migrants
is linked, the dynamics between recent migrants and older migrant generations/
Canadian-born people of color has revealed many divisions. One major tension
is the "model minority" syndrome. Vijay Prashad has written about what he
describes as immigrants "license to accumulate economic wealth through hard
work" in exchange for their willingness to be used as a symbol of discipline
against ghettoized communities of color such as undocumented migrants (2000,
102). The ability of the state to determine who is worthy of citizenship creates
barriers between immigrants who believe they have met this test of worthiness
(and are grateful for being accepted into the colonial nation) and others who are
subverting the system in order to exert the right to reside in Canada. This is further perpetuated by the fact that many mainstream immigrant groups have become focused on multiculturalism issues, isolating themselves from more radical
anti-racist struggles. However grassroots community activists like Sid Tan of the
BC Coalition of Chinese Headtax Payers have made the links between historic
injustices of the Chinese Head Tax and today's migrant worker programs and
the need to stand in solidarity with current generations of migrants (Tan 2006).
Similarly, writing in the *Indo-Canadian Voice* about an unprecedented direct action
at the Vancouver airport to physically prevent the deportation of a paralyzed
migrant Laibar Singh, I have argued that

Instead of making declarations on what others are entitled to simply by virtue of the fact that we happen to already have immigrated to Canada or have inherited the privilege of Canadian citizenship by birth, let us support one another in being able to live a life of well-being and dignity. (2007, n.p.).

CONCLUSION

The lack of sensationalized stories about workplace raids, massive roundups, or overflowing detention centers does not point to a humane immigration policy in Canada. Rather Canadian migration policy is the result of a perfected system of social control, containment, and expulsion. R.M Unger has written that "the more people become aware of the conditionality of a context, the more likely they are able to effect meaningful change to that context" (Unger 1987, 5). While the increased reliance of the state and capital on migrant worker programs poses a formidable challenge, it also provides an opportunity for "re-imagining community beyond the bounds of citizenship, the political beyond the state, freedom beyond the market, and humanity beyond Whiteness" (Walia and Oka 2008). This involves deepening the analysis that capital has created migrant workers through the devastation of rural economies across the globe and by dividing the global labor force. We must demand total freedom of movement across borders in order to eliminate the vulnerability of migrant workers and eradicate racism against those who are believed to belong only to the "Third World". Finally, the struggle of migrant workers reveals that rather than awkwardly embracing a Canadian nationalism that emphasizes the state and capital's absolute authority, we must articulate and defend the importance of maintaining free, equal, and reciprocal relations between all human beings and the land. Such relationships and alliances, along with a more comprehensive analysis of colonialism, capitalism, and racism, create the battleground for building a powerful revolutionary grassroots movement in BC and Canada.

Note: An alternative version of this essay appears as "Transient Servitude: Migrant Labour in Canada and the Apartheid of Citizenship" in *Race and Class* 52: 71-84 (2010).

REFERENCES

Annian, H. 2006. *The Silent Spikes: Chinese Laborers and the Construction of North American Railroads.* China: China Press.

Arat-Koc, S. 1993. "Immigration Policies, Migrant Domestic Workers and the Definition of Citizenship in Canada." In *Deconstructing a Nation: Immigration, Multiculturalism and Racism in 90s Canada*, ed. Vic Satzewich. Halifax: Fernwood Publishing, 229–242.

Bannerji, H. 1995. *Thinking Through: Essays on Feminism, Marxism and Anti-racism.* Toronto: Toronto Women's Press, 24.

Bhattacharyya, B. S. Gabriel, and S. Small. 2002. *Race and Power: Global Racism in the Twenty-first Century.* New York: Routledge.

BC Federation of Labour. 2004. "Hand-harvesters of Fraser Valley Berry Crops: New Era Protection of Vulnerable Employees." http://www.bcfed.com/Where+We+Stand/Publications/Archives/2004-handharvesters.htm.

Bush, M. and Canadian Farmworkers Union. 1995. "Zindabad! BC Farmworkers Fight for Rights." http://www.vcn.bc.ca/cfu/about.htm.

Canadian Centre for Policy Alternatives. 2008. "Cultivating Farmworker Rights: Ending the Exploitation of Immigrant and Migrant Farmworkers in BC." http://www.policyalternatives.ca/documents/BC_Office_Pubs/bc_2008/bc_farmworkers_full.pdf.

Canadian Council of Refugees. 2005. "Report: Closing the Front Door on Refugees: Report on the First Year of the Safe Third Country Agreement." December 29. http://www.ccrweb.ca/closingdoordec05.pdf

CIC. 2006. *Canada's Refugee System: What You Should Know.* Ottawa: Minister of Public Works and Government Services Canada.

Collins, M. 2003. "Canada's Image as a Safe and Secure Destination for Foreign Temporary Workers is Under Fire, Critics Say." *Embassy Magazine.* http://noii-van.resist.ca/?p=702.

Dauvergne, C. 2008. *Making People Illegal: What Globalization Means for Migration and Law.* Cambridge: Cambridge University Press.

Diocson, C. 2003. "Organizing and Mobilizing Filipino Migrant Women in Canada." *Asia Pacific Research Network.* http://www.aprnet.org/index.php?option=com_content&view=article&id=163:organizing-and-mobilizing-filipino-migrant-women-in-canada&catid=97:impact-of-globalization-on-women-labor&Itemid=56.

Dobbin, M. 2003. *The Myth of the Good Corporate Citizen: Canada and Democracy in the Age of Globalization.* Toronto: James Lorimer and Company.

Filipino–Canadian Youth Alliance. N.d. "Statement on Stabbing Death of 15-year-old Deward Ponte." http://www.straight.com/article-130156/filipino-canadian-youth-alliance-links-deward-ponte-stabbing-to-displacement.

Hardt, Michael and A. Negri. 2000. *Empire.* Cambridge, MA: Harvard University Press.

Hill, G. N.d. "Stop the BC Treaty Process." *Warrior Publications.* http://www.warriorpublications.com/?q=node/21.

Hussain, S. 2004. "Canada Myths and Realities." *ZNet.* http://www.zmag.org/znet/viewArticle/7248.

International Native Youth Movement. 2007. "Statement for Anti-2010 Olympics Campaign." http://mostlywater.org/nym_calls_for_boycott_and_cancellation_of_2010_winter_olympic_games

Mata Press Service. 2008. "Broken Dreams." *Asian Pacific Post.* December 11. http://www.asianpacificpost.com/portal2/c1ee8c421e2878f6011e28a41a2e0039_Broken_Dreams.do.html.

Mackenzie King, Prime Minister William Lyon. 1947. *House of Commons Debates May 1.* 2644–2646.

McNally, D. 2006a. *Another World is Possible: Globalization and Anti-Capitalism*. Winnipeg: Arbeiter Ring.

2006b. "Canada and Empire." *New Socialist Magazine* 54. http://newsocialist.org/newsite/index.php?id=568.

Migrante–BC. 2008. "Statement on International Migrants Day." http://migrantebc.org/index.php?option=com_content&view=article&id=50:imd2008statement&catid=38:latestnews.

North American Competitiveness Council. 2007. "Enhancing Competitiveness in Canada, Mexico, and the United States: Private-Sector Priorities for the Security and Prosperity Partnership of North America (SPP)." US Chamber of Commerce. http://www.uschamber.com/NR/rdonlyres/6euc24q2zpx6ikwqzlvkkcjnnjkqilqziriwtzxuti2vur m633dh2hjgjix2doxqq3olv5v4wxdxlhxldvavpxg/070223nacc.pdf.

North–South Policy Institute. 2006. "Migrant Workers in Canada: A Review of the Canadian Seasonal Agricultural Workers Program." http://www.nsi-ins.ca/english/pdf/MigrantWorkers_Eng_Web.pdf.

Nyers, P. 2003. "Abject Cosmopolitanism: The Politics of Protection in the Anti-Deportation Movement." *Third World Quarterly* 24(6): 1069–1093.

Paz, A. 2008. "Harvest of Injustice: The Oppression of Migrant Workers on Canadian Farms." *Global Research*. June 22. http://www.globalresearch.ca/index.php?context=va&aid=9425.

Pelletier, E. 2008. "Guestworkers Under «Legal Practices similar to Slavery» in 2008 According to the U.N. Convention: The Case of Canada." Presented at International Metropolis Conference, Bonn. http://www.metropolis2008.org/pdf/20081029/workshops/w053-29_depatie-pelletier-eugenie.pdf.

Pickett, W., L. Hartling, R. Brison, and J. Guernsey. 1999. "Fatal Work-Related Farm Injuries in Canada, 1991–1995 (Canadian Agricultural Injury Surveillance Program)." *Canadian Medical Association Journal* 160(13): 1843–1848.

Prashad, V. 2000. *The Karma of Brown Folk*. Minneapolis: University of Minnesota Press.

Pratt, A. 2006. *Securing Borders: Detention And Deportation in Canada*. Vancouver: University of British Columbia Press.

Pratt, G. 2004. *Working Feminism*. Philadelphia: Temple University Press.

Preibisch, K. and L. Santamaria. 2006. "Engendering Labour Migration: The Case of Foreign Workers in Canadian Agriculture." In *Women, Migration, and Citizenship: Making Local, National, and Transnational Connections*, ed. Evangelia Tastsoglou and Alexandra Zorianna Dobrowolsky. Surrey: Ashgate Publishing, 108–130.

Robinson, W. 2007. "Globalization and the Struggle for Immigrant Rights in the United States." *ZNet*. March 2007. http://www.zmag.org/znet/viewArticle/1864.

Sandborn, T. 2008. "Foreign Farm Workers Unionize: A First in BC." *The Tyee*. August 21. http://thetyee.ca/News/2008/08/21/FarmWorkers/

Sharma, N. 2001. "On Being not Canadian: The Social Organization of Migrant Workers in Canada." *The Canadian Review of Sociology and Anthropology* 38(4): 415–439.

———Sharma, N. *Home Economics: Nationalism and the Making of 'Migrant Workers' in Canada*. Toronto: University of Toronto Press.

Stasiulis, D.K. and A.B Bakan. 2005. *Negotiating Citizenship: Migrant Women in Canada and the Global System*. Toronto: University of Toronto Press.

Tan, S. 2006. "Statement in Vancouver for National Day for Immigrant Rights and Status for All." http://www.solidarityacrossborders.org/en/node/161.

Teeple, G. 2000. "What is globalization?" In *Globalization and Its Discontents*, ed. S. McBride and J. Wiseman. London and New York: Macmillan Press and St. Martin's Press, 9–23.

Troper, H. 2004. "Commentary." In *Controlling Immigration: A Global Perspective*, ed. W. Cornelius, P. Martin, and J. Hollifield. Palo Alto: Stanford University Press, 136–138.

Unger, R.M. 1987. *Social Theory: Its Situation and Task*. Cambridge: Cambridge University Press.

Walia, H. 2003. "Resisting Displacement, North and South." *ZNet*. http://www.zmag.org/znet/viewArticle/10008

———. 2006. "Colonialism, Capitalism and the Making of the Apartheid System of Migration in Canada." *ZNet*. http://www.zmag.org/znet/viewArticle/4297.

———. "The Laibar Singh Case', The Indo-Canadian Voice." December 15. http://www.zmag.org/znet/viewArticle/15978.

Walia, H. and C. Oka. 2008. "The Security and Prosperity Partnership Agreement: NAFTA Plus Homeland Security." *Left Turn Magazine*. 28.

Wark, M. 2002. "Globalization from Below: Migration, Sovereignty, Communication." Presented at the Nation/States Conference, Adelaide. http://subsol.c3.hu/subsol_2/contributors2/warktext3.html.

CHAPTER 4. CONSUMING FEARS: NEO-LIBERAL IN/SECURITIES, CANNIBALIZATION, AND PSYCHOPOLITICS

Heidi Rimke

The chapter presents a critical theoretical framework to examine and analyze the sociopolitical role of the monster and the monstrous—specifically cannibalism and cannibalization—in the context of the post-911 so-called "war on terror." In particular it discusses several related themes: the politics of emotions and the emotions of politics; the politics of security and insecurity; and the politics of the spectacle of the screen or mass-mediated hyperconsumption of modern monsterization that serve conservative political ends. Providing a sociopolitical analysis of monstrosity through an analytic of the political technologies of neo-liberalism, the arguments highlight the productivity of a key neo-liberal characteristic of predatory capitalism (Evans 1989; Hedlund 1999; Ong 2006), or the cannibalizing society: psychopolitics[1], or the political workings of an entrenched psychocentrism, defined as the cultural domination by, and consumption of, psy discourses that simultaneously depoliticize the political while capitalizing on the emotional through the hegemony of emotional practices of power. Like Bourdieu (1998, 18), the chapter takes a position "against the narrow-minded, regressive, security-minded, protectionist, conservative, Xenophobic" State with the view to open, progressive, fluid, internationalist movements to theorize against and beyond the State.

Contemporary moral panics and discourses on dangerized souls have persistently re-emerged and been reconfigured within new discursive linkages and practices in the post-911 world. Neo-liberalism emphasizes economic freedom encouraging aggressive global capitalism and expansive privatization at the expense of the weakest sectors of the workforce; while neoconservatism calls for greater regulation of society, especially the poor and the unemployed, and immigrants (c.f. Garland 2001, 99–100). Advanced capitalism requires not only a dominant conservative political discourse—masked in the neo-liberal rhetoric on "freedom," "justice," and "equality"—it also requires a psychocentric hegemony which directs attention away from the roots of social problems instead providing individual "remedies" or "market solutions" to adapt to and cope in an increasingly insecure society. One particularly powerful and seductive neo-liberal political technology is the spectacle of screen that serves to produce and maintain public insecurities by mass-mediated representations of stranger danger, or "monsters among us" alternatively parading historically in multiple dangerized images whether as terrorist, criminal, anarchist, communist, immigrant, queer, the welfare-mother, a young man in a hoodie, the psychopath, the pedophile, or the cannibal, for example.

PSYCHOCENTRISM AND THE PSYCHOPOLITICS OF NEO-LIBERALISM

Neo-liberalism relies upon, disseminates, and reinforces a psychocentric Weltanschauung. Psychocentrism, or the outlook that all human problems are innate pathologies of the individual mind and/or body, is a chief governing rationality of neo-liberal populations. Neo-liberal culture emphasizes individualism, flexibility, enterprise, productivity, autonomy and responsibility. Individuals are held personally responsible for their physical, emotional, and mental health, and any socially structured difficulties they may experience such as poverty, illness or victimization. Contemporary self-help literature for example props up neo-liberalism by promoting an individualized rather than a collectivized understanding of responsibility celebrating personalized achievement, continuous self-assessment, hyper-productivity and self-enterprise embodying neo-liberal political technologies of the self (Rimke 2000).

Psychocentricity thrives on the human deficit model while obscuring societal deficits and social relations of power that frame, underlie, and create human struggles and difficulties. Rather than challenging social deficiencies and economic corruption, the human deficit model incites modern subjects to focus on personal or inner deficiencies of the self and others. This Western mode of understanding ourselves has not only normalized and naturalized the discourses of normalcy/abnormality; it has also had the effect of rendering its own power invisible. Psychocentric attitudes, perceptions and interpretations thus dominate the social world. Thinking of all human life in terms of "the normal" and "the pathological" is a major modern development based on what Foucault refers to as "normation" (2007)—the emergence of scientific norms as regulatory mechanisms for the official production of the "vicious" or otherwise dangerous and degenerate classes (Rimke and Hunt 2002; Rimke 2003, 2008a, 2008b, 2010b, 2011).

Six primary and related characteristics of psychocentrism are as follows: 1) reductionism: reducing human experience and problems to the individual sensory input in the self-contained body-mind model; 2) determinism: claiming that human conduct and experience are determined by their "natural" bodily make-up (genetics, personality, hormones, neurochemistry, etc); 3) essentialism: the view that humans can be classified into essential types; that groups of individuals possess an innate characteristic or essence that is permanent, unalterable, stable, static, etc; 4) presentism or ahistoricism: historical amnesia or the cultural disregard for history and its role in constituting our present understandings of ourselves individually and collectively; 5) naturalism: viewing humans as "natural" rather than "social" or socially located, shaped, and produced; 6) ethnocentrism: the belief that one's cultural practices and beliefs are normal and thus superior compared to other cultural practices and ways of being in the world.

Psychocentric discourses, of course, do not only circulate academic departments, form research programs for industry, guide institutions, and inform governmental policies. Representations of madness or mental illness have long been a staple of popular cultural media seen in a barrage of movies, documentaries, magazines, fiction and non-fiction books, television shows, newspaper articles and internet sites. Although they have a history, the psychopolitics of psychocentricity invisibilizes the taken-for-grantedness that today it has become compulsory to think of human others as "normal" or "abnormal." The compulsory ontology of pathology (Marsh 2010), or the dominating modern view of human life as normal or pathological, is now an inescapable presence in everyday life and spectacles of criminal monstrosities. As Haggerty (2009) has shown, studies of serial killing have been dominated by an individualized focus on the etiology and biography of particular offenders. As such, normative social science has tended to downplay the broader social, historical and cultural context of such acts.

Psychopolitics can be understood as those processes, relations, discourses, and practices that obscure the sociopolitics of the personalized and privatized. Psychopolitical productivity individualizes the individual by depoliticizing the political while simultaneously cannibalizing and capitalizing on emotionality, especially fear, paranoia, anger, resentment and frustration. In other words, the social production of in/security felt in the habitus or emotional embodiment demands a sociological rather than an individualized, ahistorical model of analysis.

A critique of psychocentrism also entails rejecting the anti-emotionalism characteristic of positivist social and political thought, and instead emphasizes "the emotional practices of power" underlying the insecurization of social life. The hyper-consumption of the monstrous is thus understood here as a political technology of the spectacle.

Psychopolitics is thus a concept that describes the overarching neo-liberal tendency towards adopting and reproducing the compulsory ontology of individual pathology which obscures the privatized workings of socially structured emotionality. Psychopolitics is not only the opposite of sociopolitics; it is antithetical to the classical promise of sociology to illuminate the social bases of the seemingly personal and private (Mills 1959). The asocial and ahistorical orientation of psychopolitics of neo-liberalism hinges on popularized and professional psychocentrism. The point of the analysis is not to provide a psychology of politics, a psychology of society, or a psychology of history; instead the analytical framework is a sociology of psychopolitics, which strikes at the heart of the microphysics of power of everyday contemporary practices of the individualized, hyperconsuming neo-liberal self.

A SOCIOLOGICAL TERATOLOGY: GLOBAL CAPITALISM AS CANNIBALIZATION AND CARNIVALIZATION

The political prototype of cannibalization is the image of the capitalist writ large. Many writers have commented on the monstrous nature of capitalist culture and society: Marx used metaphors of the bloodsucking vampire or werewolf to represent life-draining capitalists in *Das Kapital*; Baudrillard (2010) characterizes society as organized around carnivalization (mass-mediated spectacles) and cannibalization (hyper-consumption; hyperconsuming and consumed selves) (2010); and Neocleous has shown how the political functions of "the dead and the monstrous" promote divisive conservative ideologies (Neocleous 2005).

As Baudrillard explains:

> This "carnivalization" passes through the stages of evangelization, colonization, decolonization, and globalization, which themselves are historic. What is less visible is that his hegemony, this ascendancy on the part of the global order, whose models seems irresistible—and not just its technical and military models, but its cultural and ideological ones too—is accompanied by an extraordinary process of reversion, in which power is slowly undermined, devoured, or "cannibalized" by the very people it "carnivalizes." (2010, 4)

As such, the first victims of this evangelical masquerade, according to Baudrillard are the Indigenous where the Whites may thus said to have carnivalized—and hence cannibalized—themselves long before exporting all this to the whole world...It is this dual—carnivalesque and cannibalistic—form we see reflected in every corner of the world, with the exportation of our moral values (human rights, democracy), our principles of economic rationality, growth, performance and spectacle. (Baudrillard 2010, 5, 7, 10)

The proliferation of discourses on danger rationalizes the wider social policing of the Other. "Disorder" is emphasized to fabricate social order (Neocleous 2000) to ensure orderliness for capitalist social and economic relations. Categorizing the person in inferiorized terms, the abnormal individual provides the rationale for a style of control and colonization that requires "monsters" as the enemy or the scourge threatening Western "civilization." Neocleous notes that "monstering is a common motif" and the media frequently employs the "monstrous as a label for anything and everything it fails (though usually barely tries) to understand" (2005, 4). For example, the process of monstering can be clearly seen with relation to media portrayals of the cannibal, the terrorist, the anarchist, and the sex offender.

GENEALOGIZING THE DANGERIZED: FROM MORAL INSANITY TO MENTAL ILLNESS

What became known as "the dangerous classes" in the nineteenth century provided the very foundation for rationalizing the emergence of modern psychiatric medicine and the social regulation of deviants according to the truths professed by human scientific experts, especially in the criminal sciences (Graham and Clarke 2001; Foucault 1978b; Quinney 2001; Sheldon 2001; Taylor 1995). In particular, the category of moral insanity (Rimke 2003; Rimke and Hunt 2002) provided two essential roles in the historical process of policing the self and others at the level of the everyday: first, the doctrine provided a means to legitimate the existence of dangerization in an ill, dangerous, or degenerate social group according to the human sciences; and second, it provided a formalized scientific category to cast a net over those groups and individuals who could not be formally classified as criminal due to the existing penal codes. Dangerized and pathologized through a hybridization of Christian morality and bourgeois enlightenment science, the nineteenth century production of monstrous subjects provided the space and grid for increasing psychocentric rationalities providing for capital the social authority to regulate that which the law could not. Campaigns directed at policing the unfit included major forms of social authoritarianism that reproduced social categories of dangerousness not only according to institutionalized morality (the law) but also in terms of spiritual damnation and evil (religion), degenerate bodies and minds (science), and emotional subjectivities, especially fear, anxiety, and resentment (culture). The political history of social policing in North America entails a long list of groups by bourgeois culture and morality: foreign agitators, Reds, Jews, gays, anarchists, Indian nationalists and other "alien enemies" spectacularized as dangerous to national interests and security (c.f. Maurutto 2000; Rimke 2008a, 2009a, 2009b, 2010b; Kinsman, Buse and Steedman 2000; Kinsman and Gentile 2010). Social policing identifies risky, subversive targets as dangerous elements which threaten the moral and economic health of the social body—deflecting attention from the powerful to the marginalized as the social source of human pain and suffering. Historically and contemporarily, such broadcasts serve to create, incite, and instill moral panics over the invisibility of monsters—the unnatural, the immoral, the evil—amongst us (rather than addressing the utopian liberal claim that capitalism serves up the greatest good for the greatest number, for example).

Classical English liberal theory at the end of the eighteenth century argued that a 'medicine of the soul' should account for individual pathology, proposing the need for a "moral calculus" to measure pain and pleasure for the purpose of governing populations. Medicine and psychiatry thus played a primary historical role in legislating morality. In *Principles of the Civil Code*, Jeremy Bentham outlines the social significance of understanding the relationship between medicine, morality and the soul in governing the population. Civil society, according to the principles of utilitarianism, needed a science or art of mental pathology on which legislation ought to be based. Further, Bentham proposed the need for an instrument to measure his formulaic theory of happiness and suffering. In *The Theory of Legislation, Part 1: Objects of the Civil Law*, Chapter Six, "Propositions of Pathology on Which the Advantage of Equality is Founded" states:

> Pathology is a term used in medicine. It has not hitherto been employed in morals, but it is equally necessary there. When thus applied, moral pathology would consist in the knowledge of the feelings, affections, and passions, and their effects upon happiness. Legislation, which has hitherto been founded principally upon the quicksands of instinct and prejudice, ought at length to be placed upon the immoveable base of feelings and experience: a moral thermometer is required, which should exhibit every degree of happiness and suffering...It will be said that we must deal with generalities in human affairs, and be contented with a vague approximation. This is, however, the language of indifference or incapacity. The feelings of men are sufficiently regular to become the object of a science or an art; and till this is done, we can only grope our way by making irregular and undirected efforts. Medicine is founded upon the axioms of physical pathology: morals are the medicine of the soul: legislation is the practical branch; it ought

therefore, to be founded upon the axioms of mental pathology. (1887, 102–103)

According to Bentham's classical (Eurocentric) utilitarianism, the state of barbarism differed from civilization by two primary characteristics: first, irascible appetites, which referred to the pleasures of malevolence and second, concupiscent appetites, which refers to all other pleasure, were not to be found amongst the civilized classes (1887, 375). "Interests" thus characterized the civilized and superior while the baser "passions" defined the inferiorized and dehumanized as animalistic. The liberal psychopolitics of inferiorization intensified individualized self-formation as the standard of political and social progress. Represented as the superior "irresistible progress" in the Empire and its colonies, the rhetoric of liberalism became inherently linked with bourgeois discourses on upstanding, respectable, property-owning citizenry defined by "rational interests." This dividing practice contributed to the growing tendency to categorize social groups into the moral and normal/immoral and abnormal divide thus depoliticizing the brutalizing, alienating, and dehumanizing affects and effects of capitalism, imperialism, and patriarchy. The production, absorption and capitalization of human pain and suffering based upon individualized and psychocentric models gave rise to the now enormously profitable crime and disease industries. Consequently, and by extension, there emerged a contingent division between those at risk (presumed to be benevolent, safe and secure) versus those who endanger respectable (property-owning) citizens. Social dividing practices also fueled the fear of cities and "the strangers" that inhabited them constituting notions of insider/outsider and inside/outside necessary to the rhetoric of enemies. The sociopolitics of Othering through the image of the monster or alien occurs through the pathologization of difference in the forms of both cultural and biological racism. Social and moral contrasts thus became necessary in sustaining classism, sexism, heterosexism, racism, ethno and eurocentrism and thus channeling and absorbing resistance, defiance and rejection of dominant governing rationalities.

The myth of the dangerous individual has historically paraded as a gripping spectacle in the (de)moralizing theater of mass-mediated "crime and deviance." Popular culture has an immense and insatiable appetite when it comes to consuming monstrous images and monsterized spectacles. The cannibalization and carnivalization of the cannibal in the form of a monstrous subject is spectacularly represented and consumed as inhuman, seen in neoconservative claims that Li is an animal, a monstrous being, and thus undeserving of basic human rights and dignity.

CONCEPTUALIZING A TYPOLOGY OF CANNIBALISM

Although a complete or exhaustive cultural and historical overview of the different literal and metaphorical forms of cannibalism in society is not possible, a basic conceptual typology includes at least the following forms of cannibalism operating in the history of Western culture and society: 1) as metaphor: capitalism as multiply predatory based upon mass and hyperconsumption of self and other; 2) as a physical and/or symbolic act: survivalism, ritualism, human sacrifice, anorexia/bulimia, war practice; 3) in religion: consequence of demonic possession, and paramount in the consumption of the body and blood of Jesus Christ in "Holy Communion"; as paranormal or spiritual phenomenon seen in the Indigenous example of the windigo, believed to be a superhuman force that possesses and compels human to commit heinous acts of violence and murder; 4) in common law as a defense of necessity based on a lottery in life or death emergencies such as a shipwreck or plane-crash scenario; 5) as anthropophagy in science (anthropology) as either a pathos or human evolutionary trait; 6) in sexual terms: vorephilia defined as the fantasy to physically consume or be consumed by one's lover; sexual slang seen for example in a t-shirt slogan stating "support cannibalism: eat me"; 7) the so-called historical "discovery of the Americas" justifying and legitimating colonialism and imperializing the Other as savage, barbaric, uncivilized, seen in both "natural law" philosophical writings (e.g. Malthus, Rousseau, Montaigne), and literary traditions (e.g. Conrad, Melville, Poe, Dickens, Swift, Twain); and 8) in multiple cultural forms: as "infotainment" (information/entertainment) (c.f. Kohm 2009; Peelo 2005), in fairy tales such as Brother Grimm's *Hansel and Gretel*; in popular (and gothic) culture (e.g. *Southpark* and the human chili episode, *Silence of the Lambs*, *Texas Chainsaw Massacre*), in "true crime stories" (e.g. Jeffrey Dalmer and Albert Fish) and other movies such as *Eating Raoul*, *Sweeney Todd*, *The Butcher, His Wife and Her Lover*, and so forth. As such, the social production and productivity of cannibalism and cannibalization can be said to occupy many social sites, discourses, and imagery demonstrating its fundamental place in human society.

In March of 2009, Vince Weiguang Li stood trial for the stabbing, beheading and cannibalization of 22 year-old Tim Mclean and was found not criminally responsible on account of a mental disorder (NCRMD)—specifically, a diagnosis of schizophrenia. The ruling sparked public demands for reinstating the death penalty and abolishing human rights for the mentally ill, the main lobbyist being the mother of the victim, Carol deDelley. Having taken center stage in the push for legislative memorialization of her son's violent death with the proposed (and shifting) "Tim's Law," she and her followers are demanding legislation that would essentially treat those determined to be suffering from an illness in the same manner as those found guilty of murder—either by execution or involuntary hospitalization for life without possibility of release (paralleling parole criminal convictions). Other racist, xenophobic, and anti-immigrant discourses circulating internet media comments and blogs have called for Li's expulsion from Canada, on the grounds that he is an "alien," a foreigner, or "not one of us." Hundreds of facebook groups with tens of thousands of members have emerged in digital culture literally calling for "an eye for an eye." At a public vigil in Winnipeg, Manitoba at the provincial legislature in July 2009, on the one-year anniversary, a man who suggested that perhaps Li, too, was a victim was met with collective rage. The fact that the first words uttered by Li in court were to "please kill me" complicates matters more and demonstrates the social and political complexity about the politics over the right to life and the right to death in advanced capitalism.

GOVERNING THROUGH INSECURITY: POLICING THE PRODUCTION OF DISORDER

A vast collection of critical scholarship has now amassed documenting the rise of profit-driven, consumer-oriented products and services in the field of security, especially the commodification of policing. The proliferation of for-profit-masked-in-morality policing apparatuses include the following: private policing, security firms, parasecurity forces, and rent-a-cops (Haggerty 2003; Neocleous 2000, 2008; Rigakos 2002; Sanders 2005; Shearing and Stenning 1983, 1987); for-profit correctional services (Lynch 2004); gated residential enclaves for the wealthy (Lynch 2001); publicly accessible and privately secured properties like shopping malls (Hermer et al. 2005; Hutchinson and O'Connor 2005); nightclubs and "bouncers" (Rigakos 2008); and not least of all the growth of criminal sciences, such as criminal justice programs and security studies in the post-secondary education industry (Neocleous 2008).

As many have shown, crime control and the growing security apparatuses are financially lucrative sectors private industries (Christie 2000; Davis 2003; Garland 2001; Neocleous 2008; Rigakos 2002; Taylor 1999). It is within that context that the current "war on terror" and its accompanying rhetoric of democracy, freedom, and security must be situated. The Canadian Security Certificate, like the US Patriot Act, relies upon the globalized spectacle of terrorism to maintain and reproduce a neoconservative global economy based on a permanent war industry of so called enemy combatants and patriots (c.f. Aiken 2007; Pue 2003; Jackson 2005; Rothe and Muzzatti. 2004). The increasing fetishization of Canadian "border security" and concomitant erosion of civil and constitutional rights (Larsen 2008; Larsen and Piché 2009a, 2009b; Bell 2006; Pue 2003) in the name of "the war on terror' should be contextualized and understood as an extension of the Canadian authorities' increasing harmonization with the neoconservativism of US law and border policies (Aiken 2007).

Most notable in the context of the psychopolitics of neo-liberal insecuritza-tion is the anti-security research provided by Mark Neocleous in the UK and George Rigakos in Canada who build upon one of Foucault's key insights, that reveals liberalism's central thematic is not Liberty, but Security showing how rather than resist the push to security in the name of liberty, liberalism in fact enacts another form of political rationality that sets in place mechanisms for a "society of security" based on social policing (c.f. Neocleous 2000). Challenging the notion of a "balance" between security and liberty, Neocleous (2007) argues that the idea of balance is a liberal myth that masks the fact that liberalism's key category is not liberty, but security. For example, one can go for days without reading in the newspapers about issues pertaining to equality, but one can barely turn a page (or a corner, for that matter) without coming up against the question of security. In seeking security, states need to constantly limit the liberties of citi-zens, and that the democratic society is one which has always aimed to strike the right "balance" between liberty and security, a question that has received a new lease on life following the 911 World Trade Centre attacks and the subsequent "war on terror" (Neocleous 2007:131-132). "Security" and "insecurity" here strad-dles law and economy, policing and political economy, and power/knowledge that becomes the dominant mode of what Foucault calls "governmental rational-ity." Implicit in this dominant mode of governing is a "governmental emotionality" that further underpins the rationalization of growing security apparatuses.

Contemporary North American society is more deeply divided than ever on principles of security-seeking and the sources of our insecurities. The figure of the inhuman criminal as a permanent threat provides images that increase the probability of fear of victimization, trumpeting calls for more police, more se-curity measures, harsher criminal laws and more criminalization through "new and improved" legislation. Multidimensional social systems and tactics are in-cited and promoted on the bases of social suspicion and distrust of Others. These practices produce rearrangements of the population not only on the basis of se-cure and non-secure areas; coupled with the image of unsafe individuals citizens are encouraged police themselves and others. Furthermore, modern subjects are compelled to understand their insecurities as either rooted in their "psychology or biology" or produced by dangerized strangers in their midst. As a result, con-temporary discourses of security omit discussions on the necessity of securing basic human needs (such as job security, food security, sexual security, etc). Psychopolitics operates when individual insecurities are seen as either rooted within the person's own constitution; similarly, the capitalization of fear is promoted in the images of dangerous strangers. Rather than view insecurity ontologically, as part of the human condition, or as the effects of the current organization of social arrangements and unequal social relations, dominant discourses deflect attention to "the monstrous criminal." Emotional governance thus not only represses but it produces emotional subjectivities necessary to the organization of a certain social and geopolitical divisions and ordering of human populations. When emotions are taken seriously as a form of human experience and communication, rather than as an expression of abnormality, disorder or uncivil conduct, a practical dialogue about the social affects and effects of the dominant social and political order becomes possible. The benefit of taking the social production and ordering of emotional subjectivity seriously is that it interrogates the emotional practices of power, thus highlighting the affectivity of socially constituted and maintained injustices in all domains of social life.

DANGERIZATION, RISK, AND VICTIMIZATION

Many have argued that risk has become the basic social guide for understanding our world in late modernity (Beck 1986; Giddens; Liaszos and Douglas 2000). Media, experts, and politicians insist on the advent of a newly dangerous, uncertain world, associated with environmental problems and to technologies which produce them, chemical, nuclear and biotechnical. The idea of *dangerization* is useful to introduce the idea that feelings of threat and the perception of risk are built by cultural means (c.f. Liaszos and Douglas 2000). In contemporary social life we are incited to continuously scan and assess public and private spaces in terms of potential threats by certain dangerized Others.

Dangerization is thus the tendency to perceive and define the world and others through and according to socially scripted categories of menace. It leads to a prevalence of defensive perceptions over optimistic ones and to the dominance of fear, paranoia and anxiety over solidarity and interconnectedness. Larsen and Piché (2009b:188) demonstrate in their study on post-911 public vigilance campaigns how the dynamics of social control in late modern societies reflect an attempt by governing authorities to reformulate a relationship with the population in efforts to obtain actionable information in order "to prevent terrorism" thus enlisting citizens to view other citizens rather than authorities with distrust and suspicion. Such public campaigns of resentment and anger also exemplify how governance through uncertainty, suspicion, and risk may (re)produce a form of normativized citizenship while simultaneously encouraging the imaginary iden-tification of threatening others.

Socially structured perceptions entail rule-governed interpretations of what is and is not important to see. Feelings and sensations of danger, risk, anxiety, and vulnerability are thus sharpened and directed through dominant social discourses of inevitability and unpredictability—thus socially prescribing and scripting expectations of social dangers and enemies everywhere (Rothe and Muzzatti. 2004). The spectacle of "stranger danger" can be seen most forceful-ly in the mass-mediated representations of the Greyhound case. Discourses of "mental illness" or madness are based on a social judgment and moral evaluation of a person's belief system, highlighting the political nature of truth claims that can be used to justify and rationalize anything—however rare—as "dangerous."

The history of psychiatry is replete with examples of human rights abuses in the name of conformity with the governing modes of normation. Instead of asking questions or providing terms of reference to promote means for overcom-ing fears of otherness and difference, the xenophobia underlying contemporary Canadian popular and expert discourses highlighting risk, safety, and security masked in the democratic rhetoric of citizenship, nationality, nationalism and nation ("us" versus "them") encourages citizens to redefine and dread monster-ized Others. The social productivity of modern spectacles of monstrosity inse-cures subjects while securing growing regulatory powers of the state and the norm police (citizens) in what has amounted to a "perpetual war against fear—a war that seems to be anything but winnable" (Bauman 2007:53). Fearing danger has become normativized and naturalized in modern society. "Everywhere you see this stimulation of the fear of danger which is...the condition, the internal psychological and cultural correlative of liberalism. There is no liberalism with-out a culture of danger" (Foucault 2008, 66–67).

Neocleous (2005) makes the insightful observation that fear is the very life-blood of conservative thinking. As a result, conservatism *needs* monsters, it is pre-cisely these monsters that generate and embody the social fear on which conser-vatism thrives. Conservatism functions by "mobilizing fear for its own politics of order." Thus, it is a matter of course for conservatives to portray anything or anyone who threatens, challenges or undermines social order as monsters, be-cause without the fear such monsters produce "there can be no rule" (Neocleous 2005:29). Robert Castel writes of the current anxieties feeding the security fetish in the West that we "live undoubtedly in some of the most secure societies that ever existed, and yet, contrary to the objective evidence we, the most cosseted and pampered people of all—feel more threatened, insecure and frightened, more inclined to panic, and more passionate about everything related to security and safety than the people of most other societies on record" (cited in Bauman 2007, 101).

As many have shown the political economics of the globalized industries of war, terror, and security profit from the very enemies they prop up, combat, and "protect" us from. Just like the so-called "criminal justice" system ensures its continuation by not working or delivering its promises, so to do the apparatuses of security interlocking with the war economies built upon death, disease and decay industries. In medicine and psychiatry, for example, profit hinges on treatment rather than cure; similarly the crime control industry or prison industrial complex is sustained by the spectacularly represented and social production of criminalities. The usefulness of the notion of psychocentrism is that it provides an entry point for analyzing emotional subjectivities without falling into the political trappings of psychocentrism, outlined earlier. As such the politics of emotions and the emotions of politics—against and beyond the state—acknowledges the necessity of analyzing the psychopolitics of individualized states of in/security as always already tied to the sociopolitics of life and living in the carnivalesque and cannibalistic society.

CONCLUSION

Modernity was hailed and glorified as that period in history when the irrational fears that permeated previous historical periods would be conquered, if not eradicated; and yet, at the end of the first decade of the twenty-first century, the dangerization riddling neo-liberalism has not only resulted in the growth of social insecurities witnessed in the proliferation of discourses, imageries, and practices of fear: the fear of ecological decay and disaster, the fear of terrorism, the fear of natural catastrophes, the fear of pandemics and epidemics, the fear of strangers, the fear of crime, the fear of the apocalypse, and so forth—all of which point to, of course, the fear of the inevitable—death, the inescapable material finality we all must bear. Thus, in today's cannibalizing society of insecurity, "the phenomenon to be manipulated and capitalized on is the fear of death—one 'natural resource' that can boast infinite supplies and complete renewability" (Bauman 2007, 52).

The psychopolitical affectivity and effectivity of neo-liberal dehumanization serves to not only "make up" and "disorder" monsterized subjects through a matrix of individualizing technologies and myths; it also reinforces normative expert discourses and dominant governing institutions as a given. Rather than normalizing psychocentrism or reproducing the longstanding social and political theoretical tendency to anti-emotionalism or positivism, a genealogical approach to the psychopolitics of emotional practices and relations of power critically interrogates the psychocentricity of dominant and dominating neo-liberal discourses of in/security. This perspective allows something new to be thought, and as Foucault announced, "to learn to what extent the effort to think one's own history can free thought from what it silently thinks, and so enable it to think differently" (1986, 9). After all, the purpose and promise of the sociological imagination is to produce theories and research methods, as well as new forms of knowledge, useful for understanding the link between private troubles and public issues. Understanding the force of psychopolitical practices and discourses thus necessarily entails critiquing the psychocentricity territorializing mental and emotional states that (re)produce and mask the social, political, economic, cultural, and historical conditions of human pain and struggle.

NOTES

1. While Parenti (1999) mentions this concept in his critical text on the politics of history, I develop the concept further. Peter Sedgwick (1950) also used the term to highlight the politics of anti-psychiatry discourses that fed the deinstitutionalization movement. While clearly linked to the current conceptualization, the contours of the conceptual relationship exceed the focus of the current problematic of neo-liberal monsterization.

REFERENCES

Aiken, Sharryn J. 2007. "Risking Rights: An Assessment of Canadian Border Security Policies." In *Whose Canada? Continental Integration, Fortress North America, and the Corporate Agenda,Ricardo Grinspun and Yasmine Shamsie*, eds. Ricardo Grinspun and Yasmine Shamsie. McGill–Queen's Press, 180–208.

Beck, Ulrich. 1986. *The Risk Society.* London: Sage.

Bentham, Jeremy. 1887. *The Theory of Legislation.* London: Trubner and Company.

Baudrillard, Jean. 2010. *Carnival and Cannibal or The Play of Global Antagonism.* Translated by Chris Turner. Calcutta: Seagull Books.

Bauman, Zygmunt. 2001. *The Individualized Society.* Cambridge: Polity Press.

———. 2007. *Liquid Fear.* Cambridge: Polity Press.

Becker, Howard. 1967. "Whose Side Are We On?" *Social Problems* 14(Winter): 239–247.

Bell, Colleen. 2006. "Subject to Exception: Security Certificates, National Security and Canada's Role in the 'War on Terror.'" *Canadian Journal of Law and Society* 21(1): 63–83.

Bourdieu, Pierre. 1998. *Acts of Resistance: Against the New Myths of Our Time.* Translated by Richard Nice. Cambridge: Polity Press.

Bourdieu, Pierre and Loic J. D. Wacquant. 2001. "Neoliberal Newspeak: Notes on the New Planetary Vulgate." *Radical Philosophy* 105: 2–5.

Bourdieu, Pierre and Loic J.D. Wacquant. 1999. "On the Cunning of Imperialist Reason." *Theory, Culture and Society* 16(1): 41–58.

Castel, Robert. 1991. "From Dangerousness to Risk" In *The Foucault Effect: Studies in Governmentality*, eds. G. Burchell, C. Gordon, and P. Miller. Chicago: University of Chicago Press.

Christie, Nils. 2000. *Crime Control as Industry: Towards Gulags, Modern Style*. London: Routledge.

Davis, Angela Y. 2003. *Are Prisons Obsolete?* New York: Seven Stories Press.

Debord, Guy. 1970. *The Society of the Spectacle*. Detroit: Black and Red

Evans, Peter. 1989. "Predatory, Developmental and Other Apparatuses." *Sociological Forum*, 561–587.

Foucault, Michel. 1978a. "Governmentality." In *The Foucault Effect: Studies in Governmentality*, eds. G. Burchell, C. Gordon, and P. Miller. Chicago: University of Chicago Press, 87–104.

———. 1978b. "About the Concept of the 'Dangerous Individual' in Nineteenth-Century Legal Psychiatry." *International Journal of Law and Psychiatry* 1: 1–18.

———. 1979. *Discipline and Punish: The Birth of the Prison*. New York: Vintage Books.

———. 2007. *Security, Territory, Population. Lectures at the College de France 1977–1978*. New York: Palgrave.

———. 2008. *The Birth of Biopolitics. Lectures at the College de France 1978-1979*. New York: Palgrave.

Garland, David. 2001. *Mass Imprisonment: Social Causes and Consequences*. London: Sage.

Graham, P. and J. Clarke. 2001. "Dangerous Places: Crime and the City" In *The Problem of Crime*, eds. J. Muncie and E. McLaughlin. London: Sage, 151–190.

Haggerty, K. D. 2003. "From Risk to Precaution: The Rationalities of Personal Crime Prevention" In *Risk and Morality*, eds. Richard Ericson and Aaron Doyle. Toronto: University of Toronto Press, 193–214.

———. 2009. "Modern Serial Killers" *Crime, Media, Culture* 5(2): 168–187.

Hermer, Joe, Michael Kempa, Clifford Shearing, Philip Stenning, and Jennifer Wood. 2005 "Policing in Canada in the Twenty-first Century: Directions for Law Reform" In *Reimagining Policing in Canada*, ed. Denis Cooley. Toronto: University of Toronto Press, 22–91.

Hutchinson, Steven and Daniel O'Connor. 2005. "Policing The New Commons: Corporate Security Governance on a Mass Private Property in Canada." *Policing and Society* 15(2): 125–144.

Hedlund, Stefan. 1999. *Russia's "Market" Economy: A Bad Case of Predatory Capitalism*. London. University College London.

Hier, Sean P., Kevin Walby, Josh Greenberg, and Dan Lett. 2007. "Media, Communication, and the Establishment of Public Camera Surveillance Programs in Canada." *Media, Culture, and Society* 29(5): 727–751.

Jackson, R. 2005. "Security, Democracy, and the Rhetoric of Counter-Terrorism." *Democracy and Security* 1(2): 147–171.

Kinsman, Gary, Dieter K. Buse and Mercedes Steedman, eds. 2000. *Whose National Security? Canadian State Surveillance and the Creation of Enemies*. Toronto: Between the Lines.

Kinsman, Gary and Patricia Gentile. 2010. *The Canadian War Against Queers: National Security as Sexual Regulation*. Vancouver: University of British Columbia Press.

Kohm, Steven A. 2009. "Naming, Shaming and Criminal Justice: Mass-Mediated Humiliation As Entertainment And Punishment." *Crime, Media, Culture* 5(2): 188–205.

Larsen, Mike. 2008. "Governing Non-Citizens as Security Threats: Canada's Security Certificate Regime." In *Violent Interventions: Selected Proceedings of the Fifteenth Annual Conference of the York Centre for International and Security Studies*, eds. M. Ayyash and C. Hendershot. Toronto: YCISS, 21–38.

Larsen, Mike and Justin Piché. 2009a. "Exceptional State, Pragmatic Bureaucracy, and Indefinite Detention: The Case of the Kingston Immigration Holding Centre." *Canadian Journal of Law and Society* 24(2): 203–229.

———. 2009b. "Public Vigilance Campaigns and Participatory Surveillance after 11 September 2001." In *Surveillance: Power, Problems, and Politics*, eds. Sean Hier and Josh Greenberg. Vancouver: UBC Press, 187–202.

Lefebvre, Martin. 2005. "Conspicuous Consumption: The Figure of the Serial Killer as Cannibal in the Age of Capitalism." *Theory, Culture and Society* 22: 43–62.

Lianos, M. and M. Douglas. 2000. "Dangerization and the End of Deviance." *British Journal of Criminology* 40: 261–278.

Lynch, Mona. 2001. "From the Punitive City to the Gated Community: Security and Segregation Across the Social and Penal Landscape." *Miami Law Review* 56(1): 601–623.

Lynch, Mona. 2004. "Punishing Images: Jail Cam and the Changing Penal Enterprise." *Punishment and Society* 6(3): 255–270.

Mauer, M. and M. Chesney-Lind. 2002. *Invisible Punishment: The Collateral Consequences of Mass Imprisonment*. New York: The New Press.

Maurutto, Paula. 2000. "Private Policing and the Surveillance of Catholics: Anti-Communism in the Roman Archdiocese of Toronto, 1920–1960." In *Whose National Security? Canadian State Surveillance and the Creation of Enemies*, Gary Kinsman, Dieter K. Buse, and Mercedes Steedman Toronto: Between the Lines, 36–54.

Mills, C. W. 1959. *The Sociological Imagination*. London: Oxford University Press.

Neocleous, Mark. 2000. *The Fabrication of Social Order: A Critical Theory of Police Power*. London: Pluto Press.

———. 2003. *Imagining the State*. Maidenhead: Open University Press.

———. 2005. *The Monstrous and the Dead: Marx, Burke, Fascism*. Cardiff: University of Wales Press.

———. 2007. "Security, Liberty and the Myth of Balance: Towards a Critique of Security Politics." *Contemporary Political Theory* 6: 131–149.

———. 2008. *Critique of Security*. Montreal: McGill-Queen's University.

Ong, A. 2006. *Neoliberalism as Exception: Mutations in Citizenship and Sovereignty*. Durham: Duke University Press.

Parenti, Michael. 1999. *History as Mystery*. San Francisco: City Light Books.

Parenti, Christian. 1999. *Lockdown America: Police and Prisons in an Age of Crisis*. NY: Verso.

Peelo, Moira. 2005. "Crime and the Media: Public Narratives and Private Consumption." In *Questioning Crime and Criminology*, eds. M. Peelo and K. Soothill. Portland, Oregon: Willan, 20–36.

Pue, Wesley. 2003. "The War on Terror: Constitutional Governance in a State of Permanent Warfare?" *Osgoode Hall Law Journal* 41: 267–292.

Quinney, Richard. 2001. "Introduction." In *Controlling the Dangerous Classes: A Critical Introduction to the History of Criminal Justice*, by Randall G. Sheldon. Boston: Allyn and Bacon.

Razack, Sherene H. 2008. *Casting Out: The Eviction of Muslims from Western Law and Politics*. Toronto: University of Toronto Press.

Rigakos, George. 2002. *The New Parapolice: Risk Markets and Commoditized Social Control*. Toronto: University of Toronto Press.

———. 2008. *Nightclub: Bouncers, Risk, and the Spectacle of Consumption*. Montreal: McGill-Queen's University Press.

Rimke, Heidi. 2000. "Governing Citizens through Self-Help Literature." *Cultural Studies*, 14(1): 61–78.

———. 2003. "Constituting Transgressive Interiorities: C19th Psychiatric Readings of Morally Mad Bodies." In *Violence and the Body: Race, Gender and the State*, ed. A. Arturo. South Bend, Indiana: Indiana University Press, 403–428.

———. 2008a. "Social Psychological Epidemics." In *Encyclopedia of Plague, Pestilence and Pandemics*, ed. Joseph Byrne. Westport: Greenwood Press, 681–683.

———. 2008b. "The Developing Science of the Mind." In *Research and Discovery: Landmarks and Pioneers in American Science*, ed. Russell Lawson. New York: M.E. Sharpe, 526–529.

———. 2009b. "The Haymarket Tragedy." In *The International Encyclopedia of Revolution and Protest: 1500 to Present*, ed. Immanuel Ness. Cambridge: Blackwell-Wiley, 1568–1570.

———. 2010a. "Remembering the Sociological Imagination: Transdisciplinarity, the Genealogical Method, and Epistemological Politics." *International Journal of Interdisciplinary Social Sciences*. Forthcoming.

———. 2010b "Genealogy of Positivism: Pathological Theories of Crime and Criminality." In *Canadian Criminology*, ed. Kirsten Kramar. Toronto: Pearson Education Canada. Forthcoming.

———. 2010c. "From the Spectacle of the Scaffold to the Spectacle of the Screen: Security Politics, Bloodlust Justice, and the Mass Consumption of Criminalized Cannibalism." Presented at the Canadian Law and Society Association Meetings, Concordia University, Montréal, Canada.

Rimke, Heidi and Alan Hunt. 2002. "From Sinners to Degenerates: The Medicalization of Morality in the C19th." *History of the Human Sciences* 15(1): 59–88.

Rothe, Dawn and Stephen Muzzatti. 2004. "Enemies Everywhere: Terrorism, Moral Panic and US Civil Society." *Critical Criminology* 12(3): 327–350.

Sanders, Trevor. 2005. 'The Rise of Rent-A-Cop: Private Security in Canada, 1991–2001." *Canadian Journal of Criminology and Criminal Justice* 47(1): 175–190.

Sedgwick, Peter. 1950. *Psychopolitics*. London: Lightning Source Publishers.

Shearing, Clifford and Philip Stenning. 1983. "Private Security: Implications for Social Control." *Social Problems* 30(5): 493–506.

Shearing, Clifford and Philip Stenning. 1987. *Private Policing*. Beverly Hills: Sage.

Sheldon, Randall G. 2001. *Controlling the Dangerous Classes: A Critical Introduction to the History of Criminal Justice*. Boston: Allyn and Bacon.

Smith, Dorothy E. 1990. *The Conceptual Practices of Power: A Feminist Sociology of Knowledge*. Toronto: University Of Toronto Press.

Taylor, Ian. 1999. *Crime in Context: A Critical Criminology of Market Societies*. Cambridge: Polity Press.

Taylor, J.M. 1995. "The Resurrection of the Dangerous Classes." In *Writing as Resistance*, ed. Robert Gaucher. Toronto: Canadian Scholars' Press, 99–109.

CHAPTER 5. "BORDER PANIC" AND THE BOUNDS OF RACIAL IDENTITY

Dr. David E. Magill

Robert Frost opens his second poetic collection *North of Boston* (1914) with "Mending Wall," a poem that crystallizes the boundary issues I explore in this article. Frost introduces the text with a backward glance to his previous work: "'Mending Wall' takes up the theme where 'A Tuft of Flowers' in *A Boy's Will* laid it down" (1914, 10). Frost prefaces "Mending Wall" with its own textual revenant, allowing us to understand the poem as a continued rumination on the fellowship of man, summarized in the narrator's comment, "Something there is that doesn't love a wall" and the neighbor's response, "Good fences make good neighbors" (1914, 11, 13). Yet this revenant also destabilizes the distinct textual borders associated with the poems. The two poems comment on one another in a way that further undermines the question of borders.

As the two interlocuters "work together" to rebuild their fence, the narrator argues against the unnecessary effort: "There where it is we do not need the wall: / He is all pine and I am apple orchard. / My apple trees will never get across / And eat the cones under his pines" (Frost 1914, 12). Frost presents a naturalized allegory of difference within a moment of fraternal exchange that captures the desire/repulsion at the heart of 1920s identity politics. Apples and cones mark the physical difference between the men as a naturalized element in their identities. When the narrator suggests dismantling the border, recognizing its futility against the various onslaughts captured in the "something" that dislikes the wall, the neighbor responds with his father's aphorism, invoking nostalgically authori-

113

tative patrilineal logic to undermine the narrator's vague promises of benevolent separation. Borders, claims the neighbor, must exist to stem the natural chaos and to order life; the fence creates their partnered identities through shared spatial demarcation, yet the continued springtime efforts of the narrator and neighbor undermine the argument for the fence's stabilizing function through its continual need for maintenance. Frost taps into the anxieties that demand such maintenance, articulating them as particularly American through the symbolic import of apple and pine. For Frost, borders become a marker of generalized difference between "you" and "me"; however, his side of the fence contains the "apples" that fruitfully symbolize American identity. And importantly, Frost's poem highlights the border as the defining symbol of the poem, demarcating groupings through its existence. Frost, then, represents a general ideal of identity division at work in the United States in a variety of cultural arenas. In what follows, I will examine a more specific formulation of this border problem as a means of understanding how the 1920s were a flashpoint for questions of national borders and racial identities.

Frost's poem highlights a central problematic that we also see in the formation of American racial identity: "border panic," to adapt Eve Sedgwick's terms, an anxiety formation based in the perception of eroding boundaries that permeated the Twenties' literary and cultural landscape as a continuing psychological response to early twentieth century physical and social border penetrations by various groups.[1] Hybridity, or what Robert J.C. Young termed "the jarrings of a differentiated culture" (1995, 23), and passing become central anxieties of white men precisely because they reflect the contradictions in binary logic that undergird the claims to power of whiteness. Nativism, delineated culturally by John Higham and traced literarily by Walter Benn Michaels, is a particularly virulent reaction to "border panic"; however, we see a multitude of responses designed to assuage spatial anxieties by restricting mobility through legal statutes and cultural practices that determine power relations in the modern United States across race, gender, and class lines. This chapter, however, examines the problem of the US Southwest, with its external and internal border issues, as a crucial location for the construction of 1920s racial identities. George Owen Baxter's *Tigerman* (1929) and Harold Bell Wright's *The Mine with the Iron Door* (1923) are popular fictions that register the "border panic" driving debates over access to the national polity. In particular, I argue that the racialized figures of the Mexican and the Indian become registers for the anxieties of whiteness and symbols for the attempted resolution of those fears through physical displacement and social dismissal. Such texts reveal how whiteness defines its purity through racial abjection in a process that redefines national boundaries, both spatial and social, and creates "natural" divisions between racial identities. Yet these texts also highlight the constructedness of these divisions through the processes by which they assuage white anxieties. As such, they reveal the contradictions of racial ideologies in the 1920s as constituted through national identity.

BORDER PANIC

The United States encountered an unprecedented era of geographic and demographic population shifts during the 1920s that radically altered the cultural and economic landscape.[2] Mexico's geographical continuity combined with its state separation to present an anxious challenge to American exceptionalism, with only politically created borders dividing racialized and nationalized people who were, nonetheless, neighbors a la Frost's characters. Such challenges revealed the nation's artificially constructed borders to be easily permeable in practice despite their theoretical rigidity. Migrations into and across the United States exacerbate racial tensions because those fluid spatial movements reflect materially the social mobility claimed by disenfranchised groups and physically the ways migration undermines the distinct borders constructed as a property claim on national identities. Thus, mobility became a key term of power as well as a marker of modernity. 1920s legislative mandates, judicial rulings, and social policies strategically re-defined America's "imagined community" as exclusively white and male through vigorous assertions of spatial boundaries, assertions that simultaneously point up these boundaries' constructedness. Read against the backdrop of immigration restriction, eugenic improvement, and cultural negotiation, 1920s literary and popular texts register a form of anxiety I term "border panic" and suggest the psychic strategies by which whiteness contained the perceived threat.

"Border panic" describes the structural and psychic anxiety formation arising from a fear of fluidity and leading to strict regulatory boundaries for determining identities and mobilities, such as national and local borders. These borders are nostalgic creations of political division, a historicized claiming of landscape as a means of enforcing power. Marc Redfield notes:

> [Benedict] Anderson's narrative about nationalism thus encourages us to understand the experience of the nation as grounded in and produced by a systematic misrecognition of its origins. The nation is a hallucinated limit to iterability. Made possible by difference, deferral, and technological shock, the nation homogenizes time and space, draws and polices borders, historicizes itself as the continuous arc of an unfolding identity. (1999, 66)

The performative/pedagogical split upon which Homi Bhabha theorizes the ambivalent instability of the nation is an anxious split; nostalgia, however, eases that tension through a revisionist historical narrative that erases the national performance and bridges the gulf between the nation and the individual.[3] Nostalgia links individuals to the nation by imagining "the people" as always and naturally embodied in the landscape, thus extending into the past a desire for group identity.

Lauren Berlant notes: "The implicit whiteness and maleness of the original American citizen is thus itself protected by national identity" (1991: 113). Yet at certain times, that prophylactic shield falters as the connections between national identity and white masculinity come under scrutiny from externalized groups demanding access, thus creating a "post-national" moment.[4] As Priscilla Wald argues in Constituting Americans, narrative shapings of identity, of the national through the individual, always produce anxiety through the slippage between the individual story and the larger narrative into which it tries to fit. Randolph Bourne's essay "Trans-National America," for example, allows us one opportunity to see the separation of that national ideology from its state apparatuses as he defines a differently accessible form of "Americanism." 1920s Congressional meetings and their legislative mandate of "American" identity in such statutes as the 1924 National Origins Act further suggest that the state saw its "nation," its ideological counterpart, becoming "something not ourselves."

The response, Charles Scruggs and Lee VandeMarr have shown, "demanded that racial or ethnic memory be erased, that history dissolve into nostalgia, and that intelligence succumb to the eternal moment of emotional patriotism" (1998, 81). As Pease notes:

> National narratives' power as instruments of psychic governance is best evidenced perhaps in the panic that has accompanied the de-symbolization and subversion of nationalist narratives at this postnational site. Surrogate abjection and unanimous violence have accompanied the wholesale delinkages of "national peoples" from the imagined communities in which they had previously "experienced" their imagined wholeness. The loss of national narrativity as an imaginative cushion has released the unmitigated force of the state's repressive apparatus as a collectively shared experience. (1997: 8)

Transnational anxieties fueled by "border panic" defined the 1920s in just this manner, leading individuals to reclaim national identity as the purview of whiteness through such abjections and violence. This more general anxiety about foreign incursion translated into specific cultural discourses aimed at particular racial groups as a means of excluding them from the nation. The United States' claims of autonomy served, then, to defend whiteness. As part of this reclamation, the turn-of-the-century "closing of the frontier" brought about a conflation of the individual and the national mapped onto the white male body. Yet this mapping is not uni-directional, as Mark Seltzer notes: "Anxieties about agency, identity, and the integrity of the natural body are distributed across physical landscapes" (1992: 150). In other words, a dialectical tension exists between the white body and the national body, such that the anxieties of one get translated and diffused into the other through the intertwined construction of whiteness and national identity.

SOUTH OF THE BORDER

Relatively neglected but important to our understanding of identity politics in the 1920s are the anxieties posed by Mexican immigration. Jose David Saldivar's *Border Matters* does argue for this type of discussion to occur: "by examining the contact zones of the US–Mexico border, the spaces where the nation either ends or begins, we can begin to problematize the notion that the nation is 'naturally' there" informs this chapter (1997, 14). While he does not particularly focus on 1920s Mexican immigration, his insight allows us to move beyond typical black-white understandings of 1920s racial debates. This shift in focus is important, for hemispheric immigration was just as much a threat to national borders as transatlantic arrivals, bringing into question US spheres of control in the post-war era. The period between 1890 and 1930 marked the beginning of a large-scale movement across the border as Mexicans sought economic and political freedoms not afforded them. Porfirio Diaz's open policies exploited poor Mexican workers and encouraged them to leave for the United States (Archdeacon 1983, 138). In addition, the Mexican Revolution threatened US business in Mexico and affected Southwestern stability, sending yet more refugee Mexicans to the United States. War preparations and need for cheap labor in the United States pulled Mexican migrants across the border as well (Lorey 1999, 69).

While contemporary critics may have avoided discussion of the Mexican immigration issue, 1920s white supremacists writers were far more cognizant of its perceived dangers. Madison Grant warned that the melting pot's evil effects were best exemplified by "the racial mixture which we call Mexican, and which is now engaged in demonstrating its incapacity for self-government" (1922, 81). He rationalized US military control in Mexico through an argument comprised of "a compounding of the elements of Manifest Destiny and the white man's burden" that supported one-way permeability of the border as a means of economic and cultural exploitation (Robinson 1997, 177). Similarly, in *The Rising Tide of Color*, Lothrop Stoddard argues for closing the Southern border in order to prevent the influx of "Mexican peons," whom bring "ignorance, dirt, disease, and vice, which infect cities with slum plague-spots, depress wages, and lower the general tone of the community" (1921, 214–215). Stoddard sees Mexicans as carriers of dirt and disease, and implicates them in communal depression within a turn of phrase. The verb "infect" associates the Mexican with contagion invading the body politic and depressing its immunities through weakness and degradation. The same metaphors used to attack European immigration recur in diatribes against the Mexican influx.

The Mexican border conflict provided a different set of circumstances from European immigration because of the Mexican Revolution's threat to US businesses, creating anxieties that circulate in the cultural imaginary. Nell Irvin Painter notes: "American investments in Mexico had doubled between 1900 and 1910, so that by 1910 Americans owned about 43 percent of the property in Mexico" (1987, 286). In addition, David Lorey notes that the United States developed the Mexican border, including the building of a railroad between the two countries, as a means of increasing resource and labor movement into Mexico and product movement out of Mexico (1999, 40–69). 1910 saw those production lines threatened, for Mexico was in civil war. General Victoriano Huerta overthrew Madero and seized control of the government. Woodrow Wilson opposed the coup and amassed troops on the border and warships in the Gulf as a prelude to invasion. As Painter notes: "To many Americans and Mexicans, occupation to protect American investments seemed inevitable" (1987, 311). Mexicans thought the American army would take over and reduce Mexico to protectorate status. Senator Albert B. Fall of New Mexico, a supporter of intervention, argued that the US had to maintain financial and social order, resurrecting Grant's racialized assumptions about fitness for self-government (Painter 1987, 287). The Revolution disrupted traditional goods movements between the two countries, although a black market border economy developed in Mexico to ship illegal goods into the US, particularly with the advent of Prohibition (Lorey 1999, 40–41). While border town economies boomed, corporations based in Mexican–US trade found the Revolution damaging to profits.

BORDER BUSINESS AND RACIAL VALUES

Southwestern "border panic," then, stemmed from worries over lessening capital and lost business as well as the increasing population and its accompanying racialist fears of "miscegenation" and disease. 1920s fictions became a key site for locating expressions of these tensions. Cedric Robinson states: "A number of American writers have used the Mexican very specifically as a foil by which to emphasize the demoralizing and dehumanizing effects of industrialism and commercialism" (1997, 225). Yet the Mexican also serves as a racial repository for the abjection of whiteness's distasteful desires and attributes. Popular fictions relied on mixed-race figures and hidden identity plots to work through border anxieties prevalent in US culture and whitewash national identity.

George Owen Baxter's *Tigerman* (1929), for example, portrays and manages such border anxieties through a hidden identity plot. *Tigerman* relates the story of Blas Lavera, a poor Mexican raised to avenge his father Enrique's digital mutilation at the hands of Senor Teofilo Dial. What Enrique (the former Guido Forseno) does not tell Blas is that Guido kidnapped him from the daughter of Señor Dial as retribution. After receiving Enrique's help in turning a desert valley into a lush paradise through landscape engineering, Dial refused Enrique's price: the hand of Dial's daughter. Instead, he tortured Forseno, crushing his hands and rendering him useless as a worker, then sent him off after allowing him to witness the daughter's marriage to a white man. Forseno retaliates by stealing the couple's baby and raising it as Mexican.

Blas Lavera, then, is a white man masquerading unknowingly as "colored." But his racial biology asserts itself in gendered terms. Blas is presented as an extremely virile figure: strong, handsome, talented, intelligent. In short, he has the wits and the physical acumen to outsmart and outfight the best men around him. Vega, the novel's villain, wants to capture Lavera for shooting several of his men and stealing money. Yet Blas attends a dance on the Vega compound and manages to escape from under their noses, stealing not only their revenge but also the heart of Liseta, Vega's dancing girl and fiancée. Blas's biology surfaces again in the revenge plot. Forseno tells Blas of the wrongs done by Dial and sends Blas to enact familial retribution. As he becomes part of the Dial household, Blas senses his connection to the family, such that Christopher (the younger brother, we discover) treats him as a brother even before the revelations come out. His refusal to kill Señor Dial in cold blood demonstrates his "civilized" (and therefore "white") instincts. Through such machinations, the novel rescues whiteness from racial degradation.

Blas Lavera regains his white identity through his father's revelations at the end of the novel. Lavera's adeptness with guns and knives, superior strength, and vast intelligence are all the outcome of biological superiority, not the environmental product of a madman bent on revenge. The text thus supports a biological determinism that tallies with eugenic and pseudo-scientific notions of racial superiority. *Tigerman*, however, diverges from the traditional plot in that Lavera marries a Mexican girl (Liseta). Thus Baxter's novel reverses the conventional pattern, in that it evolves from a "pure" union to a "miscegenative" one. The narrator tells us that Blas and Liseta live in America, where the valley of Dial lies, but that they travel into Mexico twice a year to visit Guido and "hear his plans, and look into his half-mad eyes" (1929, 308), as Guido restores yet another barren area with his engineering feats. Interestingly, though, the description of this final arrangement downplays Blas's time in America. Though he spends time there, it is with little mention of Liseta. Baxter minimizes mention of Lavera's wife, keeping her connected with Mexico so as to elide the "miscegenation" and keep it outside of US land.

More importantly, Blas regains his position and his heritage from the Dial family. The novel closes with this notation from the narrator: "And when the restless fit comes, and Blas finds himself yearning for some wilder, fiercer action, he goes to seek out old, white-headed Dial, and he drinks in the smooth, wise current of his speech; and then he learns what life can be" (1929, 309). Lavera travels to the Dial ranch in order to bond with his counterparts in a fantasy of renewal where Senor Dial, despite his crimes against Forseno, becomes the restored patriarch. Dial pays Forseno a large sum of money to expiate Dial's crimes, and Forseno leaves for Mexico. Blas, meanwhile, imports his new wife to America and is restored as rightful heir to Dial's kingdom. This novel thus enacts a vision of border relations that brings talent and technology north as well as admiration and wifely love. Whiteness, as exemplified in Blas Lavera, becomes another valuable asset rescued from theft by Mexico and protected from Southern encroachment. Though Forseno is responsible for the restoration of the valley, his contributions are elided in the restoration of the family. Instead, Forseno remains below the border, transforming another valley to add to Dial's riches. Baxter's resolution diminishes the fortune paid to Forseno so he will leave, focusing on Forseno's madness and Blas's discovery of wisdom in the old American. The regained white paternity allows Lavera to become whole, and while honor bids him visit Forseno, common bond with white Americans brings him back to the United States. Whiteness (as a property with value) does not travel beyond the border, remaining fixed on US soil. *Tigerman*, then, registers and contains white border anxieties and restores national purity through a fantastic narrative of regeneration. Yet these machinations also reveal the constructedness of that pure whiteness so as to undermine its invisible efficacy.

BORDER POLITICS AND THE PROPERTIES OF WHITENESS

While the disruption to business flows between the nations was one problem, actual border penetrations caused by civil unrest was another. As the Revolution escalated, border skirmishes and conflicts grew more frequent, causing

Americans to advocate intervention (Painter 1987, 283). Victories by rebel generals Emiliano Zapata and Francisco 'Pancho' Villa also enhanced the drive for US intrusion. Villa in particular captured American imaginations. He resembled Theodore Roosevelt and was often pictured on horseback. What is more important, he aligned himself with American interests; he protected Americans when capturing villages and welcomed invasion (Painter 1987, 289–290). Wilson eventually intervened in Mexico, holding the city of Veracruz. But intervention did not lead to the eventual removal of Huerta, accomplished by Mexican generals, and the US withdrew after seven months. The fighting continued between Zapata and Villa and the new leader, Carranza (Painter 1987, 291–292).

Pancho Villa started as a revolutionary hero in American minds. He exploited romantic notions of the rebel, espousing pro-American sentiments to assuage anti-Mexican fears. As the revolution continued, however, and US assistance was not forthcoming, Villa decided to force the United States to take action in Mexico. On January 10, 1916, Villa entered the United States, stopped a train, and robbed and killed fifteen American engineers and miners. He then attacked the United States Thirteenth Cavalry on March 9, 1916, killing 17 US citizens (Stout 1999, 33–38). These attacks infuriated Americans and caused Woodrow Wilson to send troops into Mexico to hunt down Villa and protect US business interests without permission, an act that escalated tensions. Joseph Stout relates that in addition to the massive influx of troops sent to hunt Villa and his cohorts: "Soldiers and civilians had dragged the bodies of sixty-seven Villistas to the outskirts of town, poured kerosene on them, and set them afire" (1999, 38). The virulent response to these attacks suggests "border panic"; the removal of bodies outside the town limits spatially restores boundaries, while the burning would have occurred as a ritual to prevent the spread of disease. In addition, Wilson posted 130,000 men along the border to prevent further Villista raids (Stout 1999, 123). The visual picture of white men physically guarding the invisible line marking US territory vividly displays the connections between the nation-space and racial identities. Men guarded these spaces with violence as a means of protecting their own identities and the privileges that accompanied them.

In addition, Mexican insurgents unhappy with the United States' annexation of Southwestern lands plotted to recoup their losses in violent attacks on US soil. The creation of the Texas Rangers and the increased border patrols in response to these attacks reveals the border's constructedness. While US citizens wanted to see the demarcated boundaries as absolute and unchanging, the insurgents' alternative historical narrative portrayed the borders as recently shifted in a US imperialistic annexation they wished to reverse. These penetrations of US space to murder soldiers and civilians showed the ease by which "insidious elements" could violate these boundaries. The physical attacks cemented already anxious notions of the Mexico–US border as inwardly permeable. While the US had sent soldiers into Mexico on several occasions, incursions into US space defied traditional power relations along the border and exposed the artificiality of national structures. As a result, border anxieties about Mexico continued into the 1920s, augmented by increased Mexican migration during the decade. Columnists advocated for Villa's capture, and Hollywood films portrayed that event in multiple scenarios.[5]

Harold Bell Wright's *The Mine With the Iron Door* responds to such developments, assuaging anxieties over Mexican border raids through a plotting of symbolic conquest that metaphorically legitimates US imperialist actions against its Southern neighbor.[6] It represents external "border panic" in its Sonora Jack plot, figuring racial anxieties over the removal of value from US geographical territories. At the same time, it resolves the Indian question as well in order to quell internal boundary conflicts and support white supremacy. National identity qua whiteness becomes a property to be protected from theft by border figures and from claims by native peoples.

Sonora Jack is the villain of *The Mine With the Iron Door*. Repeatedly described as half-Mexican, Sonora Jack derives his racial heritage from his mother, a fact that defines him as "colored" under the one-drop rule while simultaneously excusing the 'miscegenation' by removing the white father from view. He further incriminates himself by teaming up with Mexican outlaws and living south of the US border. Sonora Jack crosses the border between the United States and Mexico at will, demonstrating the permeability of the imaginary line as he attempts to steal the gold from the Mine with the Iron Door. He attacks the Indian Natachee and tortures him for information, echoing the Villa attacks (1923, 235–243). Thus, he represents the dissolution of mixed-race identity in the racial cathexis of 1920s America. In addition, contemporary fears of white women being sold into slavery circulate through the novel. Lee Mitchell notes of Zane Grey, "One of the standard ploys invoked by many of Grey's novels is to have Mexicans, outlaws, Mormons, or other supposedly unsavory groups succeed in enslaving white women" (1996, 237). Wright similarly capitalizes on this worry in the kidnap plot: Sonora Jack seizes the even more valuable treasure of white womanhood. He kidnaps Marta Hillgrove and threatens to sell her into ransom, forcing Natachee and Edwards to travel into Mexico to rescue Marta and kill the villain. Various characters speak fearfully of Sonora Jack's appearances, bespeaking the anxieties border crossings represent through the stereotypical imagining of Mexican characters as militant villains. When Edwards expresses disbelief in the Mexican's capability for murder, Natachee responds: "It is evident my friend, that you do not know Sonora

Jack and his methods" (1923, 250). The implication is clear: Sonora Jack's racial identity (created by his "miscegenative" biology) causes a degeneracy that white minds cannot fathom. Sonora Jack thus represents the anxiety of fluidity that would feminize America. He must be symbolically expunged by the white male and the Native American, destroyed in an act that re-establishes border control spatially and genealogically even as his existence recalls the *mestizo* mixture of white European and American Indian. Thus, similar to racial logics of slavery that denied interracial desire even as plantation owners raped slaves, the text denies the implications of its own partnerships in creating the mixed-blood identities it fears, instead creating a fantasy of purity undermined by its own anxieties.

Wright's narrative thus presents and then eases "border panic" through Marta's retrieval and Sonora Jack's death at Natachee's hand. This resolution reaffirms boundary control through the villain's dispatch and the woman's return to US soil and to her true identity. The fluidic, "miscegenated" identities are eliminated and the patrimony/genealogy of whiteness is restored through the teaming of white man and Native American as representative Americans defending the geographical borders of the landscape and the theoretical borders that encircle national identity and whiteness as linked identities. Wright's novel seeks to re-territorialize the American West as white domain through the violent enactment of borders, external and internal. Yet the landscape of Wright's novel betrays its own constructedness. While the novel begins with multiple cultures coming together, the narrative slowly engineers the construction of a white paradise through the removal of border threats.

While *The Mine With the Iron Door* satisfactorily resolves its romantic Mexican immigration plot, far more ambiguous is its treatment of the Native American issue. The white paradise imagined at the novel's close may be free of Mexican influences, but it is haunted by the lone figure of Natachee: "Lifting his dark face toward the mountain peaks that towered above his lonely hut, Natachee the Indian—mystic guardian of the Mine With the Iron Door—smiled" (1923, 339). Wright's liberal treatment of Native American affairs subordinates solutions for the "Indian problem" to the much more pressing desire to protect external borders and re-solidify whiteness's claims on American resources. Nevertheless, the Indian becomes a problem within the novel's characterological structure, as in the United States as a whole. Wright's ambiguous treatment of Natachee mirrors national attitudes toward US internal policies regarding the Native American. In particular, *The Mine With the Iron Door* registers anxieties about United States resource accessibility and control of lands, then assuages them through a fantasy that restores the value of whiteness while setting clear bounds between national and Native identities.

Wright's novel evinces the contradictory beliefs at the heart of white anxiety toward the Native American. Natachee, the novel's only Indian character, has been educated by white men and yet has returned to his Native American roots, renouncing the white culture that has given him such knowledge. He is alternately a hero and a villain, mentally torturing the white hero Hugh Edwards yet also willing to help save Marta Hillgrove from Mexican bandits. A liminal figure in the novel, he migrates between two worlds. Natachee can exist in white and Indian cultures, though the novel makes clear that biology determines his "true" identity. Given such contradictions, Wright's narrative must appease the anxieties caused by the Native American. Wright's portrayal of Natachee suggests that while the Native American might be able to take on the trappings of white culture, the biological imperative toward primitivism will win out. As a result, the Indian must be contained socially as well as geographically. Natachee, living free of the reservation, arrives unseen and departs unheard. He represents movement unfettered, and his arrivals and departures cause uneasiness and even haunt the white settlers who live there, as even he admits. After Wright describes him as "the living spirit of the untamed deserts and mountains," Natachee says, "You say that I, Natachee, come and go as a ghost. Well, perhaps I am a ghost" (1923, 115).

Wright's narrative displays at once a belief in white superiority (morally and intellectually) and guilt over the treatment of Native Americans. When Natachee tells Edwards of the Native American's demise at the hands of white settlers, Edwards can feel pity and sympathy even though Natachee tortures him. And after Natachee's capture by the Mexican bandits, Edwards rescues him without a thought as to his race—and in a chapter entitled "The Way of a White Man" (1923, 241). The title compares Edwards's humanitarian aid with Natachee's selfish torture, judging white virtue more pure. Edwards's actions demonstrate the moral value of whiteness, earning him not only respect but financial reward. Natachee's assistance in regaining Marta Hillgrove and his decision to give Edwards gold from the hidden mine combine to enact a transference of value onto whiteness. The resources of the land become Edwards's and the Indian his willing partner.

While Wright may sympathize with the Native American's plight, his heart lies with the ideology of white superiority. He dissipates the Native threat first through geographic relocation and then through a display of superior white cultural behavior. Edwards's rescue of Natachee places him in the white man's debt, allowing Wright to enact yet another symbolic pairing of Native American assistant and white man, mirroring James Fenimore Cooper and similar American authors. Yet Edwards neither tortures Natachee nor seeks revenge against George Clinton, the man who drove him to the borderlands with false accusations of embezzlement. Natachee converts to Edwards's companion after the rescue, an act that translates narrative anxiety from internal questions of "American" identity to external notions of border panic. But Natachee, though subdued by gratitude for Edwards's unselfish act, nevertheless remains behind in the valley. Contained geographically by his duty in guarding the ancient mine of his people, he further haunts the book in intriguing ways. What is clear, however, is that the virile Edwards has taken the gold and Marta as his deserved treasure. The bestowal grants him legitimacy and restores him to his former identity, allowing him to leave the borderlands for his home in the central United States. Yet Wright cannot resolve his Indian plot so neatly, and leaves Natachee watching the wilderness in solitude as a symbol of the Vanishing American. Wright cannot imagine truly including the Native American in American culture, depicting him instead as willingly separate in a primitive world apart, soon to fade away. Wright's novel thus removes the threats posed by internal and external border figures, leaving only the romance of whiteness to define American identities and values. Yet while Sonora Jack can be dismissed as villainous, Natachee is not so easily contained. His visage haunts the landscape of the novel as the Native American haunted the Twenties' social landscape, another melancholic revenant destabilizing boundaries as social constructions delimiting power to whiteness.

THE MONGREL TWENTIES

"Border panic" manifested itself across the United States, influencing local practices and national debates. White masculine anxieties over decreasing autonomy and control of the body politic led to a national dialogue on the means by which to define the nation and its inhabitants. Against such challenges, however, white men instituted national and regional borders in order to cement their claims to "American" identity and to defend whiteness against perceived contamination. The compartmentalization of races and ethnicities across the late nineteenth and early twentieth centuries contributed to the ongoing power of whiteness. The Twenties, then, hosts a debate between those who saw what Ann Douglas calls "Mongrel Manhattan" as exemplifying the present and future United States and those who resisted that pronouncement in a nostalgic return to a purer white identity which denied hybridity and fluidity through claims to purity that undergirded its power and assuaged its "border panic." The "color line" in the Southwest became a social marker of the uneven power flows at work in the US terrain and a site of contest over definitions of American whiteness.

NOTES

1. I adapt this term from Eve Sedgwick's notion of "male homosexual panic," which she outlines in *Between Men* and further expostulates in *Epistemology of the Closet* "Male homosexual panic" is, as Sedgwick describes,

> a secularized and psychologized homophobia which has excluded certain shiftingly and more or less arbitrarily defined segments of the [male homosocial] continuum from participating in the overarching male entitlement–in the complex web of male power over the production, reproduction, and exchange of goods, persons, and meanings. (1985, 185)

   The problem, however, lies in the shifting and contradictory notions of homosexuality that undermine and disrupt strict binaristic identifications. The stringent exclusion of one section of the male homosocial continuum paradoxically demonstrates the constructedness of all masculine homosocial behaviors, thus undermining the ideology that would rigidly determine power relations. Border panic similarly restricts a defined set of persons from accessing full citizenship because of certain identificatory parameters.

2. John Higham's *Strangers in the Land* remains the definitive account of this period in US history. Gary Gerstle's *American Crucible* provides a useful update, however, combining Higham's archival work with insights derived from racial theorists. See also Cedric Robinson's *Black Movements in America* and Brian Dippie's *Vanishing Americans* for discussions of internal migration.

3. See Bhabha's *The Location of Culture*, and particularly his essay "Dissemination."

4. Donald Pease argues for the emergence of transnationalism in our current "postmodern" age, marking it as a divergence of the "nation," or ideologically imagined community, from the "state," or bureaucratic organization of government:

   > Recharacterizing this display of state power as the national people's desire to recover a lost origin, national narratives have enchained a series of events as the unfolding of this collectively shared desire. But as the demarcations of its limits, postnational narrations have struggled to make visible the incoherence, contingency, and transitoriness of the national narratives and to reveal this paradoxical space (1997, 8).

   > Rather than envision the present as a historically progressive moment where "nations" have gone out of favor as we move into a globalized and digitized economy, I argue that the United States has gone through a series of trans-national moments as the ideologies of nation and the actions of the state become more or less synchronous, with the 1920s a particularly apt example.

5. For a catalog of such films, see Keller 37-110.

6. The title's reference to Dumas' *The Man in the Iron Mask* further accentuates the text's connection to ideas of masked or hidden identities.

REFERENCES

Archdeacon, Thomas J. 1983. *Becoming American: An Ethnic History*. New York: Free Press.

Baxter, George Owen. 1929. *Tigerman*. Boston: G.K. Hall.

Berlant, Lauren. 1991. "National Brands/National Body: *Imitation of Life*." In

Comparative American Identities: Race, Sex, and Nationality in the Modern Text, Ed. Hortense J. Spillers. New York: Routledge, 110–140.

Bhabha, Homi. 1994. *The Location of Culture*. London: Routledge.

Bourne, Randolph. 1920. "Trans-National America." In *History of a Literary Radical*, ed. Van Wyck Brooks. New York: Huebsch.

Frost, Robert. 1914. *A Boy's Will*. New York: Holt.

———. 1915. *North of Boston*. New York: Holt.

Grant, Madison. 1922. *The Passing of the Great Race*. New York: Scribner's.

Higham, John. 1955. *Strangers in the Land: Patterns of American Nativism, 1860–1925*. New Brunswick: Rutgers University Press.

Keller, Gary D. 1994. *Hispanics and United States Film: An Overview and Handbook*. Tempe: Bilingual.

Lorey, David E. 1999. *The US–Mexican Border in the Twentieth Century: A History of Social and Economic Transformation*. Wilmington, DE: Scholarly Resources.

Michaels, Walter Benn. 1995. *Our America: Nativism, Modernism, and Pluralism*. Durham: Duke University Press.

Mitchell, Lee Clark. 1996. *Westerns: Making the Man in Fiction and Film*. Chicago: Chicago University Press.

Painter, Nell Irvin. 1987. *Standing at Armageddon: The United States, 1877–1919*. New York: Norton.

Pease, Donald. 1997. "National Narratives, Postnational Narration." *Modern Fiction Studies* 43(1): 1–23.

Redfield, Marc. 1999. "Imagi-Nation: The Imagined Community and the Aesthetics of Mourning." *Diacritics* 29(4): 58–83.

Robinson, Cedric. 1997. *Black Movements in America*. New York: Routledge.

Salvidar, Jose David. 1997. *Border Matters: Remapping American Cultural Studies*. Berkeley: University of California Press

Scruggs, Charles and Lee VanDeMarr. 1998. *Jean Toomer and the Terrors of American History*. Philadelphia: University of Pennsylvania Press.

Sedgwick, Eve Kosofsky. 1985. *Between Men: English Literature and Male Homosocial Desire*. New York: Columbia University Press.

———. 1990. *Epistemology of the Closet*. Berkeley: University of California Press.

Seltzer, Mark. 1992. *Bodies and Machines*. London: Routledge.

Stoddard, Lothrop. 1921. *The Rising Tide of Color Against White World Supremacy*. New York: Scribner.

Stout, Joseph A. 1999. *Border Conflict: Villistas, Carrancistas, and the Punitive Expedition, 1915–1920*. Fort Worth: Texas Christian University Press.

Wald, Priscilla. 1995. *Constituting Americans: Cultural Anxiety and Narrative Form*. Durham: Duke University Press.

Wright, Harold Bell. 1923. *The Mine With the Iron Door*. New York: Appleton.

Young, Robert J.C. 1995. *Colonial Desire: Hybridity in Theory, Culture, and Race*. New York: Routledge.

CHAPTER 6. WHITE-OUT

Peter Fine, New Mexico State University
Aaron Fine, Truman State University

Fine, Peter. *Barbed Flag*. 2008. Photograph. From the collection of the artist.

While traveling home over the Thanksgiving holiday a young man in the airport was overheard speaking on his cell phone about the election of Barack Obama. At one point in the conversation he offered the wry observation that "the problem is that most Americans aren't Americans these days." He was evidently comfortable enough in his own skin to feel assured of his own American-ness; overlooking what should be apparent to all Americans, that his ancestors were, at some point, themselves, not Americans. No doubt the story of his own origins beyond the borders of the US was negotiated through a process of acquiring wealth or "class." Though he spoke with a Texas accent, wore cowboy boots, and was headed home, his appearance, minus these signifiers, might have suggested origins as diverse as Middle Eastern, Southern European, Native American or Hispanic. All of these contradictory readings of his person were subsumed within the larger image of what it is to be an American. A single white body without borders, a body that appears to blend in with its surroundings.

Our investigation begins: "Five years after the Abu Ghraib photographs were released to the public, definitively lifting the cloak off human rights violations being perpetrated by our government, why has public response been so negligible, almost invisible?" We believe that this is because of, not in spite of, the release of these photographs and other tangible threats to our civil liberties. Documentation and publication of these crimes was implicit in them from the beginning, as these prisoners were being "made an example of." In discussing extraordinary rendition our aim will be to provide an historical vantage point from which we might compare and link these disappearances with the parallel process of racial passing in America. Our title "White-Out" defines an environment where forms become invisible. It suggests the danger of losing sight of one another, and of becoming lost by blending in. Finally, to white-out is to erase an error, a fault, or a failing.

Atzberger, Elizabeth, *Obama with Noise*, 2008. Photograph. From the collection of the artist.

How we enter into whiteness is troubled by the threat that others might shift or blur the line. Danger always lurks at the door. The man who enters the convenience store needs a host of social skills, of cultural capital, a manner of being, a disarming ensemble of cues. The same man who appears suspicious on the convenience store security monitor is granted color free status as the President-Elect on television. As a candidate, Barack Obama personified public anxiety about passing in the form of a terrorist threat, most vividly in the July 21, 2008 *New Yorker* cover in which he and his wife Michelle celebrate their victory with a "terrorist fist bump." Discussion of the cover reached far beyond the typical *New Yorker* reader through cable news outlets in what was perhaps the first truly "high-tech lynching."

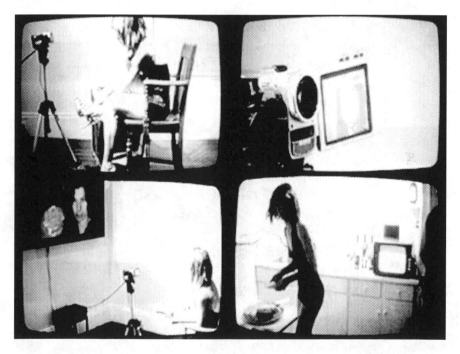

Cohen, Liz, *LIZA MINELLI a problem in translation*, 2001. Video, still. From the collection of the artist.

The logic of race, passing, human rights abuses, enemy combatants, and so on, depends on clear-cut distinctions between "us" and "them" that are often quite elusive. In her video performance "LIZA MINELLI a problem in translation," Liz Cohen plays both herself as interviewer and Liza Minelli, a transgender sex-worker she interviewed in Panama. The interviewer asks Liza a question in Spanish. Liza responds in Spanish. Her responses mimic her responses in the actual interview. The interviewer then translates Liza's response to English. The translation blends aspects of Liza's biography and Cohen's autobiography. Spanish speakers get one story. English speakers get another. The bilingual audience gets two stories to negotiate. Cohen, herself born in Colombia to a Sephardic father and a Catholic mother, emigrated to the US as a child, was raised in Phoenix, and later traveled to Panama where her Colombian family had moved. Here she began taking photographs on the edges of US society. The sex workers Cohen photographed were paid by their clients, US military personnel, in US dollars, the legal tender of Panama. Cohen's work among transgender sex workers in the Panama Canal Zone, a tiny slash that divides North from South and bridges East with West, attempts to straddle the variegated edges of American-ness. The noise in her video is all that separates the many images that modulate her own identity and those of her subjects.

To pass is to embody the paradox of race and color, to disrupt the notion of absolute racial categories. If there is pressure to pass from threats to body and soul there are also incentives to pass in terms of personal fulfillment and adventure. The threat of disappearance is both physical and psychic. The body is threatened with ruin or removal while the mind is besieged by the message of one's own inferiority. Both threats contribute to the pressure to pass. Passing is frequently treated as a deceitful, self-hating, complicit, and disloyal act. It is condemned as inauthentic, a betrayal of one's people and a self-inflicted wound on one's own psyche. But this judgment is an attempt to categorize a person who deliberately resists categorization. How can one be inauthentic or unfaithful to an identity that is both objectively uncertain and enforced by irrational and immoral racial codes?

In their graphic novel *Incognegro*, Mat Johnson and Warren Pleece play out the ways in which a black reporter passing for white details extralegal justice and its visual record of photographic trophies. These souvenirs are then used as evidence to criminalize the accepted practice of lynching. Zane, the protagonist, passes in order to slyly leverage the power of whiteness to seek justice. In this case passing is seen as empowerment—a means to subvert white privilege. What Zane calls "Assimilation as Revolution."

The danger of crossing the boundaries of whiteness are inscribed in the case of his friend Carl who, also passing for white on his first journey below the Mason–Dixon line, is lynched when he overplays his hand by affecting British speech and mannerisms. His efforts and the results chronicle the reaction to African American's middle class aspirations and the ways they were continuously ridiculed in order to guard against their entrance into full American-ness.

Johnson, Mat. *Incognegro*. Drawing, single image. Incognegro, Vertigo, 2009

The border, an arbitrary line of demarcation, provides both a concrete site for passing and a metaphor for the act of passing wherever it may occur on the map. The "illegal" migrant covertly crosses a border by traveling across it but must also cross a line in people's perceptions in order to be seen as an insider. To cross into American-ness by passing as part of the crowd. To pass by blending in.

David Taylor's photographs reevaluate the narratives that make up our understanding of the American West, with particular attention to the US/Mexico borderlands. What Taylor refers to as: "A moving target with meaning that is contingent on vantage point" (personal communication). Taylor reflects further on his work:

> The literal meaning of the word "frontier" is identical in both English and Spanish. However, its vernacular usage in each language is strikingly different. In the American psyche the frontier is an elusive destination; the locus of such national allegories as individuality, self-reliance and freedom. It is "The-Great-Out-There-Just-Beyond-the-Horizon." Conversely, "la frontera" adheres to literal definitions—it is the border or borderline; it is a barrier. (Personal communication)

Taylor, David. *Working the line.* 2007. Photograph. From the collection of the artist.

In Taylor's photograph "Working the line," Taylor views the border near El Paso, Texas (the pass), as the line drawn in the sand, a cultural barrier that is naturalized in the media while constantly in jeopardy to the natural forces at work against it. His piece "Drag" demonstrates the constant process of marking and erasing that produces a palimpsest of the traversing of the line. Tires are literally dragged over the roads and trails along the border in order to erase the marks left by those who have come before and record the marks that will be left by those who come after. The vigilance required to guard against intrusion even from within borders is seen in "Highway Checkpoint, NM" a still of a Border Patrol checkpoint on an Interstate Highway within the borders of the US. Terrorists are commonly described as "taking advantage of the openness of our society." This turns suspicion inwards, asking us all to "report suspicious activity" and thus putting us all on guard lest our own activities come under surveillance or become suspicious.

A photograph of Taylor's like, "Detention Cell 3 (with serape), NM," appears ominous in a post 9/11 context in which border security is conflated with fighting terrorism, in a war against enemies without and within. The cell is wiped clean of the presence of the body leaving only the landscape over which the body has been carried.

Taylor, David. *Drag.* 2007. Photograph. From the collection of the artist.

The line dividing pure from impure meanwhile shifts unpredictably even as we seek to pass over it. The projection of power is a white privilege and a national military strategy. The United States has long projected power far beyond its borders. Early in our history this projection was directed at the frontier.

But since the frontier reached our borders we have carried on projecting power beyond them. Dinh Lee's "Persistence of Memory" series imagines the lasting residue of these projections in a cold war context, when the border was drawn between two superpowers. Today that border has been erased, resulting in the near-global omnipresence of US power.

The two bodies straddling the border of whiteness today are those forcibly removed and denied legal access, and undocumented immigrants seeking to enter the North. Both are in effect undocumented as neither is granted full access to economic and legal rights. In both cases the body itself may serve as the document in ascribing criminality. These bodies are often marked through bonds and torture and detained on the basis of visual evidence acquired through profiling.

David Taylor. *Highway Checkpoint*, NM. 2007. Photograph. From the collection of the artist.

David Taylor. *Detention Cell 3 (with serape)*, NM. 2007. Photograph. From the collection of the artist.

Rodriguez, Angelita. *Espejo*. 2008. Photograph. From the collection of the artist.

Angelita Rodriguez's work "Espejo" explores assimilation through codes presented and absented through dress experienced over time, across borders and on bodies. Rodriguez first crossed the border in her mother's belly, carrying with her folk traditions, language and her name. Rodriguez acts out the ways in which she crosses borders of language and labor, representing her self as seen by others. In the first image, Rodriguez, dressed in business attire, faces us with features unseen, her body populated by each name she is begotten by. In the second image she turns from us, her shoulders ringed by a Mexican folk dress, her figure inscribed with Anglo names. Rodriguez's bodily image marked through her movement over borders is a stand-in for what disappears in the dissonance created in negotiating multiple identities.

Rodriguez, Angelita. *Espejo*. 2008. Photograph. From the collection of the artist.

Jacob Munoz in his work "Color Blind" takes aim at race and stereotyping using color as the vehicle, revealing and re-visualizing information suppressed over several generations. Using a DNA test he was able to ascertain and make visible that he was 49% European, 28% Native American, 13% East Asian, and 10% Sub-Saharan African. Munoz mimics the methods employed by scientific racism i.e. using the "Color Blind" test as means for visualizing race. The viewer is engaged in an attempt to see past color while it is simultaneously presented as evidence of diversity. Assimilation is made palatable through the process of observation and its clinical associations. A detailed examination of complex identities is obscured by a fastidious obsession with seeing color. In the blind spot stands the body. The artist Kara Walker very brilliantly sheds light on this process by reducing figures to flat black silhouettes. Despite this democratizing formal device, we immediately fix the race and gender of her subjects, and find ourselves complicit in a game we might have thought ourselves above.

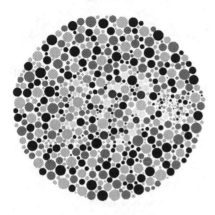

Munoz, Jacob. *Color Blind.* 2008. Digital Print. From the collection of the artist.

Munoz, Jacob. *Color Blind.* 2008. Digital Print. From the collection of the artist.

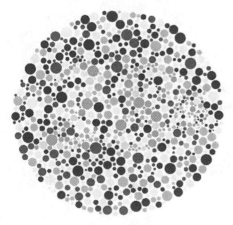

Munoz, Jacob. *Color Blind.* 2008. Digital Print. From the collection of the artist.

Munoz, Jacob. *Color Blind.* 2008. Digital Print. From the collection of the artist.

The body itself is another kind of document. It is the site where disputes over race, class, gender, nationality, etc. must be played out. It frequently bears the markers and the marks of identity. It also provides the evidence justifying either disappearance or passing.

The archive contains direct evidence of phenomena we relate to disappearance. These phenomena include lynching, beatings, forced marches, sexual abuse and humiliation, and unlawful detainment. But the archive rarely contains direct evidence of disappearance as such. One minute you are here. The next, you are gone.

The current challenge to due process, in which political dissenters face the threat of being "disappeared," is not without precedent in our nation. The United States (and its colonial forebears) has a long history of round-ups, deportations, internments, death marches, lynching and other extra-legal measures taken in response to others perceived as political and cultural threats. But this is only one side of a two-sided process of assimilation. Disappearance—of one form or another—is the stick, while access to American-ness is the carrot that encourages racial and ethnic minorities to pass over and into whiteness. Across the frontier of whiteness, the individual who fails to blend risks physical violence, while the individual who achieves whiteness, does so at the cost of their identity. Those who pass choose to become invisible rather than risk disappearing altogether.

It has been said that public outcry has been muted or absent over the recent reversal of civil liberties and human rights protections. And we are asked to seek out viable responses within the various forms of cultural production. We might first look to the history of protest against the threat of disappearance. If few spoke up it is fair to suppose that they were afraid. Who wishes to raise their hand in class when the teacher is beating a pupil? Those who are silent are calculating their own odds of going unnoticed, passing the test, or disappearing altogether. So instead of finding a record of speech we find meaning in conspicuous silences. Instead of locating visual artworks we observe the blind spots in the visual record.

CHAPTER 7. "SELF" AND "THE OTHER" A JOURNEY OF MUTUAL RECOGNITION

Graciela Susana Boruszko

Becoming...
> "Wanderer, there is no road,
> the road is made by walking."

> > *Caminante no hay camino*
> > *se hace camino al andar.*

> —Antonio Machado
> *Proverbios y cantares* XXIX

Echoing the Spanish poet Antonio Machado, it can be argued that the vocational journey follows one pathway in one direction even as the road is not always clear[1] (Machado 2006, 85; translation Craige 1978, 143). What makes the journey is not the road but rather the walk, that passionate inner drive to walk and live the adventure. If life does not present itself as a definite road, why should the vocational path allude to a clear direction? Is the direction the most important component in a vocational search? Does vocation emanate from our true meaningful identity? As Al-Sadat said:

> Without a vocation, man's existence would be meaningless...(Each man) should first recognize and be loyal to his real entity within...for it is this alone which will enable him to belong and owe allegiance to that Entity which is greater, vaster, and more permanent than his individual self (1978, 82).

Is vocation developed in each human being in a unique way or is it common to many mortals? William Wordsworth expressed this thought in this *Ode* (Wordsworth, n.d., n.p.):

> As if his whole vocation
> Were endless imitation.

As an individual sits down and starts to tell his or her story, the private story becomes public, while it has been part of the general history all along. This concept of the particular that takes place among the general is born from an inner need to be recognized in a society that treats us all as equals, regardless of our uniqueness. Our freedom and equality refer to the generalities of the references to human rights. In an era when ambiguities and changes occur at an accelerated pace, as we embark on the process of globalization we strive to find the equilibrium between freedom, acceptance and boundaries, between independence and recognition, between aliens and nationals, between integrating and excluding, between diversity and homogeneity. We are and become in relation to others but first the self needs to be. The self is molded within the community, thus reflecting its uniqueness as well as the integrative aspect of life that takes shape within a context. Those contexts are not constant anymore, responding as they do to swift world transformations that are accentuated by recurring migrations. Those seemingly parallel constructions of the self and the societies that nurture it are two complementary aspects taking place in the development of the self that require a certain balance so that they might work for the individual as well as for the community. In the collective History we find ourselves as part of society, and in our telling of our stories we find the individual with a unique voice that reaches out to be heard, to be present, to be recognized.

A few years ago I was invited to teach French to a group of advanced language students in Normandy, France. During our stay, we attended the commemoration of the landing of the American troops in Normandy during World War II. I gave the students an assignment to interview a military man and a villager. They were to capture two stories belonging to two Histories and make connections and approaches between them. It was a fascinating project as each student became captivated by the charm of the personal tangent in the linearity of History. They discovered the many worlds that lived together in a catastrophic event. By the telling of the stories and memories we analyzed the time modifiers of such traumatic events. When comparing the stories of neighbors living the same tragedy with their families, we found a window of revelations that ranged from contradictions to similarities. Coincidentally, the war in Iraq had just started and some of us had loved ones who had been deployed. We witnessed the timeless closeness of the human tragedy that shapes each individual in a unique way. Calderon de la Barca in his work *Life is a Dream* said:

> What is life? A madness.
> What is life? An illusion, a shadow, a story.
> And the greatest good is little enough: for all life is a dream, and dreams themselves are only dreams (de la Barca 1993, 1.1195).

In the same line of thought, what about the vocational pathway? How does it take shape in each life? Looking at a personal vocational journey we could find some characteristics that are common to other lives, but unavoidably it is the *person*, whether public or private, who excites interest. In the words of Sextus Propertius:

> The seaman's story is of tempest,
> the plowman's of his team of bulls;
> the soldier tells his wounds,
> the shepherd his tale of sheep (1906, 43).

We should not forget that the human character is constantly becoming, in a perpetual journey of transformation during which it declares its innermost imperfect characteristics, as Robert Frost so eloquently stated in his poem:

> And were an epitaph to be my story
> I'd have a short one ready for my own.
> I would have written of me on my stone:
> I had a lover's quarrel with the world. (Frost 1973, 87)

My life happened at the intersections of many cultures, fashioning in me a flexible comparative outlook, an inexhaustible fountain of creativity that filled in the cracks left by the absence of resources in my life in the mission field. The stage where my vocational walking played out was in conversations with those journeying with me. The constant was the presence of others rather than a familiar landscape. My personal history was being unfolded in a tight connection with the collective history of those that we served in the mission field in remote areas of South America. It is a story of love, of service and of sacrifice for the "other." A strong sense of hospitality was the axis of my relationship to the "others" that were incessantly different and to whom I was different, too. That is why conversations became the bridges that could bring us closer. I did not know the "other," but he or she was there, looking at me, and I was looking at them, at each one of them individually. A dialogue started and soon there was a conversation that led us along the road to understanding. Hospitality and conversations constituted a two-way road. I learned and practiced listening and telling, as those are the keys to life in community. We made time for both. The indigenous groups seemed comfortable in the practice of those skills that are dangerously disappearing from our post-modern society that induces us to carry on hectic, isolating and self-ish lives. A version of one of Sir Walter Raleigh's earlier poems that illustrates this thought was found, at his death, written in his Bible in the Gatehouse at Westminster.

> Even such is time, that takes in trust
> Our youth, our joys, our all we have,
> And pays us but with age and dust;
> Who in the dark and silent grave,
> When we have wandered all our ways,
> Shuts up the story of our days.
> And from which earth, and grave, and dust,
> The Lord shall raise me up, I trust (Lacey 1973, 412).

The presence of love and sacrifice as my family and I served "others" inserted my personal story into a collective story and into the sacred story. I did not decide to love these people; I was taught how to love them, and later on, love was born in me. This love was channeled through storytelling as I sat with the indigenous children and listened to "their stories," as my father told me "traditional stories," and then as I heard the "biblical stories." The fictional stories or "beautiful lies" came together with the "biblical stories." I grew to love all of the stories that in one way or another stimulated my imagination, already active, as I went from place to place discovering so many new mysteries and new things that fed my imagination constantly. Hence, my personal experiences, as well as my inner inclinations, patiently shaped my mind towards the fascination for "stories" and the languages used to communicate them. The social context of stories being recounted to me created an immediate, collective and communal scenario where stories were shared. The languages, as media to communicate directly or to suggest that which I did not understand, became magical and fascinating. Maybe it was the preparation for a future academic curiosity when this interest took the shape of an intellectual inquiry. These experiences that today have become stories, my stories, would lead me to my vocation through the personal pathway in life. As I wanted to peek behind the story and discover the little threads that moved the characters and changed the scenarios, it was life itself that challenged me to see behind the obvious, behind the known.

It was the daily connection with many different cultures and languages that created in me an enticement for the miracle of communication as a means to be a part of the never-ending kaleidoscopic relations with "the others." Therefore, letters and linguistics acted as motivators for this long journey permeated with the same passion. As I keep joining new learning communities, I can see that in the articulation of thoughts, knowledge, emotions, in the regular practice of academia, the conversation keeps on enlarging as I keep on becoming. My contribution to the academic conversation is the result of a personal journey along which I was mentored by means of direct contact with nature, by contact with the ancestral knowledge of different ethnic groups, by teachers, by elders, by spiritual leaders, by multiple voices that shaped in me a unique blend of messages and perspectives that participate in my daily practice of academia. That is how Western thought, Christian beliefs and the traces of ancestral wisdom that were transferred to me emerge as the conversations take place. The coexistence of those seemingly contradictory streams of thought and knowledge create a synergy of reflection and praxis where the comparative aspect is predominant. Not surprisingly, I became a comparatist in my academic interest as well as in my daily life. The comparative approach motivates me to keep faithful to my vocation that surfaced in "the road," as Antonio Machado says. My vocation was born, shaped and developed as I kept walking, eliciting the coincidence of the private life and the academic community life.

The praxis of a literary comparatist is to explore options, to create, to reconsider the real and imaginary worlds that overflow in conversations, where agreements and disagreements are equally important and equally valuable. The conversations create mutuality, connectivity, openness and interest for the other while cultivating a strong sense of humility as we are constantly reminded that we are all "making our way as we walk." That is why errors, pains (those self inflicted, and even those regretfully inflicted on others), joys, disappointments, and every other conceivable result of the interactions become valuable in the life of the traveler.

The practice of the conversations helps us to stay humble (close to the humus where we all come from) along with helping the development of a culture of hospitality. Hospitality is an ancestral practice and virtue that is becoming more and more rare and difficult to practice as our world is seemingly turning towards "civic rights" while becoming "less civil." Milton captures this thought in one of his poems:

> So saying, with dispatchful looks in haste
> She turns, on hospitable thoughts intent (Milton 1975, 1.331).

The well-known Benedictine hospitality underlined the complexity of the mutual adaptation of the community and the expectations of the "guests" or travelers that solicited shelter in their monasteries. Hospitality was more than a virtue; it constituted a right of the traveler rooted in the human condition. It brings to mind the ritual of *Las Posadas* of some Hispanic communities. During

Christmas time, a group of "pilgrims" goes from home to home, and at each place an ancient exchange is repeated.

> Those playing the role of Joseph approach the (house) inn, knock on the door, and say in a loud voice *En nombre del cielo, Buenos moradores, dad a unos viajeros posada esta noche* (In the name of God, we ask those who dwell here, give to some travelers lodging this evening). From inside, a chorus of voices responds, *Aquí no es mesón sigan adelante; yo no puedo abrir no sea algun tunante* (This is not an inn; move on—I cannot open lest you be a scoundrel)...For eight days, the scene is reenacted... In an outpouring of joy and festivity, those gathered on the final night celebrate the generosity of the innkeeper and the *posada* given to Mary and Joseph in song and dance, food and drink. Candy and treats from the piñata shower the children, and the community recalls anew how the stranger at one's door can be God in disguise. (Bass 1997, 30)

We can see that as the human need for hospitality is present, so is the human fear of the stranger. To be hospitable to the ideas of the others is, at once, to be sure of our own ideas while "making room" for that which is different. This practice greatly influenced my vocational journey as the revealing and shaping of my vocation was interwoven with the other that journeyed with me.

As Haughey (2004, 83) suggests: "A further idea of discerning one's vocation in life can be extrapolated from the Qur'anic concept of discernment. The Qur'an repeatedly states that God has placed signs upon the horizons and in human beings themselves, which they should attempt to read and reflect upon." Haughey continues: "These signs are known as *anfusi* (of the self) and *afaqi* (of the horizons) after a Qur'anic verse, 'We shall show them our signs in the horizons and in themselves' (41:53)" (2004, 83). Elaborating on this same thought, the Persian poet Sa'di (1292) wrote: "Every soul is created with a certain purpose and the light of that purpose has been kindled in that soul" (quoted in Khan 1973, 18). This idea can be associated with the poem of T. S. Eliot:

> With the drawing of this Love and the voice of this Calling
> We shall not cease from exploration
> And the end of all our exploring
> Will be to arrive where we started
> And know the place for the first time. (Eliot, 1963 208)

There lies the concept of knowledge being born each time that we dare to keep walking and engaging with our environments. In the Christian perspective, academicians are called to live up to their Christian values in spite of the circumstances. Tirso de Molina (pseudonym of Gabriel Téllez), the second most prolific Spanish dramatist of the seventeenth century, a friar of the Mercedarian Order, constitutes a great example of this struggle between vocations and their circumstances. Tirso combined two vocations into one: a religious man and a man of letters. His production includes most of the types of plays cultivated in the seventeenth century, among them: theological comedies, biblical comedies, comedies of the life of saints, historical comedies, comedies *costumbristas*, comedies of intrigue and *autos sacramentales*. This duality in his vocation created contradictory responses from the society of his time as he wrote comedies of a profane nature while he belonged to a religious order. Spanish society of the seventeenth century was deeply religious, so Tirso's choice of drama as a means to convey the Christian salvation message was controversial. His work was repeatedly censored while the writer defended it as he used the theater as a pulpit from which to preach Christian concepts as well as morality. His literary career was parallel to his intense religious commitment. Tirso de Molina was nonetheless the creator of one of the greatest Spanish myths, "Don Juan," which would later be turned into a more universal myth by the recurrent re-interpretations of the myth. In his drama, *El Burlador de Sevilla*, Tirso warns that only those who repent in a timely way attain the Christian salvation. Don Juan, the Spanish myth of the womanizer, gets lost in his bulimic quest for the satisfaction of his inner desires. In the story, Don Juan is finally condemned; not because of his lack of morals but because he neglected the salvation of his soul.

This is a great example of two vocations that are developed in parallel and replicated in a literary production that also reflects the dual interest of the writer: an interest to participate in a dialogue with the society of his time as well as to convey a message that represented his religious beliefs. It seems that two vocations gave place to a deeper calling, enriching each individual vocation as they stimulated the author to become intimately grounded with the society as he articulated the expression of self with the life of others. To be a Christian academician seems to be just that: to be, to live in the practice of Christianity and its values. To be a Christian academician is to believe; that is to say, to accept, to credit, to trust the Christian beliefs while making room for a hospitable atmosphere for those who do not believe. A Christian academician is the person who strives to live according to the faith in all areas of his or her life. It is not a battle against others but a standing firm on what we believe in spite of our human frailty, while keeping on the conversations, recognizing we all have a contribution to make to this world. Kindness, gentleness, compassion and all the other Christian virtues are the ones that should guide the practice of academy. This includes acknowledging and accepting legitimate conflict that leads to more conversations, conversations that help us to grow in understanding and to stay humble in attitude. I would argue that divergent perspectives do not call for reconciliation but to remain standing at ease side by side while we disagree on that issue. That is hospitality. It does not require the merging of discrepancies but seeks to let every thought stand on its own and let everyone decide in the intimacy of his or her consciousness. One of the secrets of hospitality is that it is practiced towards "strangers," so different natures are inherently included. Being different, being "a stranger," takes many shapes in society in general. It could include the elderly who are isolated from the affection and care of their loved ones; children who come to empty homes after school; those who have no voice; the differently able; the mentally ill that would seem to be excluded from moral conversations.

Another characteristic of hospitality is that it can only be learned by the practice of it. As anything else in life, it is an art by means of the ways in which we execute it. If we are going to be hospitable with those who think alike and are part of "our group," then it is only one kind of hospitality. Its importance may be recognized, but, nevertheless, there is more to it. In many academic communities, it seems that there is an urge to exhibit hospitality towards those who think differently, but in the intimacy of the community the hospitable atmosphere is not always observed. Sometimes the distinction between insiders and outsiders seems to be erased as both receive a treatment far from welcoming. Hospitality toward the "stranger," "the outsider," the "one who is different," the "one who is vulnerable," the "one who is traveling," is practiced by offering him or her a place of refuge, a place of rest, not a place of manipulation in which to convince him or her of our own perspectives. As Lindbergh affirmed: "When one is a stranger to oneself, then one is estranged from others too" (Lindbergh 1955, 43–44). The ideas and thoughts are shared in the action, "in the walk," as the poet says.

An interesting factor to consider is that hospitality flourishes at the intersection of public and private life. Academic hospitality should include both. As members of the University, both hospitalities are equally important if we are going to be contributing members of a mutually nourishing community. Hospitality does not impose any limitations, although it seems to happen at the peripheries of social and moral boundaries. It appears that this marginality makes the practicing of academic hospitality dreadfully risky and dangerous, involving the fear of failing at it; nonetheless the risk of disregarding it is greater. As a contrast we should mention that hospitality connotes a sense of being temporary. A permanent hospitality is the product of further negotiations that take place at a later stage. We are considering the initial, temporary, hospitality when in the broad practice of academia we make room for new and different ideas and opinions.

I can affirm that the most important factor in my personal growth was the participation of the many other "travelers" who shared the road with me. They are the ones who contributed to the becoming of who I am in general and in academia specifically. That is why I can see that my journey was marked by those early years when I received hospitality from those whom I was serving as well as by welcoming in a hospitable environment those who intersected our paths, "the strangers" and the "kin" alike. But hospitality has a price. It always involves generosity and the giving away of something. It requires an initiative to welcome, to include the "stranger." It also requires a proper attitude of gratitude and respect for the giver. It is at this moment of a hospitable transaction that it could be a positive exchange of mutual benefit or a broken experience when at least one party ends up losing in the material arena as well as in the emotional, cultural and spiritual realms. It involves inherently the presence of those "travelers" who are destructive to the hospitable atmosphere. If one does not understand the two-way exchange, then this member will unavoidably end up by self-excluding himself or herself from a community that operates under welcoming parameters that contrasts with the exclusionist policy that does not allow openness.

Let's make clear that it is an inappropriate behavior rather than a political, religious or ideological discrepancy that causes the break of the hospitable atmosphere. Territorialism is constituted through a series of imaginary as well as real demarcations that are sometimes hard to delineate but are instinctively clear to the individual. That is why the obligation to show hospitality to the "other" cannot be enforced. It is solely a decision of the will of each individual or of a certain community. In academia, hospitality constitutes a bridge connecting all areas of study and academic interests. The relating factor is not based on beliefs but on the practice of the virtue of hospitality that responds to a human right without necessarily creating a consensus. As a matter of fact, in an active community that is constantly seeking to reach out to the "other," disagreements are more common than agreements. Hospitality as an art has to be cultivated. It is not easy or natural, but in the challenge lies the opportunity to grow and to become more of what we can be in isolation.

STILL BECOMING NURTURED IN THE HOSPITALITY OF CONVERSATIONS

In daily conversations with our students, we continue to practice the hospitality that others previously extended to us. It becomes, in time, a modus operandi. In teaching languages, cultures, and literatures, the hospitable conversation constitutes the optimal way to convey to our students the content of such disciplines. The same atmosphere that reigns in the classroom should permeate the mentoring of our students. As the language instructor becomes a primary representative of the cultures being taught, we become an exponent of the characteristics of the culture and language that the students are learning. That is when and why our teaching and our conduct represent both our personal and academic life. As we open our offices for more extensive conversations, students seem to expect the continuation of the same cultural warmth in the course of a fine dialogue. Given the fact that in a typical language instruction class we touch on all aspects of life, as language is such a living entity, students become used to dialogue about all aspects of life, so the mentoring opportunity rises naturally beyond the personal hospitality. When we teach in one of several languages, a two-way road is created where, at times, students find themselves putting forward an evasive term. It encourages students to see a softer human side of academia.

A learning community is built through the contributions that each student makes. If the learning community is of a heterogeneous nature, then the classroom becomes a stage upon which to live the diversity and plurality of our world. This is the golden opportunity of academia to lead in conversations that shape society. Language and literature are two interwoven paths where the human expression intersects creating a voice. Conversations are the scenarios in which to meet and communicate in communion. Along with the dialogue comes the acceptance, the welcoming atmosphere that can be created. As Joseph Addison (2004, 128), in *The Spectator*, affirmed: "Good nature is more agreeable in conversation than wit, and gives a certain air to the countenance which is more amiable than beauty." That is where the instructor crafts the hospitable environment so that the student can learn the skill of cultivating a dialogue of cultures. William Somerset Maugham in his work *The Trembling of a Leaf* illustrates this thought: "Do you know that conversation is one of the greatest pleasures in life? But it wants leisure" (Maugham, 1921, 66). A community of learners is being formed. Wordsworth stated it in this poem:

> Brothers all
> In honor, as in one community,
> Scholars and gentlemen. (Wordsworth n.d., n.p.)

We can even hear resonate in our 21st century the words of President Roosevelt of his *Fourth Inaugural Address* of January 20, 1945:

> We have learned that we cannot live alone, at peace; that our own well-being is dependent on the well-being of other nations, far away. We have learned that we must live as men, and not as ostriches, nor as dogs in the manger. We have learned to be citizens of the world, members of the human community. (n.p.)

We could echo the words of Francis Bacon in his *Essays* ("Of Goodness and Goodness of Nature"), written in 1625: "If a man be gracious and courteous to strangers, it shows he is a citizen of the world, and that his heart is no island cut off from other lands, but a continent that joins to them" (n.d., n.p.). Even in our global community we can still hear the words of William Lloyd Garrison in his *Motto of the Liberator* of 1831: "Our country is the world—our country-men all mankind" (Nye 1955, 125). The evidence of our vocation, as we are called and respond to it on a daily bases, is also found in our students' lives. How are they practicing the language and literature that they studied with us? Knowledge is not stored in the memory bank of facts but in the equally important bank of living facts of shared memories. The personal calling is evidenced in the life of the professor by the passion that persists class after class and year after year. A calling or a vocation is like a marathon, a long obedience in one direction. Each stage of the race is different and presents new challenges, but overall we seem to come back to the same igniting passion that transcends the temporary and keeps us moving even further into the same calling. That is why the calling or the vocation is not a dated event but a daily decision to pursue it. The nurturing of our vocations is deeply rooted in our association with the others, being it colleagues or students or all other constituents that relate to us. The confirmation that as academicians we are contributing to a specific cause could be conveyed through many manifestations. It could come through the testimony of a student that found our mentoring stimulating and clarifying in his or her own quest for their vocation. One of the most fulfilling confirmations is when a student validates his or her own calling by "reading" our own practice of academia, through the influence of our praxis in addition to the content of our instruction. We teach in many ways, and teaching by example is the most efficient way to connect more personally with the student. The one-on-one time spent with the student is a golden opportunity when the issue of the quest for a vocation arises naturally. At the crossroad of struggle and hope, as in the *Pilgrim's Progress*, we struggle to speak honestly about our own calling. As in Bunyan's story the "being" is constantly becoming, struggling, changing, growing. Accepting this fact of ourselves will allow us to approach unassumingly the quest of our students. We confirm our vocations when we share with the learner our personal experiences, establishing a nexus of communication, even a certain communion with the student seeking to discover his or her vocation. Stories are life capsules shared in a narrative form. These stories become connectors as we are all fascinated by the story of the other; because we unavoidably will find our own story intertwined in it.

I cannot recall how many times I told my own story of how I discovered my calling and vocation when I was 16. As I grew up in the mission field, we move repeatedly from town to town and from country to country. At the age of 16, I was in Peru, having finished my high school education but not being able to continue with university studies due to my young age. I was sure that I wanted to be an astronomer as I cultivated an interest in the subject. The only constant in my migrating from place to place seemed to be in the skies while the land surrounding me was always different. I found it fascinating to learn from distant worlds and planets as the exercise of my imagination responded to the tension between the known and the unknown. Nonetheless, I felt stuck in Peru and I thought that I would be losing two years of my life waiting to be ready to continue my studies. I felt it was a very unfair predicament. Meanwhile my father, a missionary working at the time in a church located in a very marginal neighborhood of Lima, Peru, decided to appoint me the Sunday school teacher for the group of six-year-old children of the church.

That is how I found myself in front of a class of more than thirty children that had had no training on how to behave socially in an orderly manner. The first Sunday in front of the class was chaotic and I felt helpless watching the children run wildly. In my dismay, I discovered a girl of about eight years old who was standing by me. I was glad to announce to her that this was not her class and I thought that at least I could reduce my class by one. She kindly let me know that she had been appointed as my helper. Finding it hard to be thankful for such aid, and not furnished with any pedagogical training, I decided to take the children to the restroom, wash their faces and help them learn how to be presentable for a church gathering. By the time I finished with that long line in the restroom, I told them a short bible story and soon it was time for them to go home. I repeated that routine with a bad attitude since the task was imposed on me without much training or aid. After a few Sundays, when I thought I was making a very pointless effort to educate the children, one of the boys came to class with face cleaned, hair combed and shirt tucked inside his pants. He was visibly proud of his attention to personal grooming. This effort on his part was very remarkable given the fact that he lived in a precarious living accommodation without running water, in addition to being a member of a family that faced many challenges at the time. Immediately, I knew that lives could be touched and enriched by caring instruction. I asked the boy to be my helper and that Sunday there were two lines in the restroom and soon there were more. This experience changed my perception of my calling, of my vocation. I discovered the transcendental power of intersecting with a life and bringing more value to it. I then diverted my passion for the universes far away toward those who were close to me in the life of a student. I realized that I had a lot to give while still receiving much. I was fascinated by the synergy created by the intersection of the personal history, the collective history, and the sacred history all encapsulated in "stories" to be shared.

As I tell my stories, I challenge my students to "read" their own histories in an intersection with those of others in order to find the true passion of their lives. Their story takes them through different pathways but it always carries in itself a force that drives them all along. If the students can see the way we live our calling in teaching and researching, they can relate that to their own inner inclinations.

If our passion becomes unnoticeable to our students, then it might be time to redirect our vocation.

As an educator, I intentionally provide the students with as many scenarios as I can create in order to allow students to express their passions, even in a foreign language or in a literary story of the "other," so that they continue to understand the pathway toward cultural immersion in their unique social contexts that bring with them many more challenges. They also develop the skill of discernment, the ability to design a strategic, resourceful way to analyze and interpret the complex cultural paradigms. "The foreign" scenario of a different culture gives the student an opportunity to deploy many skills and discover new ones. It is in the contrasting reality of new cultures that the student finds yet another opportunity to know the intimacy of his or her being, thus allowing him or her to face the vocational decision with a more solid discernment. The skill of understanding is then elaborated and practiced in the discipline as a means to train the student to apply those methodologies to solve personal quests like the vocational discovery. Undergraduate studies constitute the stage in students' lives when they can explore and find, as individual contributors to society, where their vocations really fall. By stimulating and requiring the students to participate in service projects where they have to either be "the stranger" or reach to the "stranger," they learn that in the process of becoming closer to "the strange" it becomes familiar. This approach is not only the best way to acquire and learn the language studied, but also it is a transforming experience where the students find themselves reflected in some aspects of the life of the "other." Introducing the student to the appropriate venues that will inform their vocational discovery or vocational affirmation is a life-changing experience that parallels the language acquisition process or literary interpretation. To "read" in a foreign language, to "read" a literary work or to "read" the signs in society, even to "read" the person with whom we live day in and day out is just learning to discern the codes of communication, to let ourselves be surprised, or be wrong, or simply to be.

So "Wanderer, there is no road; the road is made by walking." It is by continuing to walk on the pathway of our vocation that we will affirm our calling and inspire and lead others in finding their own ways. The personal story reproduced into many other stories will touch still others in turn. The discernment of our calling and our mentoring will be revitalized when we hear the stories of those touched by our students. Then we will see the cycle completed.

I will leave you with the poetic thought of Antonio Machado as he has summarized this journey and my own journey in the last lines of his short poem.

>	and upon glancing behind

one sees the path
that never will be trod again.
Wanderer, there is no road—
Only wakes upon the sea.

> *y al volver la vista atrás*
> *se ve la senda que nunca*
> *se ha de volver a pisar.*
> *Caminante, no hay camino,*
> *sino estelas en la mar.*

NOTES

1. From Selected Poems of Antonio Machado

Wanderer, your footsteps are
the road, and nothing more;
wanderer, there is no road,
the road is made by walking.
By walking one makes the road,
and upon glancing behind
one sees the path
that never will be trod again.
Wanderer, there is no road--
Only wakes upon the sea.

****

> *Caminante, son tus huellas*
> *el camino, y nada más;*
> *caminante, no hay camino,*
> *se hace camino al andar.*
> *Al andar se hace camino,*
> *y al volver la vista atrás*
> *se ve la senda que nunca*
> *se ha de volver a pisar.*
> *Caminante, no hay camino,*
> *sino estelas en la mar.*

REFERENCES

Addison, J. 2004. "*The Spectator*, Number 169, September 13, 1711." In *Cato, A Tragedy and Selected Essays*, ed. Christine Dunn Henderson and Mark E.Yellin. Indianapolis: Liberty Fund Inc., 127–130.

Alonso Mendero, B. 1995. *Tirso de Molina El Burlador de Sevilla*. Madrid: Editorial Santillana.

Al-Sadat, Anwar. 1978. *In Search of Identity*. New York: Harper and Row.

Bacon, F. 1996. *Francis Bacon: Essays*. Oxford and New York: Oxford University Press.

Bass, Dorothy. 1997. *Practicing Our Faith*. San Francisco: Jossey–Bass.

Bain, K. 2004. *What the Best College Teachers Do*. Cambridge, MA: Harvard University Press.

Benhabib, S. 2004. *The Rights of Others: Aliens, Residents and Citizens*. Cambridge: Cambridge University Press.

Buechner, F. 1982. *The Sacred Journey: A Memoir of Early Days*. New York: Harper One.

Collins, L., J. Chrisler, and K. Quina. 1998. *Career Strategies for Women in Academe: Arming Athena*. Los Angeles: Sage Publications.

Connors, R. and P. McCormick. 1998. *Character, Community, and Choices*. New York: Paulist Press.

Craige, Betty Jean. 1978. *Selected Poems of Antonio Machado*. Baton Rouge: Louisiana State University Press.

De la Barca, Calderon. 1993. *Life is a Dream*. New York : Iasta Press.

Elliot, T.S. 1963. "Little Gidding." In *Collected Poems 1909–1962*. New York: Harcourt, Brace and World.

Frost, Robert. 1973. *A Witness Tree*. New York: Lenox Hill Press.

Haughey, J. 2004. *Revisiting the Idea of Vocation*. Washington, DC: The Catholic University of America Press.

Hill, J. 1979. *John Milton Poet, Priest and Prophet: A Study of Divine Vocation in Milton's Poetry and Prose*. Totowa, New Jersey: Rowman and Littlefield.

Hughes, R.. 2005. *The Vocation of a Christian Scholar*. Ann Arbor: William B. Eerdmans Publishing Company.

Jacobsen, D. and R. H. Jacobsen. 2004. *Scholarship and Christian Faith: Enlarging the Conversation*. New York: Oxford University Press.

Khan, H. 1973. *The Purpose of Life*. San Francisco: Rainbow Bridge.

Kerr, J. 2007. Monastic Hospitality: The Benedictines in England, c.1070–c.1250. Woodbridge: The Boydell Press.

Lacey, Robert. 1974. *Sir Walter Raleigh*. New York: Atheneum

Lindbergh, A. 1955. *Gift from the Sea*. New York: Pantheon.

Machado, Antonio. 2006. Madrid: Movimiento Cultural Cristiano.

Marshall, P. 1996. *A Kind of Life Imposed on Man: Vocation and Social Order from Tyndale to Locke*. Toronto: University of Toronto Press.

Milton, John. 1975. *Paradise Lost: An Authoritative Text, Backgrounds and Sources, Criticism*. New York: Norton.

Nye, R. 1955. *William Lloyd Garrison and the Humanitarian Reformers*. Boston: Little, Brown.

Palmer, P.J. 2007. *The Courage to Teach: Exploring the Inner Landscape of a Teacher's Life*. San Francisco: John Wiley and Sons.

Placher, W.C. 2005. *Callings: Twenty Centuries of Christian Wisdom on Vocation*. Ann Arbor: William B. Eerdmans Publishing Company.

Pohl, C.D. 1999. *Making Room: Recovering Hospitality in a Christian Tradition*. Ann Arbor: William B. Eerdmans Publishing Company.

Propertius, Sextus. 1906. *Elegies*. London: Oxford at the Clarendon Press.

Roosevelt, Franklin Delano. 1962. "Roosevelt, *Fourth Inaugural Address*, January 20, 1945." In *Contemporary Forum; American Speeches on Twentieth-Century Issues*, ed. J. Wrage and B. Baskerville. New York, Harper.

Smith, G.T. 1999. *Courage & Calling: Embracing Your God-Given Potential*. Illinois: Inter-Varsity Press.

Somerset Maugham, W. 1921. *The Trembling of a Leaf*. New York: George H. Doran Company

Taylor, C. 1992. *Multiculturalism and "The Politics of Recognition"*. Princeton: Princeton University Press.

Wentz, F.K. 1967. *My Job and My Faith: Twelve Christians Report on Their Work Worlds*. New York: Abingdon Press.

Wordsworth, W. N.d. *Ode: Intimations of Immortality from Recollections of Early Childhood*. The Literature Network. http://www.online-literature.com/wordsworth/523/

CHAPTER 8. NO ONE IS ILLEGAL: RESISTANCE AND BORDERS

Jeff Shantz

Much writing on capitalist globalization speaks of diminishing nation states in the face of growing trade and communications flows. Prominent analyses of contemporary movements have tended towards, on one hand, an uncritical celebration of smooth (borderless) aspects of globalism or, on the other hand, towards a "Left nationalism" that seeks to address the ills of globalization through appeals for a return to the protectionist Keynesian state. Despite apparent differences both approaches are underpinned by the same association of globalization with the decline of territorial nation states. Both perspectives fail to come to grips with the evolving role of the state in fostering or maintaining the inequalities associated with globalization.

Perhaps out of hopefulness more than analysis some social theorists have uncritically celebrated a perceived decline of nation states. Much has been made in recent social theory of the "flow" across borders supposedly characterizing the age of globalization. Thom Kuehls (1996) suggests that the emergence of "flows," notably satellite communications and the Internet, provide spaces for an enactment of politics beyond the bounded spaces of states. These emergent spaces of action "are said to offer great opportunities for activism beyond sovereign territories" (Shantz 1998, 97).

Even Left social activists have been drawn to emphasize mobility and the permeability of borders. For example, one activist and academic inspired by the works of Gramsci and Freire, suggests, perhaps hopefully, that "the complex process of globalization that has increasingly decentralized production and centralized decision-making has diminished the importance of borders and of the nation-states within them" (Barndt 1996, 243). New technologies, most notably the Internet, are credited with facilitating global communications and global networks of anti-capitalist activism. These networks have, in turn, facilitated a move beyond the nationalism that characterized earlier struggles such as those against free trade.

> Ironically, "free trade" has offered us some free space, especially opportunities to connect across borders: geopolitical borders, sectoral borders that divides [*sic*] us as social change workers, and epistemological borders, the borders within our minds that impede both our connecting and our acting together. (Barndt 1996, 243)

Certainly the last decade of capitalist globalization has seen important linkages across geopolitical and sectoral borders. Anti-capitalist activists have, since Seattle, brought about an important new phase in coalition politics. Countermovements must now attend to the difficult tasks of developing their strength among the disparate groups which when taken together form a majority increasingly excluded by the "New World Order" of global markets, transnational corporate structures and rapid financial and cultural "flows" (Shantz 2002). Great efforts have been made to connect workers and community groups around shared interests despite geographical distance. While these analyses have focused on important developments to organize global resistance to capitalist globalization, they have also tended to under-play the relevance of national state practices as part of globalization.

Recent events, most notably the criminalization, including imprisonment and killings, of anti-globalization activists, the extension of security forces since 9–11 and the military invasions and occupations of Afghanistan and Iraq, have shattered that hope and weakened this pole of analysis. At the same time the bold exposure of the truly imperialist nature of globalization sharply reminds us that struggles against borders, rather than diminishing, are perhaps the key struggles of our times.

The other side of the "state decline" coin has been a revival of Left nationalism or neo-Keynesianism which argues for a return to the social citizenship of the welfare state that, in North America, characterized the decades roughly from 1945 until the early 1980s. In Canada the perspective of resurgent Left nationalism has been most forcefully articulated theoretically by Gordon Laxer and the editors of venerable Left publication *Canadian Dimension*. Politically Left nationalism has been a central feature of trade unions like the Canadian Auto Workers (CAW) and union federations like the Ontario Federation of Labour (OFL). Nationalist approaches to globalization actually strengthen the state's claims when what is needed is a critique of emergent state practices.

Sharma (2002, 24) critiques sharply the "idea, very popular in much of the 'anti-globalization' movement, that what we need to counter the power of corporations is a strengthened national sovereignty." This neo-Keynesian approach "fails spectacularly to account for how that same 'sovereignty' is what destroyed communities of Indigenous peoples the world over and created highly exclusionary categories of membership based on ideas of "race, gender and sexual orientation" (Sharma 2002, 24). Indeed, nation states have provided the military force for the expansion and institution of capitalist ventures while organizing the very "nationalized boundaries that contain people, most obviously perhaps in the nationalized character of labour markets" which control the mobility of labor to ensure favorable conditions of exchange for capital (Sharma 2002, 24).

Against commentators who would argue that distinctions between here and there no longer mean anything in a wired world, Bauman (1998, 18) counters that "some people—in fact, quite a lot of them—still can, as before, be 'separated by physical obstacles and temporal distances,' this separation being now more merciless, and having more profound psychological effects, than ever before." Borders, and specifically state control of borders to free the transfer of capital while determining the movement of workers, maintain and extend processes of social polarization.

In fact, recent social transformations have been marked by what Bauman (1998, 23) identifies as "the extraterritoriality of the new elite and the forced territoriality of the rest." This "forced territoriality of the rest" is made more and more to resemble a prison for anyone confined to it. For growing numbers of people, the reality is quite literally a prison.

> For the inhabitants of the first world—the increasingly cosmopolitan, extraterritorial world of global businessmen, global culture managers or global academics, state borders are leveled down, as they are dismantled for the world's commodities, capital and finances. For the inhabitants of the second world, the walls built of immigration controls, of residence laws and of 'clean streets' and zero tolerance policies, grow taller; the moats separating them from the sites of their desire and of dreamed-of redemption grow deeper, while all bridges, at the first attempt to cross them, prove to be drawbridges. (Bauman 1998, 89)

This chapter re-situates the state as an active and crucial part of developing globalization processes. Rather than seeing a diminished role played by the state, this chapter highlights specific interventions by the state, especially around control of population movements, which play a crucial part in transforming social relations in the context of globalization. The chapter then focuses on emergent strategies and analyses deployed by new movements that contest transformed state practices.

These movements express what Sharma terms the "actual local," in opposition to nationalist ideas that conflate community and nation and nation state and home. Actual local movements call simultaneously for self-determination and global connectivity while confronting the new realities of statist border practices. In doing this they develop creative strategies to organize against the local agents of local capital, including nation states, while seeking to create political spaces and communities beyond appeals for state protectionism.

The chapter analyzes these emergent practices primarily through a discussion of some of the work undertaken by the Ontario Coalition Against Poverty (OCAP) and No One Is Illegal (NOII) over borders within the context of the Canadian state. It does so from the perspective of a participant in the struggles under discussion. A movement made up primarily of poor people, unemployed workers and homeless people of various backgrounds, OCAP and NOII have been poles of attraction for struggles against local regimes of neo-liberal global governance. Through direct actions, rank-and-file militance and community organizing based on a sense of solidarity of the excluded, OCAP and NOII have provided an impetus for a recomposition of class struggle forces across the borders which keep oppressed and exploited people divided. In doing so, their work provides important insights into the bridging of sectoral differences among movements of poor people, immigrants, refugees and Indigenous people.

RACIST IMMIGRATION PRACTICES IN CANADA SINCE SEPTEMBER 11

September 11 offered an excuse to openly display the cruel forces of xenophobia and racism which are ever present, if often denied, features of Canadian society.[1] Among the institutions feeding those renewed forces is the federal government with its zealous focus on "security" and manic obsession with the phantom of permeable borders. In an effort to show its allegiance to the US world order, the Canadian government has entered into discussions of joint agreements around border security and immigration controls up to and including the creation of a security perimeter around North America, a "Fortress North America."

Towards this end the Canadian government has taken a number of steps. On June 28, 2002, the Immigration and Refugee Protection Act was passed into law. The Act was passed with a number of troubling amendments, including the omission of appeal processes for refugee claimants (Zerehi 2003). Refugee claimants now have only 28 days following their interview with a Refugee Protection Officer to prepare a Personal Information Form and all required documents must be provided 20 days in advance of a hearing with the Immigration and Refugee Board. These are onerous deadlines which are difficult for many refugees to meet (Zerehi 2003). Because the decision-making panel has been reduced from two members to one, refugee protection decisions are now made by a single decision-maker with no right of appeal for applicants.

One of the most troubling changes to the immigration system has been the signing of the "safe third country" agreement with the US at the end of 2002 (CRIAW/ICREF 2003). This agreement, which was implemented in April 2004, means that refugees coming to Canada through the US will be immediately turned away at the border. In effect this will deny asylum to many people since the US refugee policies are more restrictive and require that refugee claimants apply within the first year of arrival. Return to the US also means mandatory detention (Zerehi and Scott 2003). Many of the routes for international travel to Canada go through the US (Zerehi 2003). Notably, this agreement may be extended to other countries that are deemed safe by the Canadian government. Unfortunately, the safety of a country is often gauged according to trade relations with Canada, rather than its human rights record (Zerehi 2003).

Perhaps the most disturbing immigration policy change has been the increased detention of immigrants and refugee claimants in Canada. Since September 11, 2001, alarming numbers of people have been detained in Toronto jails and detention centers, often in solitary confinement. Under Immigration Canada instructions issued at the beginning of 2003, officers can detain refugee claimants if interviewees are hesitant in responding to questions or if they fail to provide "sufficient documents" (Zerehi 2003; Zerehi and Scott 2003). Provision of sufficient documents does not ensure one's release as claimants must first post a bond in amounts averaging between $5000 and $10,000. While under detention people have been denied access to proper sanitation and medical care, and hearings often occur by video link. At the notorious Celebrity Inn, a motel near Toronto's Pearson International Airport used as a detention center, families are split up. There have been reports of denial of essential services and supplies to Canadian-born infants and children due to the (non)status of their caregivers (Zerehi 2003). Full information about people detained since September 11 has yet to be disclosed, even as late as 2009, despite the efforts of groups such as Anti-Racist Action and Colours of Resistance. In anticipation of growing numbers of detainees, Immigration Canada opened a new and expanded detention center on April 1, 2004, to replace the Celebrity Inn.

The Federal government is not alone in this. The recent neo-liberal Ontario government of Premier Ernie Eves and Minister of Public Safety and Security

Bob Runciman, has been one of the region's strongest forces for both free trade and immigration controls. Runciman called for an "Australian-style" detention system for Canada which would include a "jail first, ask questions later" policy. In Ontario alone, for 2002, $60 million was designated for public safety and security issues. That budget increased by $8 million for 2003 with more money for border policing. In the early days of the attack on Iraq, the provincial government implemented emergency plans to ensure the easy flow of corporate traffic across the border while limiting the movement of people. Part of the emergency plan for the border included closed consultations involving the Ontario Provincial Police, trucking industry representatives, business leaders, Canada Customs and US government officials.

The Great Lakes Security Summit, held in Toronto from April 7–9, 2003, brought together Canadian premiers and US governors from the Great Lakes region along with immigration officials, police representatives and business leaders for a joint conference on Canada–US "border security." Part of broader government efforts to develop a regional economic and security zone, the summit focused on integrating policing at all levels and across borders, harmonizing Canadian and US security and immigration laws and facilitating freer trade among provinces and states (Zerehi 2003). At the same time as the summit sought ways to free up the flow of goods across borders, it sought to increase restrictions on the movement of people between Canada and the United States. As Zerehi (2003, 21) notes, the summit's real agenda "was to facilitate neo-liberal globalization: the free movement of capital and goods, but zero mobility for workers."

"NO ONE IS ILLEGAL": ORGANIZING DEFENSE OF IMMIGRANTS AND REFUGEES IN CANADA

A broad coalition of anti-poverty, anarchist, socialist, labor and immigrant defense organizations, including the Ontario Coalition Against Poverty, the Canadian Union of Public Employees and Anti-Racist Action, No One is Illegal (NOII) is beginning to articulate, through public meetings and participation in actions, a mobilized resistance to the Canadian state's racist attempts to divide the working class locally and internationally. This is especially important given that the federal minister responsible for the government's newly established office of "public safety and security" has identified as his primary goal the creation of "an Australian-style detention system".

A painful illustration of the dangers facing us in this epoch is presented in microcosm by the recent experiences of three women who have been set upon by Canadian Immigration: Irma Joyles, Brendalyn MacDonald and Shirley-Ann

Charles. Despite each woman having lived in Canada for many years, working, attending school and raising families, Immigration authorities targeted them for deportation without hearings. In order to avoid having to make the awful choice between leaving her child behind without her only support or taking the child with her to a climate which will worsen her health, Irma has filed a Humanitarian and Compassionate Claim. Brenda, facing a similar impossible choice, has also filed a Humanitarian and Compassionate Claim. Unfortunately, Immigration authorities moved quickly and, with no hearing at all, Shirley-Ann was deported.

According to Canadian immigration policy, all three women were entitled to have Humanitarian and Compassionate claims heard. Instead, without explanation, officers were sent to Brendalyn's home to arrest her. In this time of war, increased "security" apparently means that government can remove women without notice or hearing. Poor immigrants and refugees now stand without a right to due legal process. Prior to September 11, none of these women would have been targeted and pursued with such viciousness. Because they have children, homes and jobs, it is likely that they would not even have been investigated.

Eventually, after much struggle, Brendalyn McDonald received a favorable decision on her application to apply for permanent residence. This was a major victory and came only after months of fighting the deportation order by Brendalyn, her family and allies. OCAP's efforts, including written correspondence and phone calls, small and large scale actions, the mobilization of unions and drawing media coverage, were critical in this victory and show the type of work that needs to be done to fight off government attacks.

These increasingly repressive practices, as outlined above, have emerged in the context of a long period of neo-liberal socio-economic transformation. Free trade agreements like the North American Free Trade Agreement (NAFTA) implemented in 1994 between Canada, the United States and Mexico, have given expanded opportunities to capital to influence social policies. Indeed the mid-1990s in Ontario were marked by economic downturn and factory closures in key industrial centers like Windsor and Hamilton. Economic shifts from mass to lean production techniques and the dismantling of the welfare state have weakened unions and community movements that have mobilized against these inequalities on a broader scale (see Sears 1999; Moody 1997).

Among the groups which have determined not to allow these practices continue and intensify is the Ontario Coalition Against Poverty (OCAP). OCAP has been at the forefront of developing new, creative and effective ways of dealing with government agencies which target for mistreatment those who are deemed to be vulnerable. One of the most successful practices pioneered by OCAP is "direct action casework." Unlike more hierarchical "client/caregiver" forms of casework, direct action casework directly involves the people facing injustice, allowing them to determine what course of action to take. Unlike more passive forms of casework, direct action casework goes directly to the source of injustice, whether a welfare office, landlord or Immigration office, mobilizing large numbers of community members (neighbors, students, unionists, activists) to get whatever is needed. Over the years, this approach has been highly successful, winning such tangible benefits as welfare and disability checks, wheelchairs, rent refunds and even stays of deportation. In three years OCAP has successfully supported over 50 families with immigration work.

In response to the increasingly inhumane treatment inflicted on immigrants and refugees,[2] OCAP, Colours of Resistance and Anti-Racist Action along with allied groups have organized a series of actions and events, including rallies outside the Celebrity Inn to draw attention to these issues and to demand rights and dignity for all detained people. In opposition to the Great Lakes Security Summit, a counter summit, "Do You Feel Secure?," was organized by various community groups under the banner, "No One is Illegal." The counter conference held a day of workshops and panel discussions on issues of defending immigrants and refugees, aboriginal self-determination, imperialism and colonialism, and solidarity against capitalism and the states system. Pickets outside the summit site at the posh Sutton Place Hotel on Bay Street (Canada's Wall Street) were held Sunday evening and Monday morning.

One important recent case that shows the mobilizing potential and political effectiveness of No One is Illegal networks in Canada involves the case of Laibar Singh. Singh came to Canada from India on a false passport in 2003, claiming he had left his country because he had been falsely accused of being a member of the terrorist Khalistan Commando Force. In 2006, while still in Canada, he suffered a debilitating aneurysm that left him a quadriplegic in 2006. The 48-year-old lost his refugee claim and all subsequent appeals and in June 2007 was ordered deported. On the eve of a July removal date, supporters, following his wishes, moved him from Vancouver's George Pearson long-term care facility where he faced certain removal by the Canada Border Services Agency (CBSA), and took him to Abbotsford's Kalgidhar Darbar temple. Singh remained there until he was transported to the airport on the orders of the CBSA.

On Monday, December 10, 2007, more than 1500 people came to the Vancouver International Airport and successfully rallied to prevent Singh's deportation. The mass turnout of supporters, mobilized on short notice, blocked traffic for hours, threatening a shutdown of the airport, and succeeded in preventing Singh's removal. CBSA said at the time that it feared for the safety of agents if they attempted to cut through the chanting mob and take Singh out of his taxi to an awaiting flight.

Following this successful defense of Laibar Singh, by members of the Sikh community in Vancouver and the No One is Illegal network, Singh took shelter in Surrey's Guru Nanak temple. Despite the temple's declaration of sanctuary for the paralyzed man, CBSA again sought his forced removal. On January 9, 2008, at 4:00 in the morning, Canadian Border Services Agency planned to break Laibar Singh's sanctuary under the cover of night. This would have been only the second violation of sanctuary in Canada. However, despite only a few hours notice, hundreds of supporters of Mr. Singh arrived at his place of sanctuary to prevent CBSA from carrying out the deportation order. A tractor-trailer truck was parked behind a locked a gate, preventing access to the grounds of the complex. This show of support forced CBSA to once again back off from deporting Laibar Singh. Singh remained at the temple for months, receiving volunteer medical care around the clock.

Although there has been tremendous support for Laibar Singh's case, NOII has also had to confront a growing and frightening racist backlash against him. Respondents to a poll by the Canadian Broadcasting Corporation (CBC) overwhelmingly supported deporting Laibar Singh, despite his medical condition and the fact that sanctuary would likely have to be breached to deport him. NOII has noted that if the government has wide public support for pulling a man in such marginalized circumstances out of sanctuary and deporting him, that will have a very serious impact on how broader immigration issues are treated in Canada.

Showing the strength of No One is Illegal as a national network, supporters of Laibar Singh including members of Toronto's Sikh Community have demonstrated at Citizenship and Immigration Canada Headquarters in Toronto to demand that Minister of Immigration Diane Finley grant Mr. Singh status and to call on the Canadian Border Services Agency to not break the sanctuary.

The No One is Illegal network has also played an important part in the development of the anti-war movements in Canada. Of great importance, the anti-war opposition has begun to target the racist attacks on immigrant and refugee communities that have played such a crucial part in the Canadian state's participation in the war in Afghanistan, which is scheduled to continue until at least 20011. As a growing underclass of migrant and refugee labor, including many people who have already fled imperialist-backed wars, faces increased exploitation and criminalization in Canada, the necessity of the No One is Illegal and anti-war campaigns coming together continues to be crucial.

These ongoing efforts are part of the growing "No One is Illegal" campaign which is building solidarity with immigrants and refugees, Indigenous communities, unionists and anti-poverty activists against the attacks on vast sectors of the working class which, under the veil of security, create miserable insecurity within our communities. As the situations facing immigrants and refugees become worse and worse and as xenophobia becomes the basis for social policy, the need to develop creative and effective means of struggle becomes more and more pressing.

FLYING SQUADS AND LABOR UNITY

One particularly effective means of struggle has been pioneered by OCAP recently in struggles against deportations. This example, borrowed from labor movement histories, is the "flying squad," a rapid response network of rank-and-file unionists that can mobilize members to take part in direct actions to defend people facing attacks from bosses, landlords or governments. Little more than an active phone tree that any member can initiate, the flying squads offer a mobile defense force and support network.

OCAP, along with allies in the Canadian Union of Public Employees (CUPE) Local 3903 flying squad, have gone directly to Pearson International Airport to demand an end to threats of deportation. Leaflets have been given to passengers alerting them to the situation and visits have been paid to the Immigration Canada deportation office in the basement of Terminal One. Deportations have been canceled. This unusual result, in which the removal dates were canceled prior to a Federal Court challenge, is a testament to the powers of direct action.

It must also be stressed that the presence of the flying squad has been crucial in the success of these ongoing actions. The flying squad, a decentralized group of rank-and-file activists, is on call to support strikes, demonstrations or casework actions; it demonstrates how labor organizations can step out of traditional concerns with the workplace to act in a broadened defense of working class interests. The expansion of union flying squads, with autonomy from union bureaucracies, could provide a substantial response to the state's efforts to isolate immigrants and refugees from the larger community. CUPE 3903 has also formed an Anti-Racism Working Group and an Anti-Poverty Working Group to work hand-in-hand with OCAP on actions or cases. These are just a few of the initiatives that organized labor can take in the here-and-now to build a global network of solidarity and support in which more secure members of the working class contribute to the defense of less secure members. The emboldened aggressiveness of Immigration Canada after September 11 make such actions in defense of people much more pressing, as the case of Shirley-Ann Charles shows with frightening clarity.

There is more that unions could do. In the Netherlands, pilots can refuse, as a health and safety issue, to transport people who have been deported. This is something which should be implemented in airline unions in North America. Instead of refusing to attend the Pearson action, as they did, the Canadian Auto Workers (CAW), which represents many airline workers, could have used the opportunity to discuss the issue with their members as a first step in actively pursuing such a policy.

A NEW UNDERGROUND RAILROAD?

The emerging circumstances of increased repression mean that unions and social movements must develop much more thorough and advanced strategies for support. Labor needs to organize outside of the limited confines of collective bargaining and the workplace to build networks of class-wide support. This must include support for unemployed workers, poor people, injured workers, immigrants and refugees among others. In effect these networks should form the basis for a new underground railroad which can secure safe travel across borders for people seeking to flee economic exploitation or political repression. As in the original underground railroad, this new network must be ready to operate outside of legal authorities. While community organizations can be expected to play a part in this, only organized labor has the resources to make this an effective and ongoing practice. Labor can help to provide transportation, safe houses and even employment, all of which will be necessary.

Recently such networks have emerged to transport conscientious objectors and deserters from the US military safely across the border into Canada. The War Resisters Support Campaign (WRSC) has established a broad-based coalition of community and labor organizations in cities including Vancouver, Toronto and Montreal to provide material support for US soldiers seeking asylum in Canada because they refuse to fight in Iraq. Among its activities the WRSC, assists war resisters in getting across the border into Canada and provides them with access to jobs and housing.

Since the attack on Iraq a growing number of US soldiers have taken the decision to come to Canada as conscientious objectors. With the US army "surge" extending its efforts against Iraq, requiring the mobilization of reservists and the recall of vets as well as initiating talk of re-instating the draft, as well as a new shift of focus towards an unwinnable war in Afghanistan, channels for bringing resisters into Canada have become, as during the Vietnam War, increasingly important. As of early 2009 upwards of 120 US army resisters are known to have crossed the border into Canada with the help of WRSC and other groups. It is believed that possibly three times that number have crossed the border without going public.

Labor must work fundamentally against the statist categories of citizenship which arbitrarily grant workers differential political and legal rights. As long as these citizenship categories exist, bosses will continue to use "illegal" labor for their own purposes. As long as there are vulnerable and hyper-exploitable categories of workers, capital will be able to use these differences against workers. Illegal workers will still be subject to harsher working conditions at lower pay without social benefits. Legal precariousness will always be a mechanism for exploiting those workers who find themselves in such a situation. Thus labor must not stop at helping the movement of illegal workers but must fundamentally work to abolish those practices which make anyone illegal. As these movements have stated: "No One Is Illegal."

Bosses have established free movement for themselves through free trade deals and other legal mechanisms while simultaneously working to limit the movement of workers. This redounds to their benefit by allowing them to pursue low wages and weak environmental regulations while limiting workers' options for seeking improved living conditions. Limiting the movement of workers makes it tougher for them to refuse the bad deals bosses offer them, which in turn weakens wages and working condition.

Of course socialists, anarchists and radical democrats have long maintained that people have the right to live, work and travel wherever they choose and to associate with whomever they choose. As internationalists, or perhaps more accurately transnationalists, we actively oppose the national borders which serve to divide and segregate people. Governments have no right to determine community participation (citizenship) and anarchists view as illegitimate any government claims to territorial sovereignty. It is important to remember that these views were once central parts of the international labor movement at the time of capitalist liberalism a century ago. It is time for labor to remember this vital part of its history.

BEGINNING TO BUILD BRIDGES TOWARDS DE-COLONIZATION

More recently transnationalists, notably Nandita Sharma, have argued that this perspective must be grounded in a respect for Indigenous self-determination and struggles against colonial states which have worked to exclude and eliminate native peoples over centuries of occupation. Movements against borders in settler societies like Canada must always address how statist appeals extend the effects of colonialism and neo-colonialism. Left nationalist approaches have little to offer Indigenous struggles for self-determination and land. As Sharma (2002, 24) notes, national states "exist in profound opposition to the self-determination of Indigenous people foremost." Indeed, Indigenous communities have long rejected strategies that rest on identifications of Canadian citizenship.

Along with No Borders movements, the most powerful challenge to the legitimacy of national states currently comes from Indigenous peoples' movements which also confront "the authority of national states over people" (Sharma 2002, 25). Through these challenges these movements also fundamentally contest the legitimacy of capitalism. According to Harsha Walia, an organizer with No One Is Illegal:

> Many immigrants have fled the colonial histories imposed from the North by imperialism, while indigenous peoples in BC were subject to the same colonialism. Aboriginal people living off-reserve face issues of status and citizenship comparable to migrant workers. Both communities face obvious racism in terms of access to services, incarceration and representation. (Lavender 2004)

According to Walia, the fundamental issue is "unceded territory and how land is developed" (Lavender 2004). Within capitalist globalization struggles for indigenous rights, the rights of migrant workers and the environment take a back seat to issues of sport, leisure and tourism. Sharma argues that what is needed is an honest and sustained discussion on how to embark on a process of de-colonization. While this is still an emerging project for most groups, OCAP has long worked in solidarity with native communities against the colonial Canadian state.

Despite the tremendous difficulties faced, this work has formed an important beginning in renewed efforts to build alliances across the barriers which are deployed to keep oppressed communities from coming together and sharing experiences and strategies, resources and ideas and struggling together in solidarity. This is, after all, what states and capital fear most.

In addition to issues of state repression and sovereignty, warriors have organized against industrial dumping and the locating of toxic production plants in and around native communities and reserves and against the horrible experiences of poverty in the communities. These are the features of the local face of corporate globalization and are the reasons for permanent connections to be forged between indigenous communities and anti-globalization movements across the country. And real connections continue to be forged in addition to the continued relations which have been built between Mohawk Warriors and OCAP. Among the more interesting examples includes an alliance between NOII in Vancouver and indigenous opponents of the 2010 Winter Olympics (see Shantz 2009).

Native communities have played a large part in organizing with the Ontario Common Front, a coalition of 80 community groups from across the province, for a series of economic and political disruptions which have taken place in Ontario since 2001. Those actions were organized with the intention of making it impossible for the local agents of capital to impose the destructive economic and political agenda which they arrogantly trumpet at international meetings such as those in Quebec City.

CONCLUSION

Class war, as modern war is always spatial, is fought over the "right to define and enforce the meaning of shared space" (Bauman 1998, 4). Thus the Canadian and US governments, under the cover provided by September 11, are devising joint agreements around border controls and immigration criteria. There has even been chilling talk from some authorities about establishing a continental perimeter, a "Fortress North America."

As many commentators have pointed out, these practices are also about strengthening the government's hand in fighting the globalization struggles at a time when many sensed it was beginning to lose its grip. This is one reason why legislation against activism has gone hand in hand with a clampdown on immigration, the global mobility of labor.

An enormous part of the work of spatializing class war has been carried out through policing and criminalization of various subject populations. This criminalization is more broadly deployed than is generally described. It also includes, fundamentally, the use of the repressive legal apparatus to keep possible forces of dissent from ever joining together in common cause: classic divide and conquer tactics. Whenever members of the working class are made to fear standing up to employers and the state, whether through threats of job loss, eviction or deportation, this acts to quell possible dissent, in effect to criminalize dissent.

When the legal state creates and perpetuates phony divisions between workers through immigration laws and the construction of "legals" and "illegals," we must recognize this as part of the spatialized class war. Likewise, when these divisions are maintained through legal repression against poor people and homeless people. Any legal mechanism which impedes the recomposition of the working class as a stronger force or which helps a decomposition of the working class to the benefit of capital must be understood as the criminalization of dissent.

This is why one must always be clear that really opposing the criminalization of dissent must mean opposing all immigration laws, all vagrancy laws, all coercive treatment of psychiatric survivors and all laws which weaken the forces of the oppressed classes in their struggles against their oppressors. This means, of course, that national borders themselves are part of the criminalization of dissent. Any time someone is turned back trying to cross from one country to another, even to visit, that is the spatialized class war.

Anti-capitalist organizations must take up the challenge of borders at local and global levels. As Nandita Sharma (2003) suggests:

> The Left needs to soundly reject nationalist endeavors on the grounds that the oppression and exploitation of Indigenous peoples, people of colour, queers and other Others occurs precisely because they are constructed as falling outside of the nation. What is needed in the place of Left nationalism is an honest and sustained debate on how to embark on a project of de-colonization.

OCAP and No One is Illegal deploy a variety of tactics to overcome the divide and conquer tactics which keep the opposition to capitalist control divided and weakened. Still, OCAP is an anti-poverty organization lacking the resources necessary to lead the fight. Organized labor must take up the challenge in a serious way, drawing on the examples offered by OCAP and No One is Illegal but extending them radically. The old labor standard, "An Injury to One is an Injury to All" must be labor's driving principle once more.

NOTES

1. While this chapter has a post-September 11 focus, I do not want to imply that the actions taken by the Canadian government since then are out of character. Canada's immigration system has always been racist, anti-worker and anti-poor.
2. In addition to the examples provided in this chapter, accounts of this increased repression abound in both the popular media and the social movement press. See Galati, 2002, Zerehi, 2003 and Zerehi and Scott, 2003. See also the websites of the Campaign to Stop Secret Trials (www.homesnotbombs.ca) and Project Threadbare (www.threadbare.tyo.ca).

REFERENCES

Barndt, D. 1996. "Free Trade Offers 'Free Space' for Connecting Across Borders." In *Local Places: In the Age of the Global City*, eds. R. Keil, G. Wekerle and D.V.J. Bell, D.V.J. Montreal: Black Rose, 243–248.

Bauman, Z. 1998. *Globalization: The Human Consequences*. New York: Columbia.

CRIAW/ICREF. 2003. "Fact Sheets: Immigrant and Refugee Women." Canadian Research Institute for the Advancement of Women/Institut Canadien de Recherche sur les Femmes website, http://www.criaw-icref.ca/ImmigrantandRefugeeWomen (Accessed January 27, 2004).

Galati, R. 2002. "Canada's Globalization, Militarization and Police State Agenda." *Briarpatch* 31(1): 5–7.

Kuehls, T. 1996. *Beyond Sovereign Territory: The Space of Ecopolitics*. Minneapolis: University of Minnesota Press.

Lavender, Harold. 2004. "Sun Peaks Aboriginal Land Dispute: Land, Freedom and Decolonization." *New Socialist* 50: 11–12.

Mertes, T. (editor). 2004. *A Movement of Movements*. London: Verso.

Sears, A. 1999. "The 'Lean' State and Capitalist Restructuring: Towards a Theoretical Account." *Studies in Political Economy* 59: 91–114.

Shantz, J. A. 1998. "'Don't Go in the Pit': *Active Resistance* and the Territories of Political Identity." *Post-Identity* 1(2): 84–103.

———. 2002. "Judi Bari and 'The Feminization of Earth First!': The Convergence of Class, Gender and Radical Environmentalism." *Feminist Review* 70: 105–122.

———. 2009. "Olympics Challenge: Indigenous Women, 'No to 2010' and the Emergence of a New Movement." *New Politics* XII(2): 73–78.

Sharma, N. 2002. "Open the Borders: Resist Nationalism, An Interview with Nandita Sharma." *New Socialist* 38: 24–25.

——— 2003. "No Borders Movements and the Rejection of Left Nationalism." *Canadian Dimension* 37(3).

Valpy, M. 2004. "The Soldier Who Refuses to Fight." The Globe and Mail. Sat., Feb. 7, F3

York, G. and Pindera, L. 1991. *People of the Pines: The Warriors and the Legacy of Oka*. Toronto: Little, Brown.

Zerehi, S. 2003. "The Racist War at Home." *New Socialist* 41: 21–23.

Zerehi, S. and Scott M. 2003. "Immigrants and Refugees Under Attack: Stand Up, Fight Back." *New Socialist* 44: 18–19.

CONTRIBUTORS

Dr. Graciela Susana Boruszko teaches in the Department of International Studies and Languages, Seaver College, Pepperdine University, Malibu, California. She obtained her degree in French Philology from the University of Madrid. She also completed a D.E.A. in Comparative Literature Studies at the University of Dijon, France. Her areas of research are: Comparative Literature and Linguistics, Comparative Culture Studies, Hispanic Studies and French and Francophone Studies.

Elvira Doghem-Rashid is currently a doctoral research student at the Kings Institute for the Study of Public Policy (KISPP), King College London. Her thesis deals with the impact of the Race Relations (Amendment) Act (2000) on social mobility, specifically the effect of the Act on ethnic differences in educational attainment in the UK. She is also a member of the government's Census Diversity Advisory Group and is one of the first members of Runnymede 360°, the UK's leading independent race equality think tank. Her research interests are firmly rooted in the areas of ethnicity and multiculturalism, more recently termed social cohesion, with the Asian and Arab ethnic groups of particular interest in her research. These interests have also developed into an interest into ethno-religious differences and a focus on Muslim communities. During her research, she has worked on a number of research projects focussed on minority ethnic/racial groups and authored the UK's first published report on the Halal Food Market (2000) published by Mintel. Outside of research, Elvira has a personal interest in promoting cultural engagement with the Arab community in the UK.

Aaron Fine received his BFA in Painting in 1993 from Ohio University in Athens, Ohio where he wrote a Philosophy honors thesis on Spinoza. Mr. Fine attended Claremont Graduate University in Los Angeles, where he studied art in an interdisciplinary environment, served as a humanities scholar, and received his MFA in Painting in 1996. In 1999 Aaron Fine accepted his current position as Professor of Art and Gallery Director at Truman State University in Kirksville Missouri. From May 2007 to August 2008 Mr. Fine was on sabbatical writing about pedagogy and pursuing a new body of work in mixed media drawing which can be seen at aaronfineart.com. Since then Mr. Fine has been adding more curatorial work and research into visual culture to his activities as a devoted academic.

Peter Fine is an Assistant Professor of Graphic Design at New Mexico State University. As a designer, artist and writer, he explores the role of the design past, present and future, seeking ways to integrate design history, theory and criticism with practice. He is currently exploring ways to make environmental concerns a vital component of the Graphic Design curriculum at NMSU. He continues work on his book, *Graphic Design Reconsidered,* an introduction to the subject of green design for students and professionals. In his course "Visualizing Race," students compare their DNA, personal identity and chosen medium to understand how race and representation operate within visual culture. Fine received his MFA from the University of Arizona in 2004.

Dr. Michael Kilburn, former IREX scholar at the Institute for Contemporary History in Prague (1999), is Assistant Professor of Political Science and Liberal Studies at Endicott College in Beverly, Massachusetts. His research interests include human rights pedagogy, democratization, and the use of music and art in political advocacy. Kilburn is currently working on an English translation of Vanek's environmental book *No Breathing Room* (1996). Dr. Kilburn has a lifelong mission to increase awareness of and engagement with politics and international affairs. He founded the Endicott Center for Oral History.

Dr. David Magill is Assistant Professor of English and Women and Gender Studies at Longwood University in Farmville, Virginia. He has published several essays in collections on masculinity and race in literature and popular culture. He is currently working on a manuscript entitled *Modern Masculinities : Nostalgic White Manhood and Jazz Age Politics* .

Dr. Heidi Rimke teaches in the Department of Sociology at The University of Winnipeg, Canada. She specializes in the areas of classical and contemporary social and political thought, historical and political sociology, criminology, cultural studies, the history of the philosophies of the social sciences, and the history of the human sciences with a focus on "psy" discourses and practices. Her publications examine the role of popular psychology/self-help in neo-liberalism; the history of psychiatry, the medicalization of morality; political biography; the history of criminal sciences; and anti-capitalist resistance movements. Some of her current projects examine the criminalization/pathologization of resistance; the psychiatrization of everyday life; the birth of psychopolitics and psychocentrism as neo-liberal political technologies; and, capitalism and cannibalism.

Jeff Shantz has been a community organizer for decades. His writings have appeared in such academic journals as *Feminist Review*, *Critical Sociology*, *Critique of Anthropology*, *Capital and Class*, *Feminist Media Studies* and *Environmental Politics*. He hosted "The Anti-Poverty Report" for several years on community radio stations in Toronto, where he was a member of the Ontario Coalition Against Poverty. He is currently a full-time faculty member in the Department of Criminology at Kwantlen Polytechnic University in Vancouver, Canada. He teaches courses on critical theory, elite deviance, human rights, and community advocacy.

Harsha Walia is a community organizer and writer active in Metro Vancouver. She is a member of No One Is Illegal (NOII). No One Is Illegal-Vancouver, Coast Salish Territories is a grassroots anti-colonial migrant justice group with leadership from members of migrant and/or racialized backgrounds. As a movement for self-determination that challenges the ideology of immigration controls, NOII members are in full confrontation with Canadian border policies; denouncing and taking action to combat racial profiling, detention and deportation, the national security apparatus, law enforcement brutality, and exploitative working conditions of migrants. They struggle for the right of our communities to maintain their livelihoods and resist war, occupation, and displacement; while supporting indigenous sisters and brothers fighting theft of land and colonization. They also place themselves within the broader movement for global social justice that struggles against capitalism, militarism, oppression, poverty, imperialism, and other systems of domination and exploitation.

Index

A

Abu Ghraib, 130
Advantage of Equality, 100
African-Americans, 2, 5, 15, 17-18, 22-23, 41, 72, 132
Age of
  Capitalism, 110
  Crisis, 110
  Globalization, 91, 157
Al-Sadat Anwar, 141, 155
Alberta Tar Sands, 73, 82
Alito, Justice Sam, 24
American
  Civil Liberties Union (ACLU), 13, 19, 22, 25, 33
  Indian (see also Native American), 123
  Justice System, 66
  Science, 111
  West, 123, 133
American-ness, 9, 129, 132-133, 140
Americanism, 116
Americanization, 8
Amnesty
  International USA, 33
  Report, 22, 29
Anthropology, 92, 102, 175
Anti-2010 Olympics Campaign, 91
Anti-Capitalism, 4, 88, 92, 158, 171, 175
Anti-colonial, 88, 175
Anti-Communism, 110

Anti-Deportation Movement, 92
Anti-Poverty
  Report, 175
  Working Group, 166
Anti-Racism Working Group, 166
Anti-Racist Action, 161-162, 164
Apartheid
  of Citizenship, 85, 90
  System of Migration, 93
Apparent Sanctioning of Formal Ethnic Profiling, 42
Arab
  Canadian, 84
  League, 52
Arbeiter Ring, 92
Armageddon, 127
Arrests, 2, 13, 28, 38-39, 42, 63, 66-68, 163
Ashcroft, John (US Attorney General), 18-19, 33
Asia Pacific Research Network, 91
Asian
  Americans, 72
  Ethnic Groups, 40, 45, 47
Asiatic Exclusion League, 87
Association of Muslim Chaplains, 65

B

Backlash Against Racial Profiling Studies, 67

F

Fact Sheets, 34, 66, 171
Fall, Senator Albert B., of New Mexico, 118
Farm Workers
  in general, 77-79, 91-92
  Foreign, and Unions, 77, 79, 91-92
  Labour Contractors, 78
  Rights, 91
Farmville, 174
Fascism, 110
Fast and Secure Trade Pass, 82
Fear, 1-2, 4, 6-8, 17, 21, 26, 59, 62, 79, 95, 97,
  100-101, 104-108, 114-115, 118, 121-123, 146,
  148, 164, 169-170
Federal
  Bureau of Investigation (US) - FBI, 27
  Law Enforcement Agencies, 18, 35
Federalism, 16
Feelings, 58, 100, 105-106
Feingold, Senator Russ, 22
Feminism, 91-92
Feminist Media Studies, 175
Feminization of
  Earth First, 172
  Migration, 80
Ferguson, Corinna, 57
Filipino-Canadian Youth Alliance of BC, 80
Filipino Migrante BC Coalition, 81
Filipinos/Filipinas, 80-81, 91
Floralia Plant Growers, 79
Flying
  Squads, 166
  While Arab, 19, 67
  While Brown, 71
FOI Legislation, 60
Foreign
  Relations, 82
  Temporary Workers, 85, 91
Forms of Racism, Contemporary, 34
Fort Worth (TX), 127
Fortress North America, 108, 160, 170
Foucault Effect, 109
Fourth Inaugural Address (of US President
  Roosevelt), 150, 156
France, 109, 142, 173
Francophone Studies, 173
Franklin, Benjamin, 32
Fraser Valley Berry Crops, 91
Free

Press, 126
Space, 158, 171
Trade Offers, 171
Freedom of Information
  Act (US) - FOI, 45-46, 59, 68-71
  Act Publication Scheme, 69-70
  Request, 71
Frost, Robert, 113, 127, 143, 155

G

Gated Communities, 110
Gatehouse, 144
Gay, 61
Gender Studies, 174
Gendered Aspects of Racial Profiling, 71
Genealogical Method, 111
Genealogizing, 99
Genealogy of Positivism, 111
Genocide, 6, 14-16, 31, 34
Gentiles, 100, 109
Geographical Perspective, 11
George H. Doran Company, 156
German, 41, 77
Gillan and Quinton v. UK, 56, 66-67
Global
  Capitalism, 76, 96, 98
  City, 171
  Perspective, 15, 29, 31, 93
  Racism, 91
  System, 92
Globalization, 4, 9-10, 74, 82, 86, 91-93, 98,
  142, 157-160, 162, 169-171
Golden Eagle Farms, 79
Good Cop, 34
Good Corporate Citizen, 91
Gore, Al, 18
Governing
  Citizens, 111
  Non-Citizens, 110
Gramsci, 157
Great Lakes Security Summit, 162, 164
Great Race, 127
Green Left Weekly, 11
Greenway Farms, 79
Greyhound, 106
Guatemala, 76
Guernsey, 77, 92
Guestworkers, 92

Sharma, Nandita, 75, 86, 168, 171-172
Shia, 15
Sikh, 165
SIKLAB, 81
Singh, 89, 93, 164-165
Sinners, 111
Situational Racism, 71
Slavery, 5, 16, 92, 122-123
Smart Border Declaration, 83
Social
    Control, 6, 62, 84, 90, 105, 111
    Order, 32, 99, 105-106, 110, 118, 155
    Organization of Migrant Workers, 92
    Psychological Epidemics, 111
    Theory, 93, 157
Soldiers, 121-122, 167
Somali, 63
South Africa, 2
South America, 143
South Asian, 20-21, 77-78
Southern European, 130
Sovereignty, 30, 85, 93, 110, 159, 168-169
Spinoza, 174
Stigmatization, 54-55
Stolen
    Labor, 87
    Land, 87-88
Stop & Search Data (see also Police Stop
    and Search), 7, 45-47, 49, 51, 53
Street Crime, 17, 71
Sub-Saharan African, 138
Success Breeds Attack, 67
Sun Peaks Aboriginal Land Dispute, 172
Sunni, 15
Surrogate, 116
Surveillance of Catholics, 110
Survivor Testimony, 34
Suspect Communities, Creation of, 70
Sweeney Todd, 102
Synthetic Paradigm, 34

T

Tastsoglou, Evangelia, 92
Targets, 14, 40, 71, 100
Temporary
    Employment Authorizations, 76
    Foreign Worker Program, 75
Tenet, George, 24
Territorialism, 149

Territory, 4, 85, 87-88, 108-109, 121-122, 149,
    157, 159, 168-169, 172, 175
Terror, 3, 5-6, 8, 15, 19-20, 24, 27, 31, 34, 39,
    82, 95, 103-104, 107-108, 110
Terrorism Act Areas, 71
Terrorism Arrests, 68
Third World, 78, 84, 90, 92
Toronto Women, 91
Trans-Canada Railways, 75
Trans-National America, 116, 127
Transgender, 61, 131-132
Transgressive Interiorities, 111
Transient, 74-75, 90
Transnational Connections, 92
Transparency, 27, 57-58
Triangulating, 29
Tutsi, 13-14
Twelve Christians Report, 156

U

UFCW, 79, 87
Underground Railroad, New, 167
Universal Declaration of Human Rights, 14,
    27, 34
United   Food, 79
United Kingdom, 66
United Nations
    Committee, 25
    Special Rapporteur, 25, 79
United States
    Chamber of Commerce, 92
    Commission, 19-21, 34
    Constitution, 24
    Constitutionalism, 22
    Department of Justice, 34
    Domestic Human Rights Program, 33
    National Security Strategy, 21
    Patriot Act, 21
    Southwest, 114
    State Department, 25
    Thirteenth Cavalry, 121
USCCR, 20-21, 34, 67, 72
Use of
    Race, 5, 18, 35, 37, 41
    Section, 69

V